T0073438

SAP Excellence

Series Editors:
Professor Dr. Dr. h.c. mult. Peter Mertens
Universität Erlangen-Nürnberg

Dr. Peter Zencke
SAP AG, Walldorf

Marco Meier · Werner Sinzig
Peter Mertens

Enterprise Management with SAP SEM™/ Business Analytics

Second Edition
with 104 Figures
and 16 Tables

 Springer

Dr. Marco Meier
FORWIN
Lange Gasse 20
90403 Nürnberg
meier@forwin.de

Dr. Werner Sinzig
SAP AG
Postfach 14 61
69185 Walldorf
werner.sinzig@sap.com

Professor Dr. Dr. h.c. mult. Peter Mertens

Friedrich-Alexander-Universität Erlangen-Nürnberg
Bereich Wirtschaftsinformatik I
Lange Gasse 20
90403 Nürnberg
mertens@wiso.uni-erlangen.de

Cataloging-in-Publication Data applied for

Library of Congress Control Number: 2004113531

A catalog record for this book is available from the Library of Congress.

Bibliographic information published by Die Deutsche Bibliothek
Die Deutsche Bibliothek lists this publication in the Deutsche Nationalbibliografie;
detailed bibliographic data available in the internet at *http://dnb.ddb.de*

ISBN 3-540-22806-3   Springer Berlin Heidelberg New York
ISBN 3-540-00253-7   1st Edition   Springer Berlin Heidelberg New York

Springer is a part of Springer Science+Business Media
springeronline.com

© Springer-Verlag Berlin Heidelberg 2003, 2005
Printed in Germany

Hardcover-Design: Erich Kirchner, Heidelberg
Production: Helmut Petri
Printing: betz-druck

SPIN 11310976   Printed on acid-free paper – 42/3130 – 5 4 3 2 1 0

In the majority of cases – we estimate 70% – the real problem isn't the high-concept boners. It's bad execution. As simple as that: not getting things done, being indecisive, not delivering on commitment.
Ram, C., Colvin, G., "Why CEO's Fail", Fortune, June 21, 1999

Foreword to the Second Edition

Soon after the first edition of this book was published it became apparent that a second edition would be needed. This demonstrates the attention being given to the search for new methods of partially automating the decision-making process at upper management levels.

The main change was to update the description of the SAP® systems in chapter 5. A new topic here is Activity-Based Costing based on the Value Network Analyzer (see section 5.3.1).

An additional case study was also added that describes how the Balanced Scorecard was implemented at Norwegian Defense. This case points to an interesting development. While in the past business organization was often modeled on that of the military (staff positions, the tripartite division into strategic, tactical, and operational management, elements of logistics, and so on), the influence is now going the other way as military organizations are being modernized by tools from business administration and information systems.

For their dedicated work in updating the contents, the authors would particularly like to thank Ute Östringer, Sabine Sänger, Dr. Martina Schuh, Dirk Braun, Thomas Fleckenstein, and Ralf Ille. Special thanks are due to Major Trond Erik Bones (Headquarters Defense Command Norway) for the additional case study. Last but not least, many thanks to Stephen Offenbacker (SAP AG) and Andrew Zeller (Department of Information Systems I, University of Erlangen-Nuremberg for their assistance in translating the amendments of the second edition.

Nuremberg and Walldorf,   Marco Meier, Werner Sinzig, and Peter Mertens
September 2004

Foreword to the First Edition

Strategic and operational management are classic areas of business administration and information systems. Recently, there has been a flood of publications on subjects such as online analytical processing (OLAP), data warehouses, and analytical application systems.

Most of the publications about enterprise management originate from the United States and concentrate on either methods, instruments, and procedures, or pure technical aspects. Companies are currently still faced with a series of stand-alone solutions for strategic and operational planning and decision support. The integration of information processing in the formulation and implementation of enterprise strategies is still in the initial stages. With this book, we will try to establish a bridge between business administration knowledge and software.

SAP AG was one of the first companies to provide the market with a complete package with their product *SAP Strategic Enterprise Management^{TM}* (SAP SEM^{TM}). For operational decision support, this was extended and became *SAP Strategic Enterprise Management/Business Analytics* (SAP SEM/BA). With this in mind, we have decided to illustrate the instruments of enterprise management and their implementation in solutions for information processing using the SAP systems as an example.

One feature of the SAP systems is the connection of functions to Business Content. This can be viewed as a new generation of standard software and suggests a new branch or even a new focus in information systems.

In some places, for example, in portraying the business methods and instruments along with the technical information basis, we had to sacrifice detailed explanations in favor of a wider view. However, in these cases we have provided suggestions for more detailed literature about controlling, planning and organization theories, and information systems.

In Chapter 1 we explain the considerable demands placed on a modern system for strategic and operational enterprise management. Chapter 2 outlines the business basis for these demands. The instruments offered by business administration to solve the problems addressed are considered in Chapter 3. Chapter 4 describes how developments in information technology contribute to the changes. Chapter 5 deals with SAP SEM/BA. A clear impression of the practical use of the system is given in Chapter 6 by case studies of companies that use SAP systems. An interview with David P. Norton, one of the fathers of the Balanced Scorecard and a summary that looks at the challenges faced by integrated information systems of strategic and operational management conclude the book.

The book is aimed at managers and employees in controlling and information processing who are concerned with the development and implementation of systems for business management information and decision support. The book can also be used in universities and technical colleges to demonstrate practical requirements.

Despite the multitude of developments, we have decided to restrict the scope of this book in the hope that this will enable us to better satisfy interested parties in our target audiences. The subject matter is developing so dynamically that an edition of a book is not designed to describe the latest system status in detail, since it would be out of date by the next software release. We will therefore look at the systems at an abstract level. Should you require more detailed technical information, we suggest you read the White Papers, presentation material, and documentation (also available via the Internet).

A special feature of the publications in this series is that they are produced in close cooperation with SAP. SAP has generously given us access to their documentation and permitted us to use both content and diagrams. Here we would particularly like to thank Ute Östringer, Maja Scholer, Dr. Martina Schuh, Thomas Fleckenstein, Matthias Heesch, Ralf Ille, Stefan Karl, Stefan Kraus, Jens Reithmann, Udo Summ, Andreas Vetter, and Marcus Wefers. We would also like to thank Alejandro Bombaci L. (Empresas Polar), Dr. Raimund Browarzik (Henkel Surface Technologies), Roland Lochner (Siemens AG), and Dr. David P. Norton (Balanced Scorecard Collaborative, Inc.). In the Bayerischen Forschungsverbund Wirtschaftsinformatik (FORWIN) we have been greatly assisted by Irina Depperschmidt, Olga Hein, Hermiona-Louise Schwarzmann, Andreas Billmeyer, Peter Bradl, and Martin Stößlein. Last but not least, many thanks to Jean Gill, Tara Lawson-Brown, Stephen Offenbacker, and Tracey Duffy for their assistance in translating this book.

Nuremberg and Walldorf,   Marco Meier, Werner Sinzig, and Peter Mertens
November 2002

Table of Contents

1 Current Problems and Requirements

With its software product SAP Strategic Enterprise Management/Business Analytics (SAP SEM/BA^{TM}), SAP has introduced a new software solution to the market for both strategic and operational enterprise planning and decision support.

Many of the more recent publications on application systems for enterprise management attempt to motivate you to continue reading with an introduction something like this: "Globalization, increasing environmental dynamics, more intensive competition, and higher cost pressures lead to ever-growing demands..." "New" problems and solutions are heralded by consultants, software producers, and even experts, in the area of finding a corporate strategy that promises success and that can be practically converted into reality. But when examined more closely, these "new" problems and solutions are not so new, and at times appear more like clichés. So what are the benefits of a new software package such as SAP SEM/BA and yet another book on this subject?

The need for new solutions arises on the one hand from still unsatisfactorily solved basic problems related to the flow of information to strategic and operational management, and on the other hand from current – in part industry-specific and business-type-specific – economic developments. Above and beyond this, the pressures of new technologies, led largely by new database technologies and the Internet, demand new information logistics.

1.1 Current Problems

Lack of Integration Between Strategic and Operational Levels of Enterprise Management

The basic problem that strategic management needs to solve involves timely recognition of opportunities and risks, while ensuring the company's long-term potential for success by means of decisions on capital investments and allocation of resources. The ultimate aim is to achieve a lasting increase in the value of the company. The goals of operational planning and Performance Measurement, on the other hand, are focused on shorter time periods. Their purpose, within the bounds of the corporate strategy, is to ensure profitability and liquidity of the firm within a fiscal year or shorter periods of time. The two areas are necessarily closely related. Operational planning concretizes the plans made in strategic management. On the other side of the coin, operational Performance Measurements provide impulses for the corporate strategy. The combination of the operational and strategic levels of management is what makes it possible to weigh short and medium term decisions against long-term goals.

According to an American study, the lack of integration between enterprise strategies and operational business processes manifests itself in actual practice above all in the following problems (Norton 1996):

1. Strategy is not operationalized. Only 40% of middle management and 5% of other employees understand the strategy of the company. The corporate strategy is not broken down into its elements.

2. Only 50% of top management and 20% of middle management have a bonus system that is directly linked to the medium to long-term strategic goals.

3. 85% of management teams spend less than one hour per month on strategy discussions.

4. 60% of resources of the company do not relate directly to the strategy.

5. The focus on financial figures is too one-sided as well as oriented toward the past, and too much stress is placed on reactive measures.

Insufficient Integration of ERP Systems

Business application systems can be divided into operational systems (administration and disposition systems) as well as planning and control systems (see figure 1.1). The focus of this book is on systems at the management level, however it is not possible to look at these systems in complete isolation.

Our aim is to demonstrate how, using the existing complement of classic and modern instruments of business and management economics, combined with the capabilities of information technology, it is possible to implement a practicable, integrated solution for strategic and operational enterprise management. Since SAP has, to a large extent, taken a leading role in this area, we will use the SAP Strategic Enterprise Management/Business Analytics (SEM/BA) system as a reference. It is based on SAP's data warehouse product, SAP Business Information Warehouse (SAP BW®). For handling operational transactions, SAP offers (along with other options) the SAP R/3® system (Wenzel 2001).

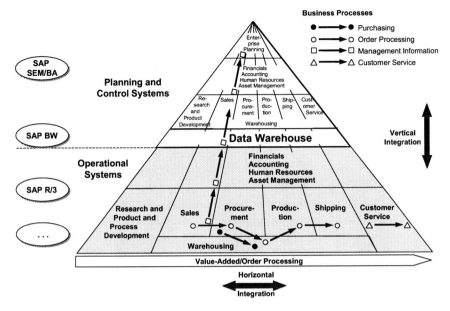

Fig. 1.1: Classification of Business Information Systems
(based on Mertens 2004, p. 7)

Operational Systems

Operational systems are geared toward rationalization of mass data processing, thereby endeavoring particularly to reduce costs and free employees from routine tasks, while at the same time speeding up processes and reducing turnaround time. Beyond the task of pure administration, disposition systems are intended to assist human decision-makers, or to make human decisions unnecessary by having the system itself make decisions automatically. Here we can differentiate between two objectives:

1. Automatic decisions should be better than decisions made by a human being; the goal is optimization.

2. We are satisfied if the information system finds solutions that are equal to those provided by human beings. In this case, the goal is rationalization of the decision-making process. The user is relieved of programmable routine tasks, and, moreover, automatic processes do not have to be interrupted for human intervention.

With operational systems, it is often relatively easy to demonstrate the superiority of the information system solely on the basis of the large number of transaction figures processed. With disposition systems, on the other hand, you have to repeatedly reassess which is better – human or automatic disposition.

Planning and Control Systems

The systems for planning and control are found in the upper part of the pyramid (see figure 1.1). If we assume that in an integrated concept, both operational and disposition systems are in place, then the next logical step in the further development of industrial information processing is to use the system, and especially its data, for planning. To this end, planning systems are developed that can be considered a continuation of the disposition models embedded in information processing. However, there are the following differences:

1. Decisions proposed by disposition models or made by information systems solve well structured problems, whereas planning models are for solving poorly structured problems.

2. Disposition models assist in decision-making related to high-volume and routine problems that usually occur in relatively short, repetitive intervals (such as planning of production processes). Planning systems, in contrast, are normally used for decision-making tasks that occur at greater intervals, and sometimes irregularly (for example, planning of capital investments or a production program).

3. Disposition systems tend to fall into the responsibility areas of middle managers, whereas planning models have been developed for top managers.

4. Operational systems work with databases in which all changes are stored in real time and in detail. Planning and control systems, however, are built on the basis of data warehouses, which contain summarized data and information that remains constant over a longer time period.

5. While disposition systems can often run fully automated (consider material requirements planning, for example), planning systems require more involvement of the user, so that human-computer interaction is the norm. Involving the human element in planning models is necessary primarily to allow enough scope for decisive entrepreneurial action, in order to correct developments that would arise if processes (such as the lifecycle of a product) were left to themselves.

Control systems are the counterpart of planning systems. Their job is to monitor adherence to the plan, and to provide indicators as to whether corrective measures should be taken. In the ideal situation, they function something like a medical problem with the sequence of events: "symptom recognition – diagnosis – proposed therapy – prognosis" (Mertens 2004, pp. 13-16).

Current practice tends heavily toward standalone solutions for the various planning and reporting tasks. Whereas day-to-day business transactions can be handled just about completely using operational systems (also called online transaction processing systems (OLTP systems), such as SAP R/3, PeopleSoft®, Oracle®, or J. D. Edwards®), most are still far from such a complete integration of data and functions for planning, budgeting, and Performance Measurement in complex organizations.

Symptomatic for this state of affairs is having numerous spreadsheet files, presentation files, and word processing files "roaming around" in different versions. Even dedicated management information systems (MIS) usually cover only limited areas. An important milestone on the road to creating some order in management information has been the introduction of central data warehouses and data marts that are coordinated with each other, in conjunction with online analytical processing systems (OLAP systems). However, this alone has not been enough to achieve an integrated solution for strategic and operational enterprise management. What are still missing are fully-developed functions for coordinating planning and Performance Measurement.

Complex and Dynamic Organizational Structures

Strategic and operational management tasks can be found at different levels of the firm, for example the corporate level or business unit level or an area of responsibility level such as the product line level. Most large companies are characterized by decentralization of decision-making competence. This results in complex organizations in matrix form that are defined by multiple dimensions such as functional areas, processes, products, projects, or regions. It also means that a large number of decision-makers are involved in planning and measurement of performance. This is further complicated by the fact that company structures are subject to dynamic changes resulting from investments by other companies or various forms of cooperation. The large number of takeovers as well as disinvestments lead to permanent changes in planning units and consolidation groups (Karl 2000). Planning and measurement of performance are also no longer limited to your own firm. In the case of Supply Chain Management (SCM), for example, they involve entire networks of companies that are not covered by a common legal umbrella (enterprise & extraprise management accounting).

Capital Market Driven Enterprise Management and Risk Management

Disappointments regarding the "New Economy" have directed the attention of the financial community (analysts, fund managers, risk capital investors) more strongly toward value-based and risk-related facts. In numerous industries and markets, capital as a production factor for realizing strategies that ensure the survival of the company has become scarcer. This intensifies competition for investor capital and results in shares becoming more and more often the subject of marketing measures. Examples of this trend are the marketing campaigns of the German telecommunications firm, Deutsche Telekom, or of Infineon. This marketing approach is not only effective for new issues, but also for enlisting the long-term commitment of shareholders (Schuler/Pfeifer 2001).

Concepts for capital market driven enterprise management have therefore become an accepted standard in recent years. Another primary reason for this is the growing concentration of shareholdings with institutional investors, with their holdings increasing from 14% to 24% within ten years (Deutsche Bundesbank

2000). For institutional investors, unlike small shareholders, national boundaries do not play a significant role. The decisive factor for investments then becomes solely the expectation related to the potential increase in the value of the concern. Analysts are demanding that company data be presented in a standardized form that allows global comparison. This increases demands for greater detail and broader scope in the information the company is expected to present, along with expectations regarding the frequency, exactness, and speed with which reports have to be delivered. Considering this situation, it is easy to explain the trend toward a merging of internal and external accounting.

In addition, a recent series of studies concludes that institutional investors and analysts do not assess companies solely on financial criteria. They base their judgments on prognoses about the development of the leading factors influencing the success of the firm. These are referred to as value drivers. According to one study, portfolio managers base 35% of their decision to invest on non-financial information. Out of 38 identified factors, the top five are listed below (Low/ Siesfeld 1998, p. 24):

1. Ability to enact corporate strategy
2. Management credibility/capabilities
3. Quality of the corporate strategy
4. Innovation
5. Ability to recruit talented individuals

In addition, there is a direct relationship between the communication of strategies by investor relations departments and the investment recommendations of analysts. For 69% of investors polled, investor relationship is an important or very important criterion for investing (Arthur Andersen 1999).

In light of certain stock market developments over which companies have no influence, such as political changes, the question arises whether focusing purely on the capital market is really the right path to success. As a result, the relations to other stakeholders (see section 2.3) increase in importance.

Technological and Legal Developments on the Commodities, Capital, and Employment Markets

The Internet plays a role in both the spiraling increase in demand and the growing pressure for improved technology. For some industries and types of business, such as the media or travel industries, the Internet creates more transparency by means of electronic marketplaces. The number of purchasing options increases vastly along with the widening circles of potential customers and employees. These in turn cause a rise in price and cost pressures, demands for higher quality, and the need for more information. The reduction of legal impediments to trade have functioned in a similar way, for example the liberalization of the telecommunication, air transportation or energy markets, in addition to shorter product lifecycles and greater speed in innovation in many industries, such as the chip, electronic entertainment, or mobile communications industries. At the same time, the Internet offers a rich source of competitive information and opens new vistas for inexpensive, at least partially automated research geared toward external information, as well as simple, worldwide distribution of reports.

Information Overload

As a consequence of the problems and developments outlined above, the individual faces ever-increasing information requirements that in turn create a bottleneck in the form of our limited human capacity for processing information. 49% of 1300 managers questioned by Reuters in Great Britain, the United States, Australia, Hong Kong, and Singapore "very often feel unable to cope with the amounts of information they receive." (Reuters 1996). Another result of the same study showed that 43% of managers are of the opinion that "important decisions are delayed ... due to too much information" and 38% "waste considerable time finding the right information" (Reuters 1996).

1.2 Requirements

Even though many of the problems mentioned are not completely new, no integrated software solution that can be implemented on a company-wide or group-wide basis has been available up to now. To ensure fast and consistent data transfer and retrieval, information systems require both horizontal and vertical integration (see figure 1.1). The requirements for this new integrated solution can be outlined as follows:

1. *Information integration*: Integration of metadata (such as definitions of data fields), master data (such as organizational structures), and transaction data (such as planned and actual values for key figures) for the whole company is a basic requirement. Added to this is the requirement for linking financial and non-financial, as well as quantitative and qualitative facts.

2. *Function integration*: Integration of functions is also essential, for example, to be able to go from a Balanced Scorecard directly to a Performance Measurement or Panning System.

3. *Module integration*: Identical functions are used in different components. For example, the same currency translation function is used in planning, consolidation, and reporting.

4. *Process integration*: The following needs to be coordinated: complex event chains when converting strategic objectives into operational standards, cooperative planning within the framework of enterprise networks, and data collection in decentralized organizational structures. Achieving this requires monitoring and control functions in the sense of a control station or workflow management system.

5. *Global access via the Internet*: Particularly for companies that act internationally, data and functions have to be consistent around the world. Here, Internet technologies in conjunction with enterprise portals offer a cost-effective solution.

6. *Multidimensional structure*: The accounting data has to be displayed in views tailored to all criteria relevant to the organization (OLAP dimensions).

7. *Easy to learn and operate*: Considering the target group – managers and cost accountants – user-friendliness is an especially important factor.

8. *Interpretation models and visualization methods*: Suitable interpretation and visualization methods provide important assistance in making the interdependencies among value drivers and their effects transparent.

9. *Business Content*: Business templates represent a considerable added value, such as alternative key figure definitions and systems in the context of value-based business management.

10. *Personalization*: Individual filter mechanisms, navigation assistance, and instruments for targeted, active information delivery (push technologies) are means of fighting information overload. The basis for this is Business Content (methods and information) that is structured based on typical employee roles.

2   Business Management Background

2.1   Tasks of Strategic and Operational Enterprise Management

The process that starts with strategy development and concludes with strategy realization also contains a series of subtasks (see figure 2.1).

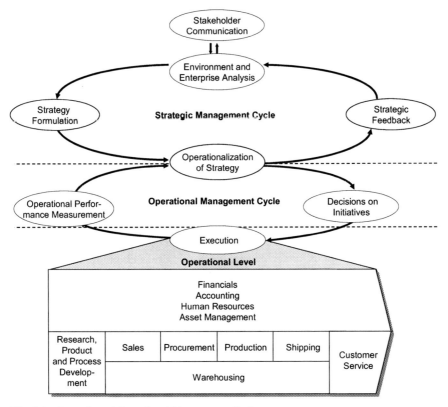

Fig. 2.1: Strategic and Operational Management Cycle

2.1.1   Environment and Enterprise Analysis

Environment analysis and enterprise analysis supply the foundation for the formulation of your strategy. The goal is to obtain a clear picture of your own position relative to the competition. Another name for this is SWOT analysis (Strengths, Weaknesses, Opportunities, Threats Analysis).

The purpose of environment analysis is to detect indications of threats (risks) and openings (opportunities) in the environment external to the company. To make this possible, there is a need for information on trends and the expectations of customers with regard to your products and services, as well as about the expectations of analysts related to financial management. The other side of the coin is enterprise analysis. It places emphasis on evaluating the strengths and weaknesses of your resources, functions, and business processes that are the source of your competitive advantages and disadvantages (Steinmann/Schreyögg 2000, p. 158).

The complexity and dynamics of the analysis fields do not allow us to explore them completely. In order to more systematically select areas to explore, we can divide the external observation areas into environmental sectors, and use the value chain to structure the internal functions (Hungenberg 2000, pp. 73-79) (see figure 2.2).

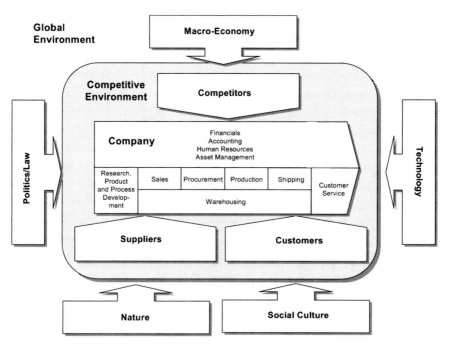

Fig. 2.2: Structuring of External and Internal Observation Areas
(Meier 2000, p. 8)

Global Environment

In the macroeconomic area, financial market data and data on the economic situation are the most relevant. Technological advances influence both the products themselves as well as the manufacturing processes. Frequently, inventions are developed in a different area than that in which the product later finds its principal use. The quartz watch, for example, originated in the aerospace industry. Sociocultural developments – demographic indicators and changes in predominant values – also affect markets. The changed position of women in society, along with related factors such as larger numbers of working women, later marriages, and an increase in divorce rates, have led to greater demand for convenience foods. Nature also has its influence. On the one hand it provides raw materials, but on the other hand the environmental effects of manufacturing processes and products are a significant factor influencing the strategy. In the political and legal realms, this manifests itself in environmental protection legislation. Other legislation such as laws governing taxes, imports and exports, and approval processes for products such as medications are additional parameters defining planning (Steinmann/Schreyögg 2000, pp. 160-169).

Competitive Environment

Analysis of the immediate surroundings, the competitive environment, is extremely important for strategic planning. This analysis is determined by company and product information about and sometimes from competitors, customers, and suppliers. According to Porter, it also makes sense to consider potential market participants and substitute products (Porter 1997, p. 26).

The dividing line between the competitive environment and the global environment is not always clearly drawn. The following terms serve as points of reference: branch of the economy, industry, market, and strategic business activities.

Company

The value chain of the company provides a structured schema for recording and evaluating the resources of the company from a strategic point of view. Not only the hard factors, but also soft factors (intangible assets), such as employee knowledge or market image, play a role in this assessment.

2.1.2 Strategy Formulation

Using the results of the environment analysis and enterprise analysis as a basis, the next tasks are to assess the current strategy, identify logical strategic alternatives, along with their elements and interrelationships, and then to evaluate them. This process should also include a comparison of expectations, target values, and defining impulses of the company as a whole with those of strategic business units and shared service departments.

Strategies are competition-related. That is, they determine the actions of the company in relation to its competitors, taking the forms of imitation, cooperation, dominance, or differentiation, for example. The strategy has considerable influence on the financial position of the company and far-reaching consequences for the commitment of resources. It involves "big" decisions. The term "vision" is also being used more often in this context. But vision usually refers to a more general path of development in the firm. The company's vision has a broader scope than its strategy; in a certain sense the vision has to precede the strategy. An example is the vision of the German telecommunications firm Deutsche Telekom: "From a national network operator to a global service provider" (Steinmann/ Schreyögg 2000, pp. 155-156). In SAP terminology, which leans heavily on the language of the Balanced Scorecard (see section 3.1.6), we understand vision to mean the overall strategy of a company.

Alongside its vision, the company often has a corporate philosophy or a mission statement (also referred to as policies). It helps in orienting the behavior of employees toward partners, and thereby contributes to making the vision a reality (Bea/Haas 2001, pp. 67-69).

The current mission (the current phase in the life cycle of the firm, for instance, start-up, merger, or restructuring) can be another framework for the strategy formulation. SAP uses this term synonymously to the term vision, i.e. as another name for the overall strategy.

In response to the question of how to accomplish a strategic reorientation, business management literature for a long time made reference to forms of creativity and entrepreneurial inspiration that do not allow empirical investigation. What followed was a series of attempts at finding alternatives using universal norm strategies that can be derived from supposed natural laws. Portfolio analysis (see section 3.1.5) may be assigned to this phase. However, it became apparent that it is not really possible to determine strategies using models based on natural phenomena. The rules found in this way often lead only to short-lived success. The answer may be to view norm strategies not as inevitable consequences but as a means of orientation that help to give a structure to a collection of strategic options. This leaves the way open for new, surprising ideas (Steinmann/Schreyögg 2000, pp. 192). Table 2.1 shows a series of classification criteria for norm strategies along with possible characteristic values for them.

Characteristic	Characteristic Values			
Participating Area	Company	Business area		Functional area
Starting Points for Competitive Advantages (Porter)	Cost leadership		Differentiation	
Reach (Porter)	Core market		Niche	
Direction of Development	Growth	Stabilization		Contraction
Product-Market Combinations (Ansoff)	Market penetration	Market development	Product development	Diversification
Regional Participating Area	Local	National	International	Global
Degree of Autonomy	Own resources	Cooperation		Acquisition

Table 2.1: Categories of Strategies (based on Bea/Haas 2001, p. 164)

Participating Area

Corporate strategies involve the highest level of the corporate hierarchy. In large firms, this is normally the parent company or the holding company. The general plan of attack (growth, stabilization, or contraction) originates here. Depending on the business activities in which managers see the most potential for success, they allocate material, personnel, and financial resources accordingly. At business area level, the task is to flesh out the corporate strategy. Business area strategies relating to business functions, such as procurement or production, become more concrete. At this point, the lowest level of strategy selection is reached, which is the interface between strategy and implementation.

Starting Points for Competitive Advantages (Porter)

Porter sees two main competitive options: pricing (cost leadership) and product policies (differentiation). The goal of a cost leadership strategy is to offer products to the market at the lowest cost. This entails rigorous cost reductions. In applying a differentiation strategy, the firm attempts to establish the uniqueness of its products and services, as a basis for charging higher prices. The distinctiveness can be founded on the technical features of the product, for example, or on the design, brand name, customer service, or the retail network.

Reach

In answer to the question of which markets should be served, Porter sees two alternatives: addressing the market for an entire industry (core market), or concentrating on one market segment or niche (Porter 1997, p. 67). A niche strategy concentrates on supplying the specific needs of a very limited consumer segment. Rolls Royce is an example of a firm employing a niche strategy within the automobile market. Within a niche, the company can strive for both product differentiation and cost leadership.

Direction of Development

Growth strategies focus on attaining or further expanding market leadership (see Product-Market Combinations below). The goal of stabilization strategies, on the other hand, is to securely hold on to the current position. Embracing these kinds of defensive strategies can be motivated in different ways. Frequently it is an attempt to gain time in order to prepare for exiting the market, for example, or to better assess the opportunities and risks of new technologies, or to build up strength for new offensives. Contraction strategies are usually a reaction to stagnation or degeneration of an entire industry, or to the company's ongoing adversities. A subform is selective contraction, a mixture of disinvestment and investment politics, whereby the company holds on to profitable niches but gives up unprofitable ones. Market exit barriers play an important role when choosing contraction strategies. These barriers could take the form of the company having strong emotional ties to the business segment, or social obligations to its employees (Bea/Haas 2001, pp. 174-176).

Product-Market Combinations (Ansoff)

The options for growing a company, according to Ansoff, are market penetration, market development, product development, and diversification (Ansoff 1966, p. 132). Using a market penetration strategy, the company aims at increasing its market share with existing products in markets in which it is already present. It attempts to win new customers or increase sales among existing customers. This alternative comes into play primarily in glutted markets, such as the detergent market in Europe. The basic idea behind a market development strategy is the search for new markets for existing products by addressing new target groups or supplying additional regions. The product development strategy introduces new products to existing markets. The replacement of video cassettes with DVD (digital versatile disks) is an example of this strategy. With diversification strategies, the potential for success lies in bringing new products to new markets. There are three types of diversification: horizontal, vertical, and conglomerate. In the case of horizontal diversification, the products are on the same step of the value chain. The aim here is achieving economies of scope by transferring core competencies to other areas. Here an example would be a watchmaker entering the market for time clocks. A vertical diversification strategy relates to prior or following steps in the value chain. An example of backward integration is when a producer of mobile devices sets up its own chip production facilities. Forward integration is when the same producer opens its own retail outlets for its products. The outstanding feature of conglomerate diversification is that there are no relationships between the new and the old markets, as for example an insurance company purchasing shares of a food producing firm. The primary argument in favor of this approach is that it spreads risk (Bea/Haas 2001, pp. 167-168).

Regional Participating Area

At the geographic level, strategies can be classified as local (confined to a town or region), national (countrywide), international (crossing national boundaries), and ultimately global (worldwide).

Degree of Autonomy

The degree of self-sufficiency indicates to what extent the company achieves growth by harnessing its own potential ("autonomy strategies"), as opposed to cooperation or acquisitions. When exploiting its own resources, those most significant to the company are research and development, along with the qualifications of its employees. Cooperation strategies hope to achieve synergistic effects for all participants by promoting cooperation between two or more firms. Depending on the value chain steps involved, cooperation can be classified as either horizontal or vertical. Similar goals are pursued when acquisition strategies are put into practice, except that in this case other companies or shares in other companies are purchased. Compared to the autonomy strategy, the advantage of the acquisition and cooperation strategies is that synergy effects can be realized much sooner. However, this has to be weighed against the considerable risks involved in coordinating and organizing these strategies (Bea/Haas 2001, pp. 171-173).

2.1.3   Operationalization of Strategies

The challenge lies in the operationalization of the strategy, in other words – breaking down the strategic plan into concrete, operational goals and detailed plans for quantities, prices, budgets, etc., for all organizational units, defining responsibilities, and communicating this internally to employees. This could also involve making changes to the current organization. The task of making strategy happen was long disregarded in the fields of business administration and management economics. Now, however, it has gradually come to be recognized that the reason for the failure of many strategies often lies exactly at this level. The goals set by management fulfill the following functions (see Table 2.2):

Function	Explanation
Coordination	Goals help in aligning sub-activities.
Decision-making	Goals supply criteria for evaluating various options for action.
Motivation	Goals should encourage a common identity, a "we" feeling, that motivates employees.
Information	Employees and the company environment are both informed about the intentions of the company.
Control	Goals form the basis for the plan/actual comparison, and thereby represent a yardstick for Performance Measurement.
Legitimation	Goals serve as a justification of actions to stakeholders outside the company. This is indicated by the fact that goals such as "retention of jobs" are often included in annual reports.

Table 2.2: Functions of Enterprise Goals (Bea/Haas 2001, pp. 72-73)

A problem, especially in complex organizations, is the amount of variety in the plans relating to different planning objects. As a result, it seems logical to talk about multidimensional planning. Table 2.3 shows an overview of some of the many possible planning objects:

Characteristic	Characteristic Values				
Basis of Planning	Liquidity	Costs	Revenue	Profit	Inventories
Timeframe	Short-term		Medium-term		Long-term
Resources	Personnel		Materials		Operating funds
Functional Area	Research/ Development	Sales	Procurement	Production	Shipping
Processes	Product launch	Purchase order handling		Order processing	Complaint processing
Products	Divisions	Product groups		Products (variants)	Replacement parts (services)
Regions	Global	Continental areas		Countries	Sales districts

Table 2.3: Examples of Focuses for Planning

Information in the planning process normally flows not only top down, but also bottom up from the lower planning levels upward, resulting in mixed top-down/bottom-up planning. This engenders problems in coordination, intensified by interdependencies among the operational subplans.

Planning lays the groundwork for making the decisions that should enable the firm to reach its goals, such as what measures to take and how to distribute resources like capital investments, or increases or reductions in personnel. This also includes training programs that help to develop the competencies needed for making the strategy a reality. These activities are usually accompanied by the specification of fixed budgets.

The practice of setting up fixed budgets is currently the subject of very critical discussions. The disadvantage of fixed budgets is that they impede quick reactions to changes in the market. As part of a "beyond budgeting initiative" a large number of concerns are taking part in the development of alternative instruments for operationalizing strategies. With this new approach, control should be more decentralized, and it should give more weight to performance while not limiting its orientation just to financial figures. Key words in connection with this initiative include self-controlling networks or resources on demand (Fraser 2001).

2.1.4   Strategy Execution

During the execution phase, the initiatives that have been specified are resolutely carried out. Strictly speaking, this area is not really a part of enterprise management but it is closely linked with planning and Performance Measurement. Business processes are largely handled with the help of transaction systems, which at the same time supply the basic actual data. The values gathered in this way are analyzed as part of operational Performance Measurement or strategic feedback.

2.1.5 Operational Performance Measurement

In order to recognize critical developments early enough, and enable management to react quickly, timely Performance Measurement is needed. Here, the emphasis is placed on cost-revenue control and budget control. The aim is to assess how effective the measures were.

The assessment relies on financial and non-financial key figures from both internal and external sources. Measurements that have an indispensable role for performance in certain areas, such as Customer Relationship Management or Supply Chain Management, are referred to as *key performance indicators* (KPI).

The causes of any deviations and their effects have to be analyzed carefully. The initial question to be answered is whether the goals can still be reached by employing additional or changed initiatives at the operational level. In other words, the original strategy remains in place but the firm tries other means of fulfilling its objectives. The central question is: "Are we doing things right?" This is also known as single loop learning.

2.1.6 Strategic Feedback

Performance Measurement (or control) is usually depicted as the last phase. However, this way of looking at things is not applicable to strategic management. Since planning begins by setting premises in order to structure the decision-making field, a large number of possible situations are removed from consideration. This is not done without a certain risk. Strategic Performance Measurement should therefore offset the selectivity that results from planning (Steinmann/Schreyögg 2000, pp. 247-248). In this context, the terms "strategic learning" or "double loop learning" are commonly heard.

Even if target and actual values largely coincide, changes in the basic conditions on which planning is based can cause the strategy to become obsolete in the long-term. The purpose of the feedback process, therefore, is to find out if the strategic objectives are still valid. In contrast to the question posed by operational Performance Measurement, strategic feedback asks: "Are we doing the right things?"

In a company in which there is a danger of plans being frequently revised – for example, because of a change on the executive board – a plan/plan comparison may also be recommended. This comparison shows how the revised plans differ from the original plans.

It is possible to distinguish between two different levels of comparison. A premise check starts with the assumptions made and attempts to determine if they were made incorrectly. Strategic monitoring, on the other hand, acts as a kind of global safety net. It takes into account the fact that there can be a large number of critical events that were not recognized when the premises were laid out. Figure 2.3 shows a summarized classification of the types of Performance Measurement.

Type of Performance Measurement / Characteristics	Strategic Feedback		Operational Performance Measurement
	Strategic Monitoring	Premise Check	
Sharpness of Focus	Little	Medium	High
Related to	Envionment/ Resources	Planning Premises	Planned Activities

Fig. 2.3: Types of Performance Measurement (based on Steinmann/Schreyögg 2000, p. 248)

All employees involved in strategy realization should participate in assessing and reporting on the strategies, offering their judgments and comments about the current results and future expectations.

2.1.7   Communication with Stakeholders

The fate of a company is not solely determined by the general conditions affecting it; nor are firms autonomous decision-making bodies that are limited only by their own resources. Large corporations particularly, in opening themselves to bidirectional communication with stakeholders, such as investors, customers, suppliers, competitors, trade unions, governments, etc., allow stakeholders the opportunity to influence the company's decisions. Good, stable relationships with stakeholder groups thereby represent an important intangible value.

Various studies also support the thesis that information and communication policies toward stakeholders influence the valuation of the company in capital markets. Active and transparent information policies, along with the use of internationally recognized accounting principles, are generally rewarded with higher valuation (Hostettler 2000, pp. 29-30).

2.2   Value-Based Management

The focus of value-based management is on the capital market driven returns earned by the shareholders of the company over the long term. The literature contains frequent references to the fact that before satisfying shareholders' demands for profit, you first have to satisfy the contractual claims of other groups. Criticism of the classic profit figures stemming from the annual financial statement, such as sales or return on investment (ROI), is the source of another prime motivation for value-based management. Perceived problems with these figures include their orientation toward the past and the potential for manipulation.

The value-based approach gained particular popularity though the book *Creating Shareholder Value* by Alfred Rappaport (Rappaport 1999).

Since then, "shareholder value" has become a term that is often interpreted differently by different groups in actual practice, and which has come to contain certain fashionable aspects. In recent years, managers and financial analysts have been confronted with a veritable flood of new concepts, figures, and terms related to value-based management. Management consultancies in particular developed a series of procedures for measuring added value. Rappaport himself focused on *discounted cash flow* (DCF); *economic value added* (EVA®) originates from the consulting firm of Stern Stewart; *economic profit* (EP) comes from McKinsey; the Boston Consulting Group (BCG) propagated the term *cash value added* (CVA) and the related *cash flow return on investment* (CFROI) (Ballwieser 2000, pp. 160-161). The origins of these models, as well as their relationships to each other, are frequently unclear. For the sake of clarity, two dimensions should be clearly delineated from each other: shareholder value as a financial figure on the one hand, and as a maxim for action on the other hand (Hostettler 2000, pp. 22-31).

As a financial measurement figure, shareholder value describes the benefits the shareholder enjoys, and is defined as the present value of all of the investor's future net income. From the point of view of the shareholder, economic profit (as opposed to accounting profit) is not attained until a certain minimum interest is earned on the invested capital (in the sense of opportunity costs). The situation can thereby arise that, despite accounting profits, the investor nonetheless experiences a loss as seen from this viewpoint (Bühner/Weinberger 1991).

Capital is seen as a constraining factor. It is essential to consider the timing of payments and the resulting effects of inflation, along with the cost of capital. The difference between the actual and the approximately determined fair share price (target share price) is referred to as the value gap. This makes it possible to determine whether the corporation is overvalued or undervalued. These estimates form an important parameter during strategy formulation. The calculation can be made in one of the following ways:

1. Number of shares multiplied by the market price (market capitalization)

2. Calculation based on the discounted payment surplus according to the DCF method (see Rappaport's approach)

3. Calculation as excess operating profit (residual net profit) (see approaches of Stewart (EVA), Copeland et al. (EP) and Lewis (CVA/ CFROI))

Using the third option, excess operating profit is the amount in excess of the cost of capital. The following elements are needed to calculate this figure:

1. Amount of profit

2. Amount of capital

3. Capital cost rate

Profit is normally the operating profit from the income statement, excluding non-operational elements. Capital is determined from assets shown in the balance sheet. The capital cost rate reflects the weighted, average earnings owed to outside investors (creditors) and providers of equity (taking opportunity costs into account) (Hostettler 2000, pp. 45-46).

When the shareholder value approach is taken as a maxim for actions, the intention is to align the objectives of the firm with the interests of the shareholders. Measures for increasing corporate value, beyond the level of simple growth in sales or profits, become of central importance.

According to Rappaport, shareholder value can be influenced in three areas with lasting effect:

1. *Operational decisions* that influence operational performance. Examples are pricing or the scope of customer services.

2. *Investment or disinvestment decisions* that are reflected on the assets side of the balance sheet. These affect both fixed and current assets. Along with purchases of machinery, this also includes increases in inventory turnover or a reduction in time allowed for customers to pay.

3. *Financing decisions* that influence the liabilities side of the balance sheet, that is, the relationship between external capital and equity. This primarily involves the sources of capital or the financing instruments used, as well as the shaping of the legal structure of the company.

Each of these decision categories has its affect on various financial figures that can be summarized in value-based key figures. Problems are caused not so much by the calculations as by the different, to some extent subjective, definitions of the basic elements: profit, capital, and capital cost rate (Hostettler 2000, pp. 23-30).

An additional parameter that intermittently has a very strong influence on shareholder value is the volatility of share prices. It is included in the calculation of capital costs in form of the beta (β) factor (comparison of the fluctuation of a share in relation to the market as a whole). As β decreases, capital costs are reduced and the corporate value rises. Measures that can reduce the volatility of the share include:

1. Continuous growth in profit

2. Early and extensive information for stakeholders (see section 2.3)

3. Efficient risk management, also communicated externally

In the following, we briefly explain some of the best-known concepts related to shareholder value and compare them with one another.

Shareholder Value Approach According to Rappaport

Shareholder value according to Rappaport is calculated using the following formula:

> Shareholder Value = Corporate value − External capital; where:
>
> Corporate value = Present value of operational cash flows
> during the forecast period
> + Residual value
> + Market value of negotiable securities

The basic elements of the corporate value are the operating cash flows, capital costs (due to discounting), the length of the forecast period, and the residual value (see below). Future operating cash flows are planned using value drivers. Rappaport sees the following value drivers:

> Cash Flow = Cash inflows − Cash outflows
> = [(Previous year's sales) x (1 + Growth rate of sales)
> x (Operational profit margin)
> x (1 − Average corporate profits tax rate)]
> − Additional investments in fixed and current assets

These are independent of the industry and type of business, and are therefore classified as generic value drivers (Rappaport 1999, pp. 39-41). They can be augmented by business-specific value drivers that are particular to a given firm. Using both together provides plannable, operational key figures. The tree diagram (figure 2.4) helps in visualizing the relationships between value drivers (which can also be qualitative) and key figures.

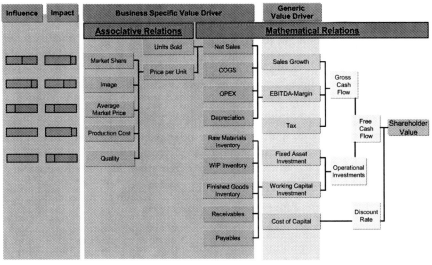

COGS: Costs of Goods Sold, OPEX: Operating Expenditure,
EBITDA: Eearnings Before Interest, Tax, Depreciation, Amortization

Fig. 2.4: Generic and Business-Specific Value Drivers © SAP AG

The figures (value drivers) that merit the most consideration are those over which the company has a large degree of control (influence) and which greatly influence the corporate value (effect).

The capital cost, with which operating cash flows are discounted, is determined by the weighted average cost of capital approach (WACC approach). This method weights the costs of equity and external investment capital according to the relationship of their market values. The problem here is that the market value of equity is the net corporate value, which is not calculated until the DCF method is applied. To avoid this problem, the book values of equity and investment capital may be used rather than their market values. Another solution, which is also proposed by Rappaport and which conforms more closely to a payment-oriented valuation methodology, is to weight capital costs in accordance with the planned target capital structure. A third option would be to use an iterative calculation. The cost of investment capital is based on one of the following: an average value, the actual interest the firm has to pay, or the average market interest rate. The cost of equity capital is calculated by adding a risk premium to the interest rate for a risk-free investment in the capital market. This risk premium is determined using the capital asset pricing model (CAPM) (Pape 2004, pp. 105-112). The example in figure 2.5 depicts these relationships. The market-specific risk premium is the difference between the average annual increase in value of the entire market, less the yield from risk-free investments.

The residual value is equal to the present value of the operating cash flow after the planning period, which normally is a period of five to ten years. Depending on the assumptions on which the calculation is based, it is either a liquidation value or a continuation value. When making this determination, it is assumed that it is no longer possible to earn above-average yields due to erosion of competitive advantages. The arrival of other competitors on the market allows just the capital costs to be earned. This means that at the free cash flow level of the last planning year, a permanent ordinary annuity can be calculated (Küting/Heiden 2000, pp. 30-31).

The key figure, shareholder value added (SVA), indicates the change in the shareholder value. The SVA is calculated in order to evaluate enterprise strategies, on the one hand, and in that case it relates to the complete planning horizon. On the other hand, it also acts as an indicator for Performance Measurement, in which case it is only determined for one period.

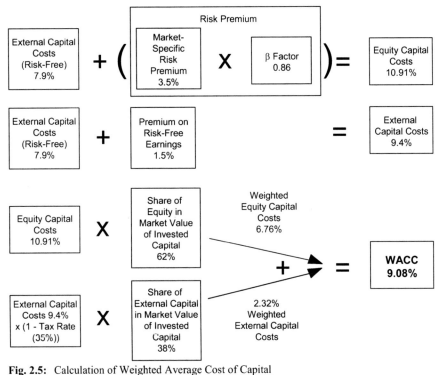

Fig. 2.5: Calculation of Weighted Average Cost of Capital
(based on Black/Wright 1998, p. 60)

Economic Value Added Approach According to Stewart

EVA is an absolute financial figure, like profit or cash flow, that is calculated annually. The formula for this calculation (in the capital charge version) is:

$$EVA = NOPAT - (NOA \times c^*)$$

Net operating profit after taxes (NOPAT) is based on accounting data, which is freed from financial, tax and valuation distortions in a series of calculations. Capital costs are determined by multiplying net operating assets (NOA) by the percentage capital cost rate, c^*. The balance sheet assets are the basis for determining the NOA. Using various adjustments, these values are converted into the market value of the invested capital. Capital costs are then calculated, as with Rappaport, using the WACC approach.

Strategy-specific EVAs are useful in assessing strategies. A positive EVA points to an increase in value, while a negative EVA indicates reduction. The overall value of the firm is calculated as the sum of the present values of the forecasted operating EVAs within the designated planning time period.

The market value added (MVA) acts as a comparison value to the mathematical corporate value, and as a measure of planning and control over multiple periods.

The MVA is calculated as the difference between the overall corporate value and the invested capital (Pape 1999, pp. 129-130).

Economic Profit Approach According to Copeland, Koller and Murrin

The concept put forward by Copeland, Koller and Murrin of McKinsey states that equity value, which corresponds to the stock market value of the company, is instrumental in evaluating the strategy. The central value in this Performance Measurement is EP, which expresses the increase in value by period. Economic profit is determined by multiplying invested capital by the difference between return on invested capital (ROIC) and the WACC. Here, ROIC is the measure for the return on investment.

> **Economic Profit = Invested Capital x (ROIC – WACC)**

Free cash flows, which are indirectly derived on the basis of budgeted financial statements, are discounted. In addition, the following are added: net operating profit less adjusted taxes (NOPLAT) and expenses not affecting payments. Investments in fixed assets and net current assets are deducted. Or free cash flows can be determined using value drivers (Copeland/Koller 1998, p. 199). In this case, the capital costs of the company are also determined using the WACC approach with the target capital structure as a weighting factor. The residual value after the explicit planning time period is calculated either as a liquidation value or a continuation value. In the case of continuation, Copeland et al. take future growth into account by including a growth rate in the perpetual bond formula.

Cash Flow Return on Investment Approach According to Lewis

CFROI serves as a central yardstick in evaluating individual strategies and business areas. Along the lines of a key figure for yield, the CFROI calculates the average interest earned on the entire invested capital at a given point in time. Unlike the other methods, which are oriented toward the capital value method, CFROI is calculated using the internal rate of return method.

The following elements form the basis of Lewis' approach: gross cash flow as a periodic profit figure, the gross investment basis (acquisition costs of assets) for the amount of capital, the useful life of fixed assets, and the net book value of non-depreciable assets at the end of their useful life. The CFROI is compared with the average overall capital costs of the firm with the effects of taxes and inflation removed. Lewis rejects the idea of calculating capital costs using CAPM. Instead, he derives the equity costs adjusted to risk empirically by using a stock portfolio.

Cash value added (CVA), as an absolute periodic profit figure, is used for Performance Measurement. It is the result of multiplying the difference between CFROI and the average capital costs of the period by the gross investment basis. A positive CVA points to an increase in value, while a negative CVA indicates a reduction.

> **CVA = (CFROI – WACC) * Gross Investment Basis**

Summary and Critique

These concepts all share the fact that they are based on dynamic investment calculation procedures and that they include the expectations of the investor in the valuation logic. Their differences lie in the valuation methods used as well as in the elements considered part of the company's value. Some of the key figures determined for measuring performance are absolute, while others are relative. EP is an absolute figure, to which ROIC, as a percentage value, is added. EVA is also an absolute value. SVA (per period), according to Rappaport, however, is an absolute difference amount. CFROI, on the other hand, is a percentage value related to periodic Performance Measurement, but also complemented by the CVA as an absolute key figure (Pape 1999, p. 125). Table 2.4 compares the different approaches in summarized form.

	Rappaport's Approach	EVA Approach of Stewart	EP Approach of Copeland et al.	CFROI Approach of Lewis
Central Profit Figure	Operational Cash Flow	EVA	Free Cash Flow	Gross Cash Flow
Basis of Valuation	Payment values	Book values	Book values (possibly market values)	Book value, inflated
Periods Considered	Multiple periods	One period	One period	Multiple periods
Future Strategy Planning	SHV	MVA	Equity value	Market value of shareholder interest
Retrospective Performance Measurement	SVA	EVA	EP	CVA
Capital Costs	WACC with target capital structure and CAPM	WACC with target capital structure and CAPM	WACC with target capital structure and CAPM	Average capital costs (stock portfolio)
Determination of Residual Value	Perpetual bond or liquidation value	Perpetual bond (continuation value)	Perpetual bond with growth or liquidation value	Sum of non-depreciable assets

Table 2.4: Comparison of Value-Based Approaches
(based on Hostettler 1997, p. 78 and Pape 1999, p.133)

Looking at the table, it becomes apparent that there are many parallels in the different approaches. For example, each method uses a key figure that is designed for measuring profit (SVA, EVA, EP, CVA).

The uses of value-based management are twofold: first, to judge the continuous success of an individual company (or a group or sub-area) while simultaneously assessing the performance of management retrospectively; second, to evaluate the future perspectives of alternative strategies or projects, in the sense of opportunities for investment. This is done by considering control figures that are uniform for all areas of the company or group. Not only that, but trying to link value-based figures to remuneration should increase the motivation of all managers and employees. Finally, a value-based controlling system is compatible with internationally recognized accounting standards such as Generally Accepted Accounting Principles in the United States (US GAAP) or International Accounting Standards (IAS).

In recent years, many organizations have adopted these concepts related to assets, profit, and earnings. However, it is conspicuous that these concepts are usually not adopted in their entirety. Not just the large number of different definitions of the term *cash flow* has contributed to the widely held view that these models are often too complex, time-consuming, and impracticable (Hostettler 2000, p. 3). Many corporations still place a high value on key figures based on the balance sheet, which are precisely the values Rappaport criticizes. DaimlerChrysler, for example, controls its industry business areas using return on net assets (RONA). This is calculated by dividing operating profit (before taxes according to US GAAP) by net assets (from the balance sheet) (Ballwieser 2000, pp. 160-161).

The advantages of DCF concepts are found in their analysis of long-term questions and in the formulation of strategies. Procedures based on residual net profit, such as EVA and CVA, on the other hand, are stronger in solving problems that are more short-term, and in assessing operational tasks. They are also easier to implement. Therefore it seems advisable for firms not to depend too much on one variant. Instead, they should calculate a number of value-based key figures (Küting/Heiden 2000, p. 37).

Compared to the other concepts, the shareholder value approach promulgated by Rappaport has the advantage of being close to actual practice in its orientation, while also being comparatively easy to employ (Bühner 1996, S. 392). One of the main features of the method of Copeland, Koller and Murrin is that it can be employed quite well by externals, since free cash flows can be determined on the basis of the profit and loss statement. According to the literature, it is also relatively easy to implement the EVA approach. However, certain inconsistencies in the method during value determination are viewed more critically (Schneider 1998, p. 1476).

All of the classic concepts discussed here are unable to take into account the exact point in time at which shareholders invest or disinvest capital on the stock market. For this reason, they can only have a limited significance for investors. The total shareholder return (TSR) method tries to address this problem. Precisely in the area of effective communication with shareholders, TSR is becoming more and more important. For more information, refer to (VBM Resources Center 2002), for example.

2.3   Stakeholder Approach

The stakeholder approach, which takes into consideration the interests of all parties having some claim on the company, is the opposite pole from the shareholder approach. The term *stakeholder* was introduced in strategic management by Freeman in the early 1960's. For Freeman, stakeholders are the people, groups, and institutions, both internal and external, that have a well-founded and clearly articulated interest with regard to the company in the form of claims or obligations. Therefore, they can either actively influence the decisions of management or are passively influenced by the actions of the management (Freeman 1984, p. 46). He argues that the one-sided orientation of the shareholder value approach toward the interests of investors is too limited. Table 2.5 compares these two schools of thought.

Criteria	Shareholder Approach	Stakeholder Approach
Relevant Entitlement Groups	Investors	All stakeholders
Goals	Maximizing benefits of investors	Maximizing benefits of all stakeholders
Targeted Amounts	Gross corporate value (market value of total capital)	Quantified benefits through benefits analysis
Level of Analysis	Enterprise as a whole, enterprise areas	Enterprise as a whole

Table 2.5: Shareholder versus Stakeholder Approach (based on Pape 1999, p. 143)

The ties between management and the various stakeholders differ in type and intensity. The relationship to long-term investors, for example, is very different from that to protest groups, who try to address a special environmental problem with ad hoc demands, petitions, and threats. There are also a series of legal restrictions that more closely govern the interaction between the firm and the various stakeholders. In Germany, for example, there are a series of laws, including one controlling the transparency in corporations (see section 2.5). Other laws include labor legislation, employee co-determination, or disclosure laws (Steinmann/Schreyögg 2000, pp. 75-76).

According to the stakeholder approach, the interests of the stakeholders always have to be considered as a factor when formulating strategies and when putting operational measures into practice. Stakeholder analysis can follow these phases, for example (see table 2.6).

Phase	Tasks
Scanning	Identification of stakeholders
Monitoring	Recognition of intentions and the instruments used to achieve them
Forecasting	Examination of potential threats using methods such as scenario analysis and surveys of experts
Assessment	Evaluation of the results of scanning, monitoring and forecasting, with the goal of determining how to meet the risks/opportunities

Table 2.6: Phases of Stakeholder Analysis (based on Bea/Haas 2001, pp. 103-104)

The complex relationships can be categorized and prioritized in light of their potential for influence using the roles listed in table 2.7.

Role	Characteristics
Affected Groups	Power over management and the determination to exercise it are extremely limited; examples are churches or universities.
Interest Groups	More intense determination to exercise power, but at the same time the company is less dependent on them; examples are customers in monopolistic or oligopolistic market structures.
Strategic Stakeholders	Have the will and effective power (sanctions) to influence company goals and activities; examples are trade unions or financial analysts.

Table 2.7: Classification of Stakeholders by Potential to Influence
           (based on Janisch 1993, pp. 126-128)

2.4   Customer Relationship Management

One of the most important stakeholder groups for companies is their customers. Sinzig points out that customer relationship management (CRM) can be more significant than internal accounting for products, when he cites Paul Riebel: "Products come and go; customer relationships stay" (Sinzig 2001a).

The aim of CRM is to identify, among the range of potential consumers, those who are likely to provide the largest contribution to the success of the company, and to build up lasting relationships with those customers. One goal is prevent the most profitable customers from churning to the competition. CRM is directed toward increasing the overall value of customer relationships. With this in mind, individual and personal communication with the customer is important, on the one hand, since it is intended to inspire the customer to make more purchases. On the other hand, the aim is to focus the resources in marketing, sales, and customer service departments in such a way as to increase the return on customer relationship (RCR). Somewhat analogous to ROI, return on customer relationship is considered to be the profit that the company earns through the customer in relation to the amount invested in building up the customer relationship. In practice, these costs fall under the category of overhead for the most part, so that it is difficult to make a precise calculation. The exactness of the calculation can be improved by combining Activity-Based Costing (see section 3.3.1) with contribution margin calculations (see section 3.2.2).

The general aim of CRM is to provide procedures suitable for discovering tendencies in customer behavior and that also enable firms to determine customer value along with the factors influencing it. The following are some of CRM's most important goals:

1. *Higher market penetration* by wooing new and profitable customers

2. *Securing the relationships* to the most important regular customers

3. *Building relationships* through a targeted increase in profitability. Effective measures here include increasing the share of profit – and thereby the share of customer potential (share of wallet) – or recognizing options for cross-selling. An example would be selling accessories or more valuable products (up-selling) to existing customers.

In order to reach these goals, companies have to be able to answer questions such as the following:

Higher market penetration
   a)   What type of customers would you like to win over?
   b)   What type of customers will drive future growth?
   c)   What new customers might be interested in the products?

Securing relationships
   a)   Which customers would you like to retain?
   b)   Which customers will bring the largest block of profits?
   c)   Which customers are likely to churn to competitors?
   d)   Which customers are dissatisfied with products and services?

Building relationships
   a)   With which customers is it possible to increase sales and/or profits?
   b)   Which products are usually purchased together?
   c)   What cross-selling opportunities are available?

To answer these questions, you need a comprehensive and consistent customer knowledge base that provides all relevant information to employees who plan campaigns and have direct customer contacts.

In keeping with the nature of CRM, the main emphasis lies on gathering key figures from the sales sector (including marketing) and customer service, and then considering this data in an integrated form. Once an integrated information system is in place, it is relatively easy, as well as interesting, to view information on progress and setbacks with customers with whom the firm has had relationships over different periods of time. In this way, it is possible to assess how successful the company has been with new customers, or how many customers have defected in the recent past.

To be able to decide in which customer relationships the firm should make a higher or lower investment, integrated information processing is needed to determine customer value. Contribution margin II (contribution margin I less direct customer costs) can be especially helpful in this context. This information can be supplemented by the results of Activity-Based Costing, like expenses involved in the complaint process (Mertens/Griese 2002).

Although customer retention rate, and its counterpart customer churn rate, possess general validity for the sales sector, they also play a significant role particularly in CRM (Knauer 1999). The retention rate indicates the percentage of business partners at the end of a period who were customers at the beginning of the period.

Since CRM encourages companies to base their organizational structure on customers and customer groups (such as through key account management), the results of cost center accounting can be utilized as well.

2.5   Risk Management

A risk is the possibility that desired results will not be achieved, or that unexpected effects will be experienced instead (Laitko 1999). In the case of business decisions, risk is understood to be events that have a strong effect on the target system of the company (Gerke/Bank 2003). If there are a number of factors subject to risk, simply adding up all the risks does not reflect the situation. Much more important is their correlation: whether the overall effect is greater than, less than, or the same as the sum of individual risks.

Laws such as the 1998 German law regarding control and transparency in corporations (KonTraG) place special demands on planning and risk management. According to this law, the executive board is required to take suitable measures to set up a monitoring system to ensure that developments that threaten the continued operation of the company are recognized early enough. Information processing is therefore confronted with the task of helping to anticipate possible changes in the environment and their effects on the success of the company. Risks such as market slumps or procurement bottlenecks have to be analyzed with regard to their likelihood and potential harmful effects. To substantiate the relevance of a risk, risk management requires at least a rudimentary hierarchy of goals that can be documented in a Balanced Scorecard. Then the attempt is made to examine how risks affect different key figures. The steps in the risk management process are outlined in table 2.8 (Bitz 2000).

It is also possible to categorize areas of risk according to criteria such as problem categories representing possible causes of bankruptcy (liquidity risks and profitability risks), or by origin (global effects, market changes, etc.) or by their position in the value chain (see table 2.9).

Phase	Activities
Risk Identification	a) Record potential risks for all business units b) Store them in a company-wide risk catalog c) Categorize risks and enter their detailed description
Risk Analysis and Risk Assessment	a) Focus on relevant risks per business unit b) Quantify affects of risks on targets and key figures
Risk Handling	a) Control risks by taking measures for avoiding, reducing or transferring risks b) Observe the overall risk situation before and after risk measures
Risk Controlling	a) Continuously monitor early risk indicators b) Record effects on key figures, goals, and strategies c) Risk manager makes decisions supported by the system d) Describe risk situation graphically and textually e) Adjust risk measures

Table 2.8: Phases and Activities of Risk Management

Function	Example Risks
Research and Development (Product and Processes)	Failed experiments, legal/political risks (such as curtailment of genetic research), late replacement of old product, rejected patent requests
Sales	Price crash, decline in sales
Procurement	Price increases, supplier problems
Warehousing	Obsolescence, shrinkage
Production	Machinery malfunctions, ill-chosen technologies, accidents
Shipping	Lateness, incorrect deliveries, contractual penalties
Customer Service	Warranty demands, recalls
Financials	Reduction in value of shares in other companies, changes in interest, currency fluctuations, liquidity risks
Accounting	Miscalculations, inadequate reserves
Personnel	Lack of suitable candidates, costs of severance
Asset Management	Fire, flooding, theft

Table 2.9: Examples of Risks by Functional Area

Various concepts first developed in the banking sector have emerged for measuring the threat from these areas. Büschgen and Schierenbeck, for example, provide a detailed overview of these concepts (Büschgen 1999; Schierenbeck 2001).

The critical factor in these approaches is always the determination of the margin of fluctuation (for example, of market prices, interest, or currency exchange rates). The fluctuation margins can either be calculated from historical data, or else the decision-maker has to make an estimation. At the level of individual risk, it is possible to use the following formula:

> **Amount of Risk = Potential Amount of Damage x Probability of Occurrence**

This calculation is often used in risk literature, but putting it into practice proves to be difficult when individual risks are aggregated hierarchically. Based on SAP's experience, it is also problematic for many firms to estimate these parameters. SAP therefore implemented the following procedure: Only the expected value of the probability function for the deviation of a key figure from its planned value is watched. This method works without entering an explicit probability, since the expected value, by definition, is the sum of the values of the random variable, weighted according to their probability. This means, for instance, there could be an expected value of 12 million dollars for a drop in sales for product A1 and 18 million dollars for product A2. As a result, the overall risk amount for product group A would be 30 million dollars.

The *value at risk'* (VaR) concept, which was later extended to include key figures such as cash flow or equity, also arose in the banking sector. VaR indicates (with a probability of approximately 95%) what level of loss resulting from a risk factor, such as an investment in shares, will not be exceeded. In other words, VaR specifies the absolute monetary amount that has to be set aside in order to absorb this loss with a given certainty, in this example 95%. If this concept is applied to the equity of a company, it is possible to use it to determine the amount of equity necessary to hold the probability of bankruptcy below x%.

Capital market theory also provides key risk figures such as the beta factor of a (subsidiary) company, if the corporation is interpreted as the portfolio of its shares in its subsidiaries. The beta factor measures the volatility of the returns of individual investments relative to the returns of a comparative portfolio. It serves as a means of estimating the risk of the overall corporation. It is calculated using this formula:

> **Beta factor = Covariance of Company and Market Return / Variance of Market Return**

The covariance is the measure for the relationship or independence between two random variables. The variance, on the other hand, shows how much the value of a random variable deviates from a mean. The beta factor thereby indicates by how many percentage points the value of a company fluctuates when the value of the whole market changes by one percentage point. Using this basis, it is possible to formulate risk-adequate minimum interest rates for equity. If a subsidiary has highly volatile returns (high beta factor), then this business area places higher demands on profitability. The risk manager has a number of different options at his disposal for controlling the risk (see table 2.10):

Type of Measure	Example
Risk Avoidance	Withdraw from high-risk areas, choose own local currency for contracts
Risk Reduction	Credit checks, gathering information, interest rate guarantees
Risk Sharing	Participation in cooperative development projects, coverage by government securities or bank guarantees
Risk Offsetting	Higher mark-up for high-risk business activities, customers, or countries
Risk Diversification	Regional diversification, various industry branches, supplying multiple, independent customers rather than one major customer
Risk Limitation	Upper limits for receivables per customer, limits for open currency exchange items
Risk Compensation	Making countertrade agreements with the opposite currency direction, e.g. purchases in US $ currency when a firm has strong dependence on the US $ region as sales market
Risk Redistribution	Insuring operational risk, exports insurance

Table 2.10: Examples of Measures for Handling Risks

Particularly for financial risks, there are systems that are strongly quantitative in their orientation. However, these do not lend themselves to application in the company as a whole, especially if all potential interactions among the various risk factors should be included. For this reason, risk portfolios offer graphical visualization that provides valuable assistance in identifying the areas that are most in need of management's attention.

3 Business Management Instruments

3.1 Instruments for Strategic Enterprise Management

3.1.1 Enterprise and Competition Analysis

The analysis of the firm has the objective of determining a capability profile that depicts the relative competitive strength of the firm. The value chain (see figure 3.1) is often used for structuring the internal areas for analysis. Porter distinguishes between primary activities, which are directly related to production and the sale of products, and secondary activities, which support the primary activities. Competitive advantages arise if a firm is able to conduct individual activities more efficiently than its competitors.

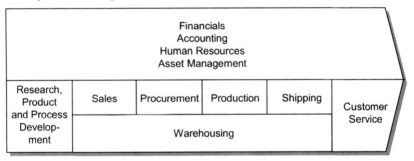

Fig. 3.1: Value Chain (based on Mertens 2004, p. 7 and Porter 2000, p. 62, see figure 1.1)

One problem with this concept is that it is heavily oriented toward functions, and therefore does not provide a suitable basis for a multidimensional consideration of values.

The performance of competitors serves as a yardstick for evaluating the strengths and weaknesses of a company. When looking at competitors, it is not only their current behavior that is significant. More important, in fact, are forecasts of future behavior. Comparing the profiles of your firm with those of the others in the same field provides insights into your position (see figure 3.2). Although the amount of disclosure has increased considerably in recent years, gathering relevant information is still a significant problem in analyzing the competition.

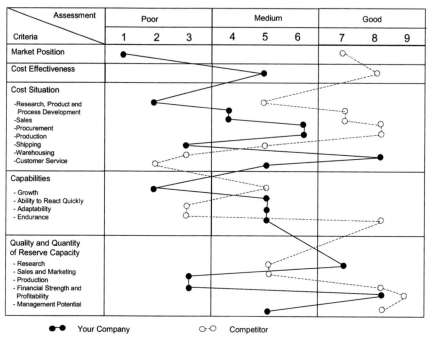

Assessment / Criteria	Poor			Medium			Good		
	1	2	3	4	5	6	7	8	9
Market Position									
Cost Effectiveness									
Cost Situation									
-Research, Product and Process Development									
-Sales									
-Procurement									
-Production									
-Shipping									
-Warehousing									
-Customer Service									
Capabilities									
- Growth									
- Ability to React Quickly									
- Adaptability									
- Endurance									
Quality and Quantity of Reserve Capacity									
- Research									
- Sales and Marketing									
- Production									
- Financial Strength and Profitability									
- Management Potential									

●—● Your Company   ○—○ Competitor

Fig. 3.2: Strengths/Weaknesses Profiles of Two Competitors
(based on ZVEI 1993, p. 48)

3.1.2 Benchmarking

Benchmarking is closely related to the analysis of competitors. By continuously comparing products, services, processes, and methods with those of other businesses, benchmarking attempts to ascertain the performance gap separating the firm from the "best in class." At the same time, it should help to find ways of reducing this performance gap. The central figures here are productivity figures, turnaround times, costs, and quality. Benchmarking is not limited just to competitors. The following variants have been identified:

Internal benchmarking: Internal benchmarking compares functions and areas within the company. Data collection in this case is relatively simple. However, there is a danger of organizational blindness.

Benchmarking of competitors: Here the comparison is made with the strongest competitors. Usually it is extremely difficult to obtain the necessary data about the competition. In addition, limiting benchmarking to a particular branch or market can sometimes make it impossible to identify world class performers. This puts the company in danger of simply copying methods or processes within a branch of industry, thereby merely gaining equal footing with competitors rather than surpassing them.

General benchmarking: General benchmarking lifts the focus from an individual industry and instead seeks out top performers in all segments of the economy. Gathering data in this case is usually less difficult than for benchmarking of competitors. However, identifying suitable objects for comparison can be problematic.

3.1.3 Early Warning Systems

Early warning systems are commonly based on the *weak signal* concept of Ansoff. He puts forward the thesis that no event occurs completely without warning, since discontinuities are hinted at by vague information before they actually occur. An example would be increasing environmental awareness that is reflected later in changed legislation, making certain investments unprofitable. These systems are therefore intended to sound the alarm when parameters in the firm's surroundings change significantly. This early information should give users the chance to take preventive measures in order to fend off or reduce the effects of signaled threats. Table 3.1 shows examples of some discontinuities in recent years and decades.

Areas	Discontinuities
Politics	• Expansion of the European Union • Social revolutions (Iran, the Eastern Bloc, Ethiopia) • Rise of Green parties in Western Europe
Economy	• Opening of Eastern European markets • Insolvency of developing countries • Legal restrictions of free market access (e.g. Japan and USA: automobiles) • Introduction of the euro
Ecology	• Increase in toxic chemicals • Environmental catastrophes (e.g. Chernobyl, various oil tankers)
Technology	• DRAM chip technology • Artificial intelligence • Internet
Cognitive Orientation	• Change in attitudes (post-materialistic values) in western industrialized countries • Growing fundamentalism in the Arab world

Table 3.1: Discontinuities Catalog (based on Macharzina 2003)

It is apparent, therefore, that not only hard figures are involved, but also soft indicators. The hard and soft factors influence each other. For example, a higher average age in the population might influence the values of a society, or a political change can alter overall economic development.

3.1.4 Scenario Analysis

Scenario analysis consciously attempts to draft various scenarios relating to the future. Starting from the current situation, it examines how possible constellations originate. In this effort, various plausibly related chains of external events are constructed. This is often represented using cones, where the trend scenario forms the center (see figure 3.3).

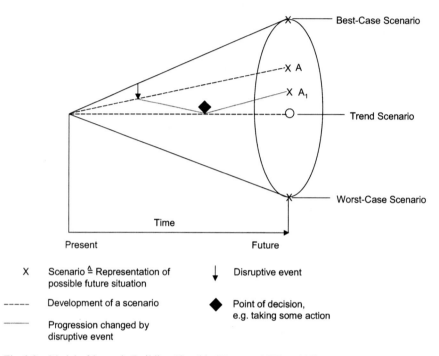

Fig. 3.3: Model of Scenario Building (Geschka/Hammer 1990, p. 315)

Scenario analysis can be broken down into the following phases:

1. Analysis

    a)   Decision about separate object of study (such as division or region)

    b)   Definition of relevant environment areas (such as macroeconomy, technology, politics, or social demographics)

2. Projection

    a)   Specification of indicators for describing the environmental areas (such as the unemployment rate or interest level)

    b)   Determination of actual values and trends (such as a projection of market volume for the next five years)

    c)   Specification of consistent group of assumptions for indicators that could develop differently

d) Building scenarios by monitoring these critical indicators over multiple blocks of time

e) Analysis of the effects of potential disruptive events on goals and key figures

3. Evaluation

a) Assessment of the effects of the determined scenarios on the object being examined (confrontation with the strengths/weaknesses profile of the company)

b) Development of reaction strategies for each scenario

With regard to decisions about strategies and measures, this makes it possible to consider adaptivity as a criterion. Hanssmann recommends the following procedure: for the robust first step along the path to realization, the planner should include the broadest possible spectrum of options in his considerations, but decide on one of them immediately. In making this decision, he should choose the option that allows him to react most readily (compared with the other options) to events that deviate from the trend scenario. This is how flexibility gains an economic value (Hanssmann 1996).

3.1.5   Portfolio Analysis

Portfolio analysis (see figure 3.4) is a combination of environment analysis and enterprise analysis.

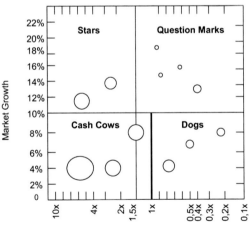

Fig. 3.4: BCG Portfolio (Steinmann/Schreyögg 2000, p. 210)

Environment indicators are shown on the ordinate axis. Amounts related to enterprise analysis are rated on the abscissa. The strategic business activities are positioned in the matrix formed in this way. It is possible to derive norm strategies from the fields of the matrix. The best-known variant is the market growth/market share matrix of the Boston Consulting Group (BCG). It represents the influence of the environment in market growth, while depicting the internal situation through the relative market share. To quantify market growth, the increase in sales in the given market is used. The relative market share represents the relationship between the company's own market share and that of its largest competitor. The matrix consists of four fields:

1.   Question marks
2.   Stars
3.   Cash cows
4.   Dogs

The diameter of the circles in figure 3.4 helps to visualize the amount of sales in a strategic business activity or product. Comparing the actual portfolio with a target portfolio can identify gaps that should be closed by appropriate strategies. The aim is to set up a portfolio so that products that "eat up" cash flow (question marks and stars) are "fed" by products that produce cash flow (cash cows) (see figure 3.5).

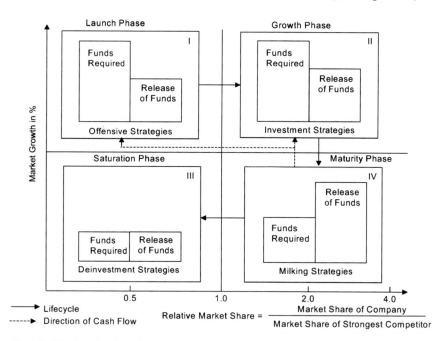

Fig. 3.5: Need for Funds and Release of Funds in Market Share/Market Growth Portfolio
            (Horváth 2002, p. 396)

3.1.6   Balanced Scorecard

The concept of the Balanced Scorecard (BSC), developed by Robert S. Kaplan and David P. Norton, links enterprise strategy to operational business processes, forming a framework for the distribution of resources in a firm. The BSC is often misunderstood as simply a grouping of key figures in four perspectives, where purely financial figures are augmented by non-financial ones. Key figures are certainly an important component of the BSC, but they do not comprise its backbone. Kaplan and Norton see the BSC as a strategic management system with the following aspects (Kaplan/Norton 1996a, also refer to the interview with David P. Norton in section 7.1):

1. Transparently formulated strategies
2. Communication of the strategy throughout the whole organization
3. Alignment of the strategy with the goals of employees
4. Linking objectives to the annual budget
5. Pinpointing of and agreement on strategic initiatives
6. Regular Performance Measurement with confirmations, and any strategy changes

Balanced Scorecards that cascade over several organizational levels, dynamic drilldown analyses, and strategy maps (see section 5.2.3.1) all assist in making this possible.

Elements

A Balanced Scorecard system is comprised of the following elements:

Perspective: Perspectives are the various viewpoints from which it is possible to consider the modeled connections. Usually there are four perspectives. However, the number of perspectives can vary depending on the business requirements.

Scorecard: Scorecards assist in monitoring the success achieved in making the overall strategy a reality. They encompass both current and planned key figures, as well as initiatives that are tied to objectives, and therefore also to strategies.

Strategy: A strategy is the top element of a scorecard. It is a part of the overall enterprise strategy, which is divided into sub-strategies for the sake of modeling.

Strategy category: Strategy categories are a means of classifying the defined strategies into groups. The basis is a *one to many* relationship: one strategy category groups together multiple strategies. Strategy categories help a user keep an overview when modeling.

Objective: An objective describes a strategic goal within the framework of a perspective. Objectives are joined together into an overall strategy by means of cause-effect chains. The extent to which objectives are reached is determined by comparing the actual and planned values of the key figures that are assigned to the objective.

Initiative: Initiatives are a set of activities that share the realization of one or more objectives as their purpose. A responsible person, a timeframe, and specific resources are allocated to each initiative.

Key figure: Key figures assist in measuring the degree to which the strategy has been put into effect. They are assigned to objectives and also receive a status that allows a qualitative pronouncement to be made on the current value of the key figure as compared with the plan value (unsatisfactory, satisfactory, good, excellent, and so on). In addition, a firm may organize the key figures in a Value Driver Tree (see section 5.2.3.2).

Risk: Risk can be seen as a completing factor to the other elements. There is the option of assigning risk to the key figures of a Balanced Scorecard and of quantifying the effects of key figures on risk. This opens up the possibility of integrated management of opportunities and risks. Certain companies have a legal obligation to set up a risk management system (see section 2.5), and these are thereby assisted to that end. Along with its verbal definition, a risk receives any number of value fields for a comprehensive and qualitative description of the risk situation.

Figure 3.6 clarifies how the elements of the Balanced Scorecard are related to one another. In the example, the "Drive Innovation" strategy contains the element "Exceed Growth in Key Segments." The objectives are linked across the cause-effect chain by the four perspectives. The objectives are realized by means of initiatives, such as a new marketing campaign. In the example shown in figure 3.6, Anne Miller is responsible for this initiative. She receives a budget of US$ 150,000. In order to measure the success of the initiative, several key figures are assigned to the objective, such as sales, contribution margin, and market share. Under the "risk" element, Anne records the extent to which she considers attaining the goal to be endangered.

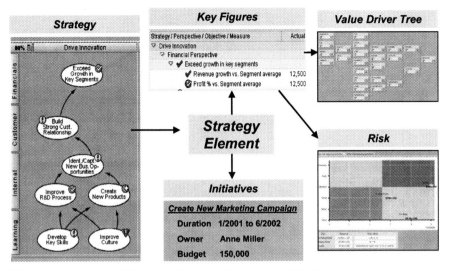

Fig. 3.6: Relationships of Elements of Balanced Scorecard © SAP AG

Procedure

First the overall strategy is divided into substrategies that consist of objectives. Very often there is also a further division into four perspectives: Financials, Customers, Internal Processes, and Innovation and Learning (see figure 3.7). However, you can also make divisions that suit your individual needs. For example, you can add a supplier or product perspective, if procurement or product development are critical success factors for the company (see section 7.1).

The use of various perspectives ensures that, along with the financial objectives and key figures, other areas are also included. At the same time this means that both long and short term aspects are considered.

At regular intervals, the responsible persons analyze the development of their objectives, initiatives, and key figures in the BSC. Statuses can either be set automatically using threshold values for key figures and aggregation rules, or they can be set manually. In many cases, the company links the attainment of given statuses of key figures, objectives, strategies, perspectives, or entire scorecards with variable, performance-based compensation of employees.

All persons and departments involved are connected to each other by a status reporting system, which allows them to exchange comments on the status and assessments. These may be called directly in the BSC. Experiences of BSC users substantiate the advantages of this openness. In contrast to traditional reporting systems, they find the benefit lies in an interpreted view of the strategy, with figures, facts, judgments and comments entered by the directly responsible persons. Kaplan and Norton also refer to this as "strategic learning by management" (Kaplan/Norton 1996b).

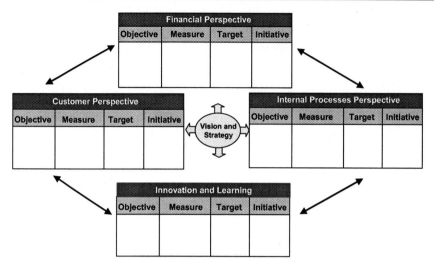

Fig. 3.7: Typical Perspectives of the Balanced Scorecard (Kaplan/Norton 1996a)

Scorecard Hierarchies

It makes sense to employ a Balanced Scorecard not only at the level of the entire company or in units that plan strategically. Instead it is beneficial to make communicating strategic objectives possible at all operational levels by setting up a scorecard hierarchy. Cascading scorecards are instrumental in making strategies transparent even at the lower levels of the organization, so that all business processes have a strategic direction.

The question of the number and integration of Balanced Scorecards is especially significant in large companies with complex structures. If we assume that companies unite multiple strategic business units (SBU) and subsidiaries under one roof in order to benefit from synergies, then cascading Balanced Scorecards are an appropriate instrument for bringing the strategies of the individual business units in line with one another. Corporate management provides a framework containing the general objectives, and these are translated into individual objectives. This enables the strategic business unit to have an individually formulated Balanced Scorecard, with contents that are in agreement with the corporation-wide objectives and that therefore allow analyses of common objectives across all areas. In practice, there are even certain cases in which scorecards are broken down as far as to the level of individual employees, and these scorecards are then used in evaluating the employee's performance (see section 7.1).

3.2 Instruments for Operational Enterprise Management

3.2.1 Target Costing

The traditional product development path consists – in very simplified form – of the following stages:

1. Design

2. Calculation of costs

3. Determination of price as a function of costs

Unlike this forward-thinking approach, target costing employs "backward thinking." The starting point is the decision to position a product in a given market segment, for instance a coupe version of a sedan. The market prices of the competition's similar (neighboring) products are known, so management has a basis for determining the price segment in which the new product will be positioned.

In the second step, the company determines what customers want regarding the attributes of the product, particularly its features. Depending on the industry, this could encompass not only the attributes of the product in the most narrow sense, but also such things as the expectations placed on customer service or financing terms (financial engineering). Collecting this data demands professional field research, since imprecise and amateurish questions give potential customers too much leeway for expressing impossible wishes: "The car should combine the performance of a Ferrari, the interior space of a large Mercedes, the passive safety potential of a tank, the noise level of a sewing machine, and the fuel consumption of a lawn mower." It is also extremely important to estimate the customers' willingness to pay for above-average performance and quality features, as well as for additional equipment. Conjoint analysis is a method that determines the level of consumers' willingness to pay for certain product attributes.

All of this information contributes to the decision regarding the target price, which usually involves intense participation of corporate management or area management. Now you subtract the desired profit from the target price. The amount of desired profit is also dependent on the strategic ideas of the company, as reflected in value-based management (see section 2.2). The result is the target value for the costs.

The responsibility then shifts to the functional area for product and process development. This is where the particular transformation problem of target costing arises. Revenue normally depends on the functionality of the product. Costs, on the other hand, are determined by the parts needed to build the product. Therefore, it is important to specify what part of the manufacturing costs can be assigned to the design engineers in the different assembly groups (bodywork, chassis, drive chain, and so on) as a kind of budget. Within these areas, it is possible to break down the budgets even further, having a separate cost budget for seats and one for upholstery, for instance. The design engineers now have to try to keep their designs within the cost budget.

Complications arise through technical interactions, but an elegant target cost system takes these into account, similarly to a product configurator. For example, when the total power requirements of optional equipment exceeds a threshold value for the electrical system, the next-largest generator or the next-largest wiring harness is selected. The reverse effect occurs if the level of optional equipment is reduced.

The procedure described up to this point is referred to as the top-down approach. If the product is a variant or successor of a known product, then a bottom-up approach can be applied: the construction elements of the existing product are changed one after the other. For example, you replace old materials with new ones or mechanical elements with electronic ones, and calculate whether these variations meet certain cost limits. Generally, these phases have to be repeated more than once.

One of the challenges for the method is to output not only average prices and average costs, but also changes over time. For example, in the automobile industry, development and warranty costs usually fall in an early phase of the product lifecycle (see section 3.3.5); revenues from repairs and sales of replacement parts, however, are usually earned in later phases. The present value of the decision is affected accordingly, similar to a dynamic investment analysis.

Another interpretation of target costing is to set allowable costs as a new, lower maximum limit. The current actual costs are compared to this limit. If the actual costs are above a level based on the market price, the firm has to take cost reduction measures. In making these decisions, the customer benefit related to individual parts of the product, as determined by market research institutes, serves as a criterion for distributing the cost reduction burden.

An even less methodically influenced development in target cost calculation correlates the expected additional benefits of modern features with the increased costs. You then try to find the optimal point in this correlation. In doing so, it has to be considered that the benefit curve for the customer declines slightly if a product is weighed down with extras. For example, the operating instructions become too long and complicated which makes it difficult to learn all the functions, or the optical signals (such as from the onboard electronics of an automobile) are more than the customer can handle. However, the costs function increases progressively due to the more expensive chips required by the electronics, for instance.

3.2.2 Contribution Margin Accounting

Contribution margin accounting is an umbrella term for different variants of multilevel gross income calculations. There are two basic types. The relative calculation of direct costs and contribution margins according to Riebel distinguishes between direct costs and overhead, whereas other types, such as direct costing, base the analysis of fixed-cost allocation or marginal costing on a separation of fixed and variable costs.

Direct costs is a relative term, since it can refer to costs on many items, including products, product groups, or units of capacity in which only certain products or product groups are manufactured. An example of product-related direct costs would be leasing costs for special-purpose machines that are only used for a single product, such as a chromium plating machine. Costs for advertising that relate to a whole product group (such as flat screen televisions) are an example of product group direct costs. Distinguishing between direct costs and overhead costs is based on the principle of identity. According to this principle, it is only possible to definitively align costs and revenues for calculating a contribution margin if they can be traced back to the same decision.

The relative calculation of direct costs and contribution margins primarily focuses on decision-making. Its main purposes are:

1. Preliminary costing

2. Control of the effect on net income of different alternatives for action

3. Profit planning related to orders, projects, and specific periods as well as across periods, and analysis of the source of profit by multidimensional evaluation objects (Riebel 1994)

Contribution margin accounting therefore offers significant support in deciding whether products should be added or removed from an existing product line. For example, less complex products in the product line may be suffering from a decline in prices, while products at the upper end may be suffering from a lack of demand, making the lot sizes too small.

Figure 3.8 shows the key figure scheme for step-by-step contribution margin accounting based on a simplified example from the pharmaceutical firm Boehringer Ingelheim GmbH.

Calc. Rules	Multistage Contribution Statement	Stock Keeping Unit	Product Group	Business Field	Business Segment	Business	Company
		A2	A1	E4	E3	E2	E1
+	Gross Sales of Goods						
-	Sales Discounts						
-	Translation/-action Difference from Receivables						
+	Royalty Income						
+	Other Income						
=	NET SALES						
-	Standard Cost of Goods Sold						
-	Direct Cost of Distribution						
-	Royalties						
=	CONTRIBUTION I						
-	Direct Promotion Cost						
-	Cost of Free Goods and Samples						
=	CONTRIBUTION I A						
-	Own Field Force						
-	Rented Field Force						
-	Commission Co.-Promotion						
=	CONTRIBUTION II						
-	General Promotion Activities						
-	Marketing and Sales Organization						
-	Indirect Cost of Distribution						
-	Research and Development I						
-	Medicine I						
-	Administration Cost						
-	Variances Cost of Goods						
-	Variances from other Int. Serv. Charges						
-	Income/Expenses I						
+	Cash Subsidies/Adjustment Payments						
-	Other Translation/Transaction Differences						
=	CONTRIBUTION III						
-	Marketing II						
-	Process Development						
-	Cost of Reserved Capacity						
-	Cost of Idle Capacity						
-	Variances Production						
-	Income/Expenses II						
-	Other Expenses in Production						
=	CONTRIBUTION IV						
-	Research and Development II						
-	Medicine II						
-	Income/Expenses III						
=	OPERATING INCOME (LOSS)						
+	Financial Income/Expenses						
+	Holding Income/Expenses						
+	Extraordinary Items						
=	INCOME (LOSS) BEFORE TAXES						
-	Taxes						
=	INCOME (LOSS) AFTER TAXES						

Fig. 3.8: Key Figure Scheme of Step-by-Step Contribution Margin Calculation at Boehringer Ingelheim (Mertens/Griese 2002)

Contribution margin I expresses whether a product should be forced or scaled back – assuming capacities are unchanged – without being completely removed from the product line. If contribution margin II is unsatisfactory or negative, the decision-maker has to consider whether production of the article should be ceased and the fixed costs (direct costs) of its production reduced by disinvestment (for example, by returning the special-purpose machine used in production, see above). In a corresponding manner, contribution margin III provides points of reference for whether an entire product group should be abandoned.

This step-by-step contribution margin calculation, if used too schematically, does not sufficiently take interactions in the market segment into account. For example, eliminating one product in a product line can endanger the entire line if customers prefer purchasing all products from one manufacturer. On the other side of the coin, the absence of one product can mean that customers instead fall back on neighboring products in your product line or group.

3.2.3 Break-even Analysis

Break-even analysis is an important tool when first considering whether an investment should be made. The question posed is a simple one: How much do we need in sales in order to move from the loss zone to the profit zone?

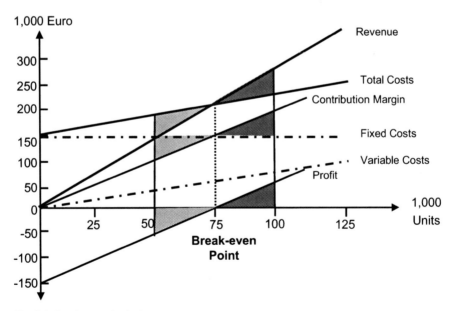

Fig. 3.9: Break-even Analysis

Figure 3.9 illustrates the principle that initially assumes constant fixed costs along with linear progression of costs and prices that are variable based on sales. It is also implicit that these are constant per unit. In other words, there is no relationship between price and number of units sold. By merging the fixed cost line and the line for variable costs, you get the total cost curve. The point at which the total cost curve crosses the price line is the break-even point. If you complete the diagram by adding the profit function and the line showing the contribution margins (difference between price and variable costs), there are more options. The graph also shows the progress of profits and contribution margins as related to different quantities sold, which also indicates different levels in utilization of capacity.

The greatest advantage of break-even analysis in decision-making is that it is relatively easily to apply "what-if" or "how-to-achieve" points of view by varying individual parameters. A decision-maker may then observe the resulting changes in the figures, particularly the movement of the break-even point. These alternative calculations can also be displayed on a computer screen. Some examples:

1. How does the break-even point change if the price can be increased by x dollars?

2. At what sales volume would the break-even point be reached if it were possible to reduce fixed costs, at the expense of variable costs, using cost management? Often this change in the cost structure can be achieved through external procurement.

3. How much do variable costs have to be reduced (such as by supplier price reductions) to be able to reach the break-even point with a 20% lower sales volume?

In actual practice, a break-even analysis is not always as unproblematic as outlined up to now. For example, as a firm gets closer to full utilization of capacity, variable costs can increase progressively (possible reasons being extra costs of overtime or increased absenteeism). Furthermore, the break-even point may not be just a function of fixed costs – the reverse might also be true. Let us assume that a company employs an external consultant for the introduction of a new product and for mastering the problems on the startup curve. The consultant's work should end when the break-even point is reached. If that point continues to lie in the future, however, the consultant has to keep working, and the fixed costs budgeted for him will rise.

3.2.4   ABC Analysis

ABC analysis is a method of classifying objects – such as customers, suppliers, products or materials – by category:

A = important, B = less important and C = unimportant

Once this assignment is made, you normally see that only a few objects fall into the "important" category. The categorization provides starting points for determining the amount of attention that should be given to the different objects.

ABC analysis originated in materials management. There, materials are divided into three classes based on their business volume measured by value or quantity, or their inventory value. To reduce time and effort in warehouse planning, objects with a high share of business volume (A objects) are planned using a more exact procedure than the medium-share B objects or low-share C objects. For instance, you make a monthly gross requirements prediction for A objects, whereas for B objects this is done quarterly and for C objects only annually (Mertens 2004, p. 79). An XYZ analysis can be used in preparation for deciding how to plan a part: whether planning is completely automatic, takes place in human-machine dialog, or is handled manually. For X parts, you can predict consumption with a high degree of certainty, while Z parts are those with requirements that fluctuate widely. Y parts are between these two extremes (Dittrich/Mertens 2003).

This concept can be applied in a similar way to customers, suppliers, or products. If most of a company's sales are generated by 10% of its customers, ABC analysis enables the company to concentrate its activities on the A customers, for instance by assigning a key account manager. In the same way, A suppliers can also receive special treatment. For products that fall into category C due to their low contribution margin, it may be worth considering removing them from the product line. However, ABC analysis supplies only basic information for such decisions. Other factors may well counterindicate removing them, for example they may be usually purchased together with A products, or capacity would otherwise be poorly utilized.

3.2.5 RFM Analysis

RFM (Recency Frequency Monetary Value) analysis is a procedure specifically for classifying customers so that the company can concentrate its marketing on those customers with whom the chances for success are the greatest. The analysis is based on the following not unproblematic assumptions (Schwedelson 2001):

1. *Recency:* Customers who recently made a purchase are more likely to place a new order than those who have not purchased for some time.

2. *Frequency:* Customers who purchase frequently are more likely to react to a new offer than those who purchase less frequently.

3. *Monetary Value:* A useful criterion here is the average contribution margin of the customer per purchase. The sales figures also include the number of units purchased and the prices of the products. This information also becomes part of the assessment of the customer.

In a typical RFM model, a simple classification code is used to divide up the customer database. The data records are initially sorted by date (Recency) and then divided further into five equal segments. The top 20% (the most recent purchases) receive the code 5, the next 20% receive a 4, and so on down to 1. The same procedure is used for the Frequency and Monetary Value criteria (Hughes 2001). The result is that each customer is assigned a code from 111 (worst customer) to 555 (best customer). There are a total of $5^3 = 125$ different possible combinations.

With this method as a basis, the firm can then develop a special advertising campaign for the code-555 customers, for example.

3.3 Instruments for Combined Strategic and Operational Enterprise Management

3.3.1 Activity-Based Costing

Today it is possible to precisely monitor the costs of manufacturing processes by combining data entry for plant, process, and machine data along with machine hour rates calculations. While this works for manufacturing, it is less true for nonproduction processes such as procurement and shipping. Especially in highly automated companies or those with low value-added and therefore significant external procurement, the share of nonproduction costs has steadily risen. Activity-Based Costing aims to allocate these overhead costs more closely in accordance with their causes and to treat activities as the cost objects rather than cost centers. Activity-Based Costing is particularly intended for assigning costs to activity chains that are important for the success of the company but at the same time may be sources of contention, such as developing a new product variant or processing complaints. Preparations for Activity-Based Costing are listed below:

1. Determine costs per unit of time, such as cost per employee hour in the external sales force. An information system can determine this kind of cost rate (such as by dividing cost center costs by output) if the work hours in the time recording system are available. Often the last recorded values are not used, but are smoothed instead.

2. Identify the most important subprocesses on the cost center and determine their time requirements. It is often difficult to find out what the costs of a process (primarily) depend on – that is, what the cost drivers are. Foster and Gupta propose a division of the overhead costs in manufacturing into three types of cost driver: volume-based, complexity-based, and efficiency-based (Foster/Gupta 1990). Renner, on the other hand, groups cost drivers into process-dependent (e.g. number of malfunctions), complexity-dependent (number of variants), and order-specific (special wishes) types (Renner 1991). Information processing support of diagnosing the influences is not simple. Exact time analyses (using a stopwatch) or activity sampling will probably run up against reservations on the part of employees (or the workers' council, if there is one). Therefore, you can try to arrive at time requirements by comparing the production per time unit of a department when involved in different spectrums of activities (Mertens 2004, p. 259).

In order to use information processing to support Activity-Based Costing, it is advisable to set up a hierarchy of master data, particularly of resource centers (to which cost centers or other areas with responsibility for costs are linked), resource accounts (to which certain resource types are assigned), and cost components (to which cost elements and the costs themselves are allocated).

In a similar way, you define a structure of activities. For example, complaints processing is part of customer service, which itself is an element of after-sales service, which in turn is a component of Customer Relationship Management.

Finally, you need to specify the cost objects (product, customer, or distribution channel, for example).

3.3.2 Forecasting Methods

Strategic enterprise management is necessarily geared toward the future. Computer-aided forecasting methods are therefore very welcome. However, it is wise not to overestimate their capabilities, particularly in supporting poorly structured decisions. In many cases, the advantage of computer-assisted forecasts does not make itself felt so much in an increase in exactness as in the rationalization of the forecast. This is the case namely when many single forecasts (for instance on sales of articles and article groups or in regions) are created and then aggregated. Figure 3.10 provides an overview of the quantitative procedures.

First, the methods can be divided into univariate and multivariate methods. With univariate forecast methods, past data for a figure are used to estimate its future values, such as issues from stock. The most important group of univariate methods are time series forecasts: An observed series of values is extrapolated into the future. Depending on the form of the time series, these are classified as constant models, trend models, seasonal models, and trend/seasonal models.

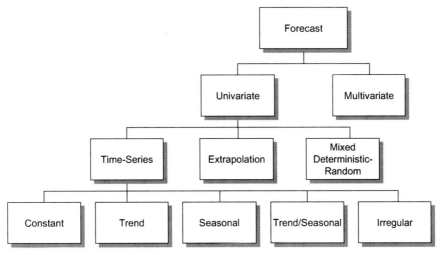

Fig. 3.10: Overview of Quantitative Forecasting Methods

We have a constant time series when the time series indicates statistical dispersion around a mean value (see figure 3.11).

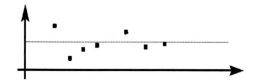

Fig. 3.11: Constant Time Series

With a trend time series, the value measured in the time series rises or falls in a steady pattern over a long period of time, with random fluctuations (see figure 3.12).

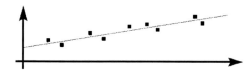

Fig. 3.12: Trend Time Series

In the case of a seasonal time series, the values differ from the mean in regular periodic intervals (see figure 3.13).

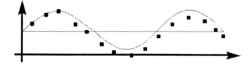

Fig. 3.13: Seasonal Time Series

A trend/seasonal time series evidences seasonal variations in a steadily rising or falling pattern (see figure 3.14).

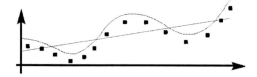

Fig. 3.14: Trend/Seasonal Time Series

Exponential smoothing can be considered the central algorithm for time series forecasts. The formula for exponential smoothing of the first order is:

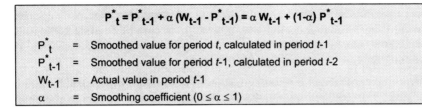

$$P^*_t = P^*_{t-1} + \alpha\,(W_{t-1} - P^*_{t-1}) = \alpha\,W_{t-1} + (1-\alpha)\,P^*_{t-1}$$

P^*_t	=	Smoothed value for period t, calculated in period t-1
P^*_{t-1}	=	Smoothed value for period t-1, calculated in period t-2
W_{t-1}	=	Actual value in period t-1
α	=	Smoothing coefficient ($0 \leq \alpha \leq 1$)

The new smoothed value P^*_t is the weighted average of the last recorded value W_{t-1} and the old smoothed value P^*_{t-1}. The smoothing coefficient (weighting factor) α plays an important role in the calculation. If we choose a large value for this coefficient, then the last observed value strongly affects the forecast. In other words, the model reacts very sensitively to the most recent actual values. If we set a small value for α, the forecast remains more stable. The effect of α can be readily seen if you set this parameter in the equation to zero (the minimum allowed value): the system then continues to update the forecast without taking notice of the real situation (W_{t-1}) (completely conservative behavior). However, if we choose the upper limit of $\alpha = 1$, the forecast is then equal to the most recently observed values (completely opportunistic behavior).

The trend, seasonal and trend/seasonal models adjust the mathematical results from the exponential smoothing of the first order by using other factors for multiplication or including other factors in the equation. Seasonal effects and the effects of trends also have to be subjected to smoothing, since they are liable to changes. If a retailer, for example, is able to sell well even outside of the season by using different pricing policies, the seasonal curves are flattened.

Making predictions for events that take an irregular course is especially difficult. In the case of an incoming order forecast or a stock issue forecast for valuable products, you can do a complete turnaround of the procedure. While with classic forecasting models the time intervals remain constant and the amount of demand or the amount shipped are the factors predicted, here you now divide the demand into classes by size, and what is forecasted after each order is when another order in this class will be received. This procedure makes sense if we assume that important customers have automatic warehouse planning models and that they order the same quantities with the same frequency as long as the economy remains stable.

The extrapolation forecast, best known from its use in political elections, operates on the basis of samples. The vote counts in the first voting districts correspond to the first orders received at trade fairs or from the first customers visited.

Mixed deterministic-random forecasts put known amounts together with those that are subject to probabilities. For example, the production program of many textile firms is based in part on outline purchase agreements or scheduling agreements that are made quite early, and partly on expectations of rush orders.

Among the multivariate methods, the indicator forecast plays a significant role in strategic planning in many companies: the course of development of one variable allows estimates to be made on the change of a second parameter, with a certain time lag. If a furniture manufacturer follows the issuing of building permits, for instance, they can draw conclusions about the increase or decrease in demand for furnishings of new buildings a few periods later.

When computer-assisted forecasting methods are used, the parameters have to be configured with special care. On the one hand, you have to be sure to choose the most suitable methods, on the other hand you need the best possible smoothing parameters. The basic options are depicted in figure 3.15.

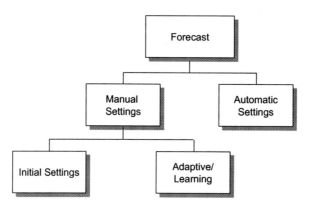

Fig. 3.15: Alternative Procedures for Setting Forecasting Parameters

The parameters are regulated either automatically or with human input. The automatic setting can be limited to the starting values. Or it can be continually repeated, in the sense of an adaptive or a learning process, if the system registers forecast/actual variances that are too large. For this purpose, we need criteria for assessing the forecast.

SAP uses a term that is calculated as follows:

$$ET = \sum_{t=1}^{n} \left[x_t - P_t \right]$$

ET = Error total
n = Number of periods
t = Period
x = Actual value
P = Forecasted value

and calls it error total. It is an indicator for whether the prediction based on the selected forecasting model is acceptable. If a model is still valid (that is, the characteristic of the series of consumption values has not changed), we can assume that the error total is distributed normally, and tends to dispersion around a mean value of zero. The error total is calculated by adding all forecast errors of a time series. These forecast errors in turn are the difference between the actual value and the forecasted value of a period.

Along with quantitative forecasts, qualitative forecasts also have a certain role in strategic enterprise management. Due to their qualitative nature, computer assistance is limited here. It is confined primarily to information retrieval, such as from internal databases or the Internet.

An exception to this rule are Delphi forecasts. Various experts first make independent predictions. These are entered into a computer that calculates the mean values and spread of the predictions. Then these mean values and the dispersion are presented to the experts. They are asked to consider these results and decide whether they want to stick to their original prediction or modify it. Based on experience, the experts usually reconsider their original estimates most intently when they see that they are quite far from the "general opinion." As a result, repeated rounds of questioning usually lead to values that lie in a more or less narrow band, which then becomes the basis for strategic planning.

A systematic procedure for forecasting comprises these steps:

1. Gather observed values.
2. Enter in suitable computer system.
3. Plot the data in graphs.
4. Trigger automatic analysis of courses of developments (events) and interrelationships, such as correlation analysis and regression analysis.
5. Simplify time series.
6. Make forecast on the basis of simplified time series.
7. Regress the simplified time series to its original form, and thereby determine the forecasted value.

3.3.3   Simulation

We consider simulation to be use of a model that represents a segment of reality and that can be calculated using a computer. The simulated model replaces actual empirical experiments in the business environment. It has therefore taken a leading role in enterprise management, since actual experiments are generally too expensive, dangerous, or simply impossible to carry out. Suppose, for example, your firm wants to introduce a new structure for shipping logistics. It would be ridiculously expensive to set up different central warehouses, distribution centers, and transport vehicle fleets in order to examine the impact of different possible variations on stock levels, tied up capital, and service level.

A leading simulation method is the Monte Carlo method. The name comes from the random numbers of roulette. Certain developments and events are represented by such numbers. They are generated in a way such that they reflect the probability of the developments actually occurring. Examples are the type and amount of customer orders and the time they are received, disruptions in procurement, production, or shipping logistics, or fluctuations in currency exchange rates.

Once new insights have been gathered from the simulation experiments, the types of questions normally posed can be essentially divided into two categories:

1. What if we...? (what-if analysis)

2. How can we achieve...? (how-to-achieve analysis)

Examples for the first type include:

a) What would the effects on the financial statement be of a change in the euro/dollar exchange rate from 0.9 to 1.2, with a simultaneous change in the euro/yen exchange rate from 110 to 150, with all other conditions remaining the same?

b) What changes in transport costs and sales would result if all distribution centers were closed, deliveries to customers were made from the central warehouse, and at the same time every fifth customer churned?

c) What changes in the tax burden could be expected if your North and South American subsidiaries were managed by a holding company with headquarters in Ireland?

Examples for "how-to-achieve?" questions include:

a) By what percentage does inventory turnover have to be increased, other factors remaining the same, if you want to increase the return on investment by 2% for foreign subsidiaries and 3% at home?

b) By what percentage do you have to increase market share with existing major customers if the company wants to attain an annual increase in sales of 2% but does not win over any new customers?

Simulation methods also allow use of the computer for representing complex relationships and are suited for situations in which exact optimization algorithms, due to their many limitations, would necessitate too much simplification. Among the disadvantages are sometimes long CPU times, and, particularly when the simulation experiments are not carefully interpreted, uncertainty as to whether you come close enough to the theoretical optimum. Improvements in the cost effectiveness of computers make it more and more possible to include simulation as a component in other decision-supporting methods. For instance in Supply Chain Event Management (SCEM) , when exception conditions occur for certain objects (such as transportation hubs, warehouses, articles, or customers), a simulation determines how the plan/actual variance can be eliminated and the process put back on track (how-to-achieve simulation).

Dynamic Simulation (System Dynamics)

Another approach is dynamic simulation, which is based on the System Dynamics method. Frequently this is also called Business Dynamics. The basis is a system theory which assumes that in a closed controlled loop (such as a company), elements are influenced by their own behavior (feedback).

The first step is to build cause-effect chains. Figure 3.16 shows an example of the dependence between the interest rate and the level of indebtedness.

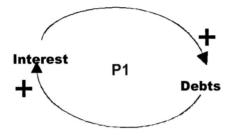

Fig. 3.16: Positive Feedback Loop

The plus signs (+) show that the values pointed to by the arrows move in the same direction. A minus sign would indicate they move in opposite directions. An increase in debt causes an increase in the interest burden, which in turn increases the amount of debt. In this case, therefore, we have a positive feedback loop. This is illustrated in the name *P1*, where *P* indicates that the loop is positive, while *1* is a reference number. A concrete example is the billion dollar bidding for UMTS rights. Due to the high capital requirements for financing the cellular network licenses, the capital structures of the mobile communication firms involved were affected. In the case of Deutsche Telekom, this led to a lowering of their credit standing. Their risk surcharge therefore increased, which also increased their capital requirements (without byline 2001). Moreover, the worse capital structure may lead to higher interest rates.

We have a "real" simulation model when we refine the cause-effect chain using a second step (see figure 3.17). The rectangles represent non-cumulative values (current debt and total payments). Their amounts are dependent on the amounts of the cumulative values (interest and monthly installment). The cloud represents a source from which the system receives data. The rhombuses stand for fixed amounts (interest rate, installment, and loan amount). Once the validity of the model has been tested, runs of the actual simulation, in which the parameters are varied, can begin. For more detailed information, refer to (Maani/Cavana 2000; Sterman 2000).

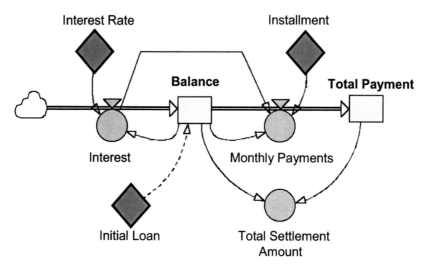

Fig. 3.17: System Dynamics Model for Development of Indebtedness

Risk Analysis According to Hertz

The following describes a special procedure that is well-suited for analyzing the risk of capital investments, or of large projects in general, using integrated information processing. It is based on a simulation using random numbers – that is, the Monte Carlo method (see above).

We start with a number of estimates from different experts regarding a capital investment calculation. As an example, we will use the development and marketing of a new product. The following profitability formula can be the criterion for the decision:

$$R = \frac{(M \cdot P) - VK - FK}{I}$$

R = Profitability
M = Quantity sold
P = Price
VK = Variable costs
FK = Fixed costs
I   = Amount of investment

A profit is made on the invested capital, and thereby the profitability of the new product can be calculated.

We start with the expected price P that we want to achieve on the market. Pessimistic experts anticipate a price of $180 per unit, optimistic ones expect $220, while still others assume $200. Now we make a different set of assumptions. Here the pessimists predict that the new product will trigger a price war on the market, and that therefore a price of $120 is the best that can be expected. Optimists, on the other hand, hope for $280, while the middle-of-the-road estimate is $200. This second constellation shows greater dispersal of estimates, which is a reflection of the considerable uncertainty in the situation.

In classic investment calculation, one would choose the middle value for *P* in both cases ($200 per unit) in the profitability formula. However, in doing so, the uncertainty indicated by the dispersal of the values would be lost. In other words, using the calculation procedure throws away information about uncertainty that was already available.

The risk analysis proposed by Hertz avoids this problem by not determining a mean value. Instead, we have the computer perform a large number of simulations using very different combinations of values, whereby each value is represented in the simulation runs with a frequency corresponding to its probability. Accordingly, the model calculates as many profitability figures as the number of simulation runs that are performed. These results may be summarized in a distribution and viewed in graphic from (see figure 3.18).

The decision-makers in the company can then see the probability that a loss will be suffered or how certain it is that the minimum profitability stated in the company's goals will be reached.

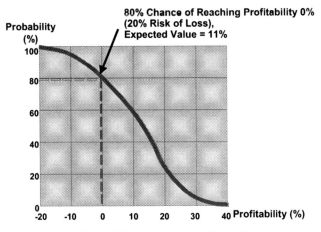

Fig. 3.18: Graphic Representation of Risk Analysis According to Hertz

3.3.4   Consolidation

A distinction is made between statutory consolidation and management consolidation. The purpose of statutory consolidation is to combine financial statements, particularly the annual statements, of corporate subsidiaries into one set of consolidated financial statements. Although certain local accounting principles sometimes (as in Germany) allow to substitute financial statements according local standards by financial statements international standards, such as IAS or US GAAP, many international corporations are nonetheless required to create them in parallel. With management consolidation, on the other hand, financial data is aggregated along the organizational structure of the corporation for internal management purposes only.

In both cases, data from the various subsidiaries of the corporate group is gathered centrally and evaluated. Different valuations as well as currencies and units of measurement are reduced to a common denominator, and internal trade relationships are eliminated. The main tasks are:

1.   Elimination of interunit revenue and expense
2.   Elimination of interunit profit and loss
3.   Elimination of interunit payables and receivables
4.   Consolidation of investments

These four steps are executed in their entirety in the case of company (statutory) consolidation. For management consolidation, however, it is possible to omit or simplify steps depending on the purpose you want to achieve (Karl 2000).

Modeling the hierarchical structures of the corporate group lays the necessary groundwork for the consolidation. The model is not limited to just depicting the corporate structure that reflects the actual legal relationships among the independent subsidiaries that make up the organization. Instead, the model can be structured using business segments that do not conform to this pattern. Other possible criteria for modeling the structure are business areas or lines of business. In large corporations, it is often impossible to establish a 1:1 relationship between divisional structures and legal entities, since the legal entity often serves a number of business segments.

Consolidation is made more difficult by frequent corporate acquisitions, divestitures, and mergers, along with other types of reorganization. Added to this, company decision-making focuses more and more on increasing value, both in theory and in practice, leading to the proliferation of various figures intended to measure this value, such as economic profit or economic value (see section 2.2). A further complicating factor is that corporate management demands financial statements at ever shorter intervals.

To avoid inconsistencies both in statutory consolidation and in the management information system, an integrated information system is needed that unifies both internal and external financial reporting. The prerequisites for this information system are:

1. *Single reporting date:* As soon as the reporting dates for internal and external financial reporting diverge, the danger of unwanted differences arises.

2. *Uniform data basis:* A common data basis for posting is required to make integration possible.

3. *Data collection:* Posting for each transaction can be made only once to each given account for internal and external reporting. This means that transactions always have to be entered only at the lowest organizational level.

4. *Scrupulous validation:* As in any integrated information system, incorrect entries also cause problems here. Therefore it is necessary to find input errors using validation checks. The effort and expense involved in correcting errors is in any case less than that for storing redundant data that increases the likelihood of inconsistencies.

5. *Matching charts of accounts:* Subsidiaries need additional assignments in order to ensure that their data can be transferred to the chart of accounts of the parent company (Schuler/Pfeifer 2001).

The investment relationships between the parent and subsidiaries are entered into a computerized consolidation system for the group. The system can then independently model the entire corporate structure, including relationships of second-tier subsidiaries or reciprocal holdings. Depending on the parameters entered, the system eliminates interunit payables and receivables, along with other redundant postings, in the consolidated statements. Currency translation uses either the current or historical exchange rate according to the parameters chosen. The system not only performs consolidation on the basis of actual data for financial reporting, but consolidated data are used in planning as well.

A high-quality system also offers options for making alternative calculations and for comparing the results of these calculations in well-designed reports. With an interactive system, common errors can be avoided using an intelligent checklist processed within a monitor.

3.3.5   Lifecycle Analysis

During the time from its development to the end of production – the product lifecycle – a product goes through a series of phases.

Development phase: The idea for a product is born and takes shape step by step. This is followed by product development, including various tests (such as market surveys or clinical studies) before the product is introduced. Such surveys attempt to determine whether the design will be accepted by potential customers. In the development phase, there is no revenue to offset the costs. During this time the firm also specifies the future costs of production, shipping, and disposal to a large degree.

Launch phase: The first few months the product is on the market are devoted to making it known and battling possible resistance, for instance due to lack of consumer confidence in new technologies. The focus in this part of the lifecycle is on intensive sales promotion, with aggressive advertising. The high costs of launching the product are therefore not compensated by initial sales, so losses are normally experienced during this phase.

Growth phase: The product experiences strong growth in sales. Competitors now try bringing similar products to the market to profit from the firm's pioneering efforts (after the patent expires, if there is one). A competitive pricing policy and attractive terms are therefore essential during this phase.

Maturity phase: Sales continue to increase, but reach their maximum at the end of this phase. The company tries to extend this period for as long as possible, since it is usually the most profitable. Maintenance marketing and product diversification are measures employed in the attempt to open up new market segments.

Saturation phase: Demand is satisfied to a large extent. The main clientele are those purchasing replacements. Price reductions are characteristic of this phase, and sales and profit steadily decline. Some companies already halt production at this point.

Degeneration phase: The product no longer meets current needs: it is either outmoded or technically obsolete. Losses start to be incurred at this point, so production is ceased.

This particular model of a lifecycle is not universal. There are cases in which a product is taken from the market during the introductory phase due to poor returns. Other products suddenly experience a new upswing after the saturation phase because of changed conditions. An example for this is when motorcycles changed from being primarily a mode of transportation to a recreational vehicle. Another factor is that the length of time for each of the phases can vary dramatically. For example, while coal has been used for centuries, the hula hoop came and went within a few years. A number of characteristic product life cycle models have developed over the years. Zingel provides detailed descriptions of these (Zingel 2000).

To make things even more difficult, there is the problem of delineating the "product" from the changes made to it over time through continued development, as well as distinguishing it from its variants. Computer systems with the right capabilities can assist with strategic planning in these cases. With the help of forecasting models, especially saturation models (Mertens 2003a), they predict the sales curves of the individual products and also merge them together. The function that thereby emerges showing total sales over time can be the starting point for income calculation, in which, based on stored or calculated cost developments, you forecast revenues, contribution margins, and liquidity.

Using the data of an automobile manufacturer, for instance, it was shown to be possible to derive cost developments from the course of sales using regression functions. The results obtained were sufficiently accurate for models of this type (Mertens/Rackelmann 1979). Sensitivity analyses can assist in readily visualizing this kind of data, especially shifts in sales profiles.

The central goal of this kind of model is to anticipate possible crises, as when a primary product enters the degeneration phase earlier than planned and its successor is not ready for the market. Figure 3.19 depicts the principle behind these planning models that represent the course of sales (costs and profit are not shown for the sake of simplicity) (Mertens/Griese 2002). Back-Hock developed her prototype of product life cycle controlling on this basis (Back-Hock 1988).

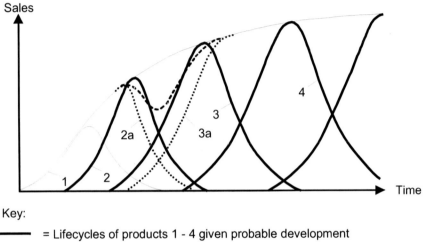

Key:

——— = Lifecycles of products 1 - 4 given probable development

――― = Sales given probable development

·········· = Lifecycles 2a and 3a of products 2 and 3 when development is
            not optimal (product 2 declines prematurely, product 3 arrives too late)

------ = Sales when development not optimal

Fig. 3.19: Product Lifecycles Superimposed (Mertens/Griese 2002)

Relatively small shifts in the cycles of individual products represent a significant danger to the company (especially if it is not able to react quickly to declining sales due to high fixed costs).

Despite the difficulties mentioned, product lifecycle analysis provides orientation for management. Table 3.2 summarizes the most important characteristics and re-commendations for the individual phases. The development phase is characterized by a large number of unique situations and requirements that are best served by special management accounting for research and development. Therefore the development phase is not included in the table. Oesterer, among others, supplies more details on this phase (Oesterer 1995).

Characteristics	Phases			
	Launch	**Growth**	**Maturity & Saturation**	**Degeneration**
Sales	Low	Rapidly increasing	Peak sales	Declining
Costs	High costs per customer	Average costs per customer	Low costs per customer	Low costs per customer
Profits	Negative	Rising	High	Falling
Customers	Innovators	Early adopters	Majority	Latecomers
Competitors	Few or none	Number of competitors and intensity of competition increases	Tendency to decrease begins	Number of competitors declines
Operational goals	Make product known, achieve initial sales	Maximum market penetration	Maximum profit, while also protecting market share	Cost reductions and skimming off last benefits
Product politics	Offer basic product	Offer variants of the product	Diversify brands and models	Eliminate articles with negative contribution margins
Pricing policy	Oriented toward maximum value for the consumer	Many alternatives, depending on the penetration strategy	Price same as competition or lower (fixed market price)	Price reductions
Distribution	Build distribution network selectively	Increase density of distribution network	Further increase density of distribution network	Selectively reduce distribution network according to contribution margin
Advertising	Make product known to early adopters and retail sector	Make product known on mass market	Emphasize distinguishing features and advantages of the brand	Advertising for holding on to the most loyal customers
Promotions	Stimulate initial sales using intensive promotions	Reduce expense of promotions, exploit high demand	Increase promotions, encourage switching brands	Reduce to a minimum

Table 3.2: Characteristics of Phases of Product Lifecycle (based on Kotler/Bliemel 2001)

4 Information Technology Instruments

4.1 Data Warehouse (Information Warehouse)

At the start of the nineties it became clear that saving data for decision-making purposes had to be done in a different way to that for operational processing purposes (Becker/Priemer 1994), and so the term *data warehouse* was coined (also called *information warehouse*). This describes an "orderly, cross-function and cross-company data collection that is aimed at business objects, for example, customers over the period of several years" (von Maur/Rieger 2001).

In addition to business data, a data warehouse contains a metadata basis and an administrative component. The metadata basis contains details on semantics, the age, source, and extraction mechanism of the information, and of changes to the data model. The administration component controls the import from the operational systems (von Maur/Rieger 2001). Inmon, who is renowned as being one of the inventors of data warehousing, specifies the following characteristic requirements (Inmon 2002):

1. *Concentration on data use:* the focus lies on using data for decisions. The way that the contents are received in the operational systems, on the other hand, is of lesser importance.

2. *Period analysis instead of time spot analysis:* the emphasis is on recognizing trends. Therefore, the time span of a data warehouse is often up to ten years, and the data is saved at different aggregation levels according to its age.

3. *Non-volatility:* The data is no longer modified, except for minor corrections. This means that data warehouses normally only allow read access, except for plan values, which are written to the data warehouse.

4. *Standardization of structure and format:* Data cleansing can be analyzed technically and semantically. Technical problems such as differing character strings, umlauts, and special characters can be solved using modern extraction tools. However, further problems are caused by groupings, key conversions, zero values, or empty fields that require an entry, while the largest challenges of all are presented by semantics:

a) *Homonyms* are terms that are spelled and pronounced the same but have different meanings. The term *silent reserve*, for example, is used in account balancing but also in the job market (where it means unemployed persons who are not registered as such).

b) *Synonyms* are different terms that have the same meaning. In the English language, *expenses* and *costs* are often used as synonyms.

c) *Equipollences* are terms that explain a concept from different angles, such as *vendor* and *creditor* which normally have the same structure. *Vendor* is used in procurement, while *creditor* is used in accounting.

Due to the extensive storage of historical transactions, the combination options provided by different types of grouping, and the integration of external data, data warehouse systems can grow to a size of several terabytes (Oehler 2000, p. 18).

Operational systems are particularly demanding when it comes to solving problems that arise when data is entered or changed. For this reason, these data structures are usually normalized, whereby they are split up into small elements that are then reassembled by the computer for evaluation. In the data warehouse, not all of this procedure is followed, in order to reduce the response times despite high volumes of data.

A basic concept in data modeling is the star schema. The main aspect of this schema is a fact table that contains key figures such as quantities, sales, costs, or contribution margins. The keys in the fact table comprise the primary keys of the dimension tables , which are ordered around the fact table. The dimension tables can have flat hierarchy structures that go against the third normal form (removal of transitive dependencies). This type of storage enables special algorithms to be used for particularly fast processing. The star schema derives its name from the star-shaped graphic (see figure 4.1). It has an enhancement, which is called the *snowflake schema* because the dimension tables are surrounded by summarization levels in further tables, thus giving the effect of a snowflake.

The requirement that all areas should be modeled centrally often led to projects running for several years or failing. Thus the data mart approach came into being, whereby sections specific to a department are dealt with separately, such as research and development, marketing, purchasing, or cost management. However, there is a risk of discrepancies between the various data marts, which in turn creates more expenses (Oehler 2000, pp. 22-24).

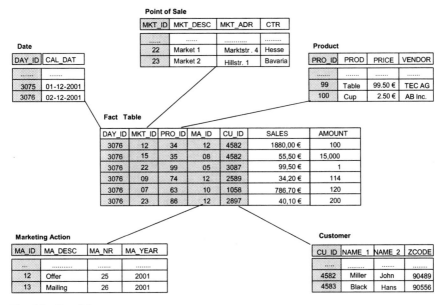

Fig. 4.1: Star Schema

4.2 Online Analytical Processing (OLAP)

The way in which information is stored in relational databases does not correspond to the way in which a typical user preparing company decisions thinks. This user requires flexible multidimensional views for which he or she can vary for different problems.

The beginnings of this arose before the invention of electronic information systems, for example in the Purpose-Neutral Data Collection (Grundrechnung) by Schmalenbach. Riebel dealt with this concept in relative unit cost and contribution margin accounting, thereby strongly influencing the development of management information systems.

At the beginning of the nineties, Codd coined the term *online analytical processing* (OLAP), which has since come into widespread use. This term basically describes twelve rules that are used for the standardization of multidimensional data modeling (Oehler, 2000, pp. 29-31):

1. *Multidimensional conceptual views:* the way that an analyst thinks is strongly influenced by evaluation dimensions such as time, product, region, or customer, and this multidimensional thinking must be directly reflected in the way in which the query is formulated.

2. *Intuitive data processing:* aggregation (drilldown) should be intuitive, as should be the exchange of column and row dimensions (slice-and-dice), for example, by dragging data with the mouse (drag-and-drop).

3. *Accessibility:* the data may originate in different places, such as in relational or file-based systems. It is managed in a special conceptual schema in the OLAP database.

4. *Batch and online access:* it should be possible to transfer data using the stacking process as well as through direct access to the basis data (drill-through).

5. *Selection provided by different analysis models:* Codd requires the following analysis models to be taken into account:

   a) The *categorical model,* which describes the comparison of historical data that comes directly from the database.

   b) The *exegetic model*, which takes into account the navigation path of a user. Exegesis is the art of explaining or interpreting texts.

   c) The *contemplative model* integrates the option of changing the structures. Therefore, it must be possible to determine the relation-ships between the elements as well as to enter data.

   d) The *formula-based model* enhances the variants mentioned so far by operations research algorithms.

6. *Client/server architecture:* the use of distributed resources is recom-mended, since OLAP systems normally manage larger amounts of data.

7. *Clarity:* the user should not have to worry about whether the OLAP functions are part of the user interface or not – the remote server applications should act in the same way as a local system.

8. *Multi-user mode:* unlike earlier systems that were designed for single users, the aim is now to serve as many users as possible.

9. *De-normalized data:* integrity problems that arise when de-normalized data is changed need to be overcome.

10. *Separate storage of OLAP and basis data:* OLAP data is kept strictly separate from the basis data of operational systems (see section 4.1). This enables faster response times and flexible simulations of different scenarios.

11. *Differentiation between missing and zero values:* this differentiation is particularly important for statistical calculations if, for example, a basic value is to be determined.

12. *Dealing with missing values:* in statistical calculations, it is necessary to deal appropriately with missing values. If, for example, out of ten business units there are three that have not transferred their sales data, a reliable sales average cannot be calculated on the basis of ten organizational units.

In practice there is not a clear difference between OLAP systems and data warehouses. Manufacturers sometimes market OLAP systems as data warehouse systems, which should be regarded with skepticism since OLAP principles encompass multidimensional data storage and evaluation whereas data warehouses provide the technology.

4.3 Business Intelligence

Business Intelligence (BI) can generally be described as a class of procedures used by companies to "get more out of basic information" to analyze their situation. Every now and then, analogies are searched for between the "intelligence" of an enterprise and a person, whereby specific facts are collected, stored appropriately, and used.

A variant of this is E-Business Intelligence, which is the evaluation of data that is recorded when websites are visited, in particular data about customers and potential customers. For example, a system may discover correlations between the sequence of "clicks" (clickstream) and purchases in the Internet. Searches that show that a large number of customers have left the page after clicking on a certain item, for example, are very informative in this context.

BI is mainly based on the collection of specific information, which differs from classic management information systems in that not only internal quantitative data (as it was transferred from the operational systems) is of importance. BI also comprises internal qualitative information, external quantitative data such as time slices bought from market research institutes for market share development, and external qualitative information from the Internet (see figure 4.2).

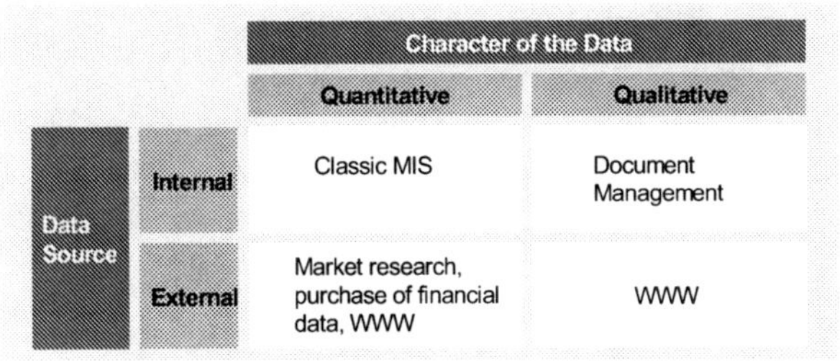

| | | **Character of the Data** | |
		Quantitative	Qualitative
Data Source	**Internal**	Classic MIS	Document Management
	External	Market research, purchase of financial data, WWW	WWW

Fig. 4.2: Example of an Information Basis used by Business Intelligence

The following examples show how BI aids decision making in different functional areas of a company:

1.   The capital investment manager of an international corporation U realizes that incoming orders for Brazilian subsidiary B are down by 10%, which is bad news. Then the manager searches for information on the Internet about the trend of the relevant market in Brazil and discovers that this market has shrunk by an average of 18%. In the light of this information, subsidiary B has done well after all, which is good news.

2.   The news service of the executive board in an industrial company C published a rumor that an important vendor L might be merging with the largest competitor of C. Since this merger would severely affect the position of C in the procurement market, an assistant to the executive board is commissioned with the task of getting data from the material management system on the purchasing business with L.

3.   A large German automobile manufacturer G knows that a Japanese competitor J wants to attack one of G's important product lines by bringing out a new product. Therefore, all test reports and test data are researched in specialist publications. Two articles about tests with a trial vehicle from competitor J arrive in the mailbox of an employee in the market surveillance department. She thinks that the first article is unimportant because it comes from an untrustworthy source, so she saves it in a document management system. However, she finds that the second article is particularly informative and gives it an appropriate valuation. It is now automatically distributed to the mailboxes of several specialist and management staff by the knowledge management system of company G.

4.   A provider of specialized gear boxes S has saved all historic orders and finds the related engineering designs from earlier orders as a result of queries. As a result of relatively minor changes to the most similar product, a quotation can be offered quickly thanks to a system of case-based reasoning.

The information nerve center for BI is often a data warehouse. Occasionally the introduction of the term *knowledge warehouse* is attempted in cases where qualitative information plays an important part.

There are certain calculations for data layout in the next level above the data warehouse. This can be illustrated by the normalization of worldwide sales using a standard currency, for example, US dollars based on the exchange rate on the key date.

This is used as a base by other methods that might be described as BI in a stricter sense. One of the first method groups is data mining, which from a broader point of view, describes the specific navigation in large datasets. If, for example, the contribution margin throughout the firm were to take a turn for the worse, the system would initially look to see if certain product or customer groups or regional markets were the cause. The system then searches among the main causes, such as sales of a particular product group to a single customer group in one region. After this "diagnosis" has been made, a specific "therapy" can be applied, such as reviewing a price list or changing the way the external sales force is managed.

The demands made on data mining are even tougher. While the paths are already marked during navigation and the system only has to select one of them, data mining is "unbiased" in its analysis method which looks for unusual data circumstances that had not previously been suspected. These types of systems are thus also known as a *suspicious circumstance generators*. In this way, for example, combinations of articles or product characteristics are identified, which can be offered to certain customer groups. Another area of use is that of early warnings, for example if the system finds conspicuous behavior of customers who are very likely to soon defect to competitors, thus providing the basis for a customer retention strategy.

The counterpart of data mining is text mining, whereby linguistic analyses are used to check whether texts match up with the information requirements profile of employees. In tests, it was found that it is possible to automatically derive the quintessence of longer texts, or for articles that are taken from different sources at different times but with the same content to be assigned to each other. This is important for compact management information, for example, individual news-letters can be created whose content and presentation style meet the information requirements and expectations of specialists and managers.

This type of active information system is supported by roles and user profiles or models. While roles tend to describe the objective side of a workplace, such as the activity of a market researcher, an accountant for Activity-Based Costing, or the head of a patenting department, user models reflect subjective preferences. Thus, managers with an engineering degree often prefer graphics while those with a business degree prefer balance sheet displays. Such personalization still requires a significant amount of research and development.

This is taken further by approaches that use intelligent agents to search for information as well as prepare and analyze it. In practical terms, the range of this type of agent goes from small, easily distinguishable program modules to expert systems with a relatively large amount of autonomy. Interesting areas of research lie in this field for business administration, information systems, and computer science, but there are still only a few running systems (Mertens 2001).

4.4 Analytical Application Systems

Analytical application systems and the approaches described in this chapter so far are more like "ready-to-use solutions" rather than "tools for generating reporting systems." Unlike data-oriented procedures in classic data warehouses, OLAP and business intelligence systems (which often produce unconnected reports), analytical application systems place the emphasis on ready-made overall solutions (closed-loop system) for typical decision-making processes. They often use elements of the concepts and systems described thus far (Hackney, 1999).

The emphasis is on all phases of decision-making support: the definition of enterprise-wide, group-based or individual targets or milestones, the identification and valuation of alternative courses of action, a performance gauge as well as feedback, which can lead to the modification of measures or targets. The need to react quickly to different issues means there are special requirements that need to be met by a flexible and simple modeling of problems. One of the most significant advantages of analytical application systems is that they are not based on inflexible structures of actual data in operational systems, thus making it possible to analyze the effects of alternative scenarios such as organizational or process variants.

When performance is measured, automatic warning functions that inform the decision-maker when certain tolerance limits are exceeded (such as via e-mail or voice mail) are increasingly important.

Analytical application systems are also required to automatically generate suggestions for improvement. For example, the system may show alternatives such as increasing the safety stock of a product by percentage X if an article is frequently sold out. Predefined metrics model the relevant key figures and dimensions for a business domain. In addition, defaulted filters restrict these solutions to certain information segments such as product lines, regions, or functional areas. The standard models can be adapted to the requirements of each user.

As well as the required functions and methods, analytical application systems include the aggregation and integration of relevant facts from different internal and external sources. An example of this would be where the software for an electronic marketplace system makes a note of the pages a customer called up and the products that she or he placed in the shopping basket. A CRM system analyzes the purchasing behavior of consumers over different periods of time, and thus calculates their value for the vendor. This data is completed by statistical analysis for population development and income distribution, which is why the term *multichannel evaluation system* is also used.

In addition to the business-oriented functions, analytical application systems normally provide a sophisticated technical infrastructure, meaning that they can quickly access data from many different sources using a performance-capable adapter, and re-import final analysis results such as plan values into operational systems. Smooth integration requires a standardized definition of the metadata throughout the company. As per this definition, SAP SEM/BA is an analytical application system.

4.5 Internet

The Internet provides a stable communication medium that is available world-wide, meaning that company headquarters that are globally distributed can be linked up in an intranet throughout the enterprise. This enables the efficient common usage of data. Other advantages of the Internet are that it does not depend on platforms (which is a prerequisite for using heterogeneous networks), it has functions for multimedia presentations, and the company plant structure is highly flexible when it comes to making changes to the organization (Schuler/ Pfeifer, 2001).

Companies and associations mainly use the Internet to gain publicity for themselves (by presenting business reports and products or services). This information is of particular interest with regard to customers, vendors, and competitors or potential collaboration partners. Suppliers from the media and market research industries are especially important, because they not only gain publicity but also provide other services that are important for research, such as access to online databases, newspaper and magazine archives, news tickers and increasingly, radio and television programs. It is also possible to access the most up-to-date scientific research from universities, research institutes, and libraries. Primary information on planned changes to legislation or on aid programs can be obtained directly from political organizations and from the government, for example, from the economics ministry (Steinhaus, 1998).

A major advantage of the Internet is that the data is already available in electronic form and thus can be integrated into a management information system without any integration gaps. Its significance has increased due to the growing numbers of preliminary and exclusive publications. Query languages are not so complex for databases in the WWW as the conventional variants, and it is not necessary to install software for each provider because standardized access is enabled by the Web browser (Jaros-Sturhan/Löffler, 1995). The quantity and quality of the data that can be used for accounting do, however, still greatly vary according to each subject area, so search results are not reliable enough to be used for decision-making until they have been checked and edited.

Despite these disadvantages, a 1998 study showed that firms rated the Internet as the main source of specialist information at 77% (CD-ROM 69%, host database 61%) (Markscheffel, 1998, p. 129). Moreover, different concepts and software tools open up new possibilities for solving or ameliorating these problems, such as *Web Farming* (Hackathorn, 1999) or an *editorial workbench* which was developed by the Bavarian Research Institute for Knowledge-Based Systems in cooperation with SAP (Meier, 2000).

4.6   Personalized Enterprise Portals

An (enterprise) portal is a user interface in a Web browser that can be used as a central point of access to information and software functions.

An intranet has a particularly large potential for integration. It may combine reports in a data warehouse, personnel data in an HR system, a newsletter from the public information office, and a mail and time management system. In addition, external modules such as electronic marketplaces or news from a press agency can be included. More recent developments now enable information to be transferred to mobile devices, such as cellular phones or Personal Digital Assistants (PDA), whereby usage needs to be examined case by case.

The main advantage of enterprise portals is that they are easy to use due to a uniform layout (look and feel) and because single sign-on is supported for multiple application systems. In addition, progressive solutions enable the drag-and-relate function to be used. For example, a user can select a delivery order from the SCM program and drag it with the mouse to the CRM software, which then presents extensive context-sensitive data on the relevant customer. These modules can even come from different manufacturers, which means that a portal can make it easier for an enterprise to combine the best offers.

It is particularly useful if the information can be prepared to meet the exact needs of the user. There are several very promising solution approaches for this concept: agent technology, content management, personalization, individualization, and knowledge management. These have a wide range of functions, from the simple display of the user name on a Web site through to complex navigation help based on extensive user models (Kramer/Noronha, 2000). The filtering, editing, and active distribution of facts relevant for decision-making especially for enterprise management is, however, still a challenge for information systems and is thus moving back into the limelight as a result of Internet technology demands.

5   Components of the SAP Solution

5.1   General Overview

SAP has committed itself to the goal of integrating and improving the flow of information within the network of strategic and operational management tasks described in section 2.1 (see figure 5.1).

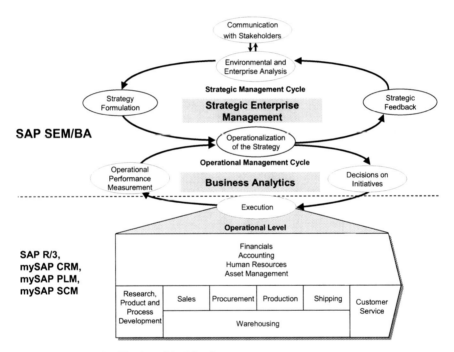

Fig. 5.1: Business Classification of SAP Products

The analytical application which SAP calls SAP SEM/BA provides a full range of functionality for corporate governance. SAP Strategic Enterprise Management (SAP SEM) supplies the functions needed for strategic decision making. SAP Business Analytics (SAP BA) controls the business processes in corporate groups and their business units. The SAP SEM and SAP BA software form a unit (SAP SEM/BA). Figure 5.2 shows its components.

Strategic Enterprise Management

Business Planning & Simulation SEM-BPS	Business Consolidation SEM-BCS	Corporate Performance Monitor SEM-CPM	Stakeholder Relationship Management SEM-SRM	Business Information Collection SEM-BIC
• Modeling Planning Structures • User Interfaces for Planning • Planning Functions and Application Systems (Including Simulation) • Coordination of Planning Processes	• Consolidation Based On Legal Requirements (Ge...	• Balanced Scorecard • Measure Builder • Measure Catalogs	• Management of Stakeholder Contacts	• Specification of Research Requests • Selection and Requests with External Information Sources • Editing and Linking Internal and External Facts

Corporate and Business Unit Management

• Working Capital Management - Analysis of Payment History - Credit Risk Analysis • Costing • Cost Center Planning • Resource Planning	• Customer Analytics - Customer Value - Customer Potential - Custom... * • Interaction Channel Analytics	• Supply Chain Management • Supply Chain	• Product Structuring • Concurrent Costing	• Personnel Planning • HR Web Cockpits • Employee Turnover Analysis • HR Benchmarking • HR Balanced Scorecard • Management by Objectives

Business Process Control

Financial Analytics	Customer Relationship Analytics CRM Analytics	Supply Chain Analytics SCM Analytics	Product Lifecycle Analytics PLM Analytics	Human Resource Analytics HR Analytics

Business Analytics

Fig. 5.2: Components and Functions of SAP SEM/BA © SAP AG

Additional elements of the package are the SAP Business Information Warehouse (SAP BW), SAP Content Management®, the mySAP Enterprise Portal®, and SAP Business Framework Architecture®. The operational level includes systems such as SAP R/3, mySAP® Customer Relationship Management® (mySAP CRM®), mySAP Supply Chain Management (mySAP SCM®), and mySAP Product Lifecycle Management (mySAP PLM®). Figure 5.3 presents an overview of the system components that will be described in greater detail below.

In addition to the software functionality, the systems also provide domain-specific information models that SAP refers to as *Business Content*. Examples of Business Content in SAP SEM/BA are measure catalogs, calculation schemas for measures in value-based management (see section 2.2), and Strategy Templates.

Application software handles business tasks, distinguishing it from the system software (operating systems for PCs and networks) and system-related software (database systems, middleware, and so on). Many software providers and consultants now use the abbreviated form *applications*, although this may not be ideal in some contexts. Since the terms *application* and *application system* have special meanings at SAP, we will briefly explain how they are used in this chapter. *Application* can refer to SAP SEM/BA as a whole, to a single component such as SEM-BPS or SCM Analytics, or to a specific task within a component (such as personnel planning). For SAP, an *application system* is always a physically installed application.

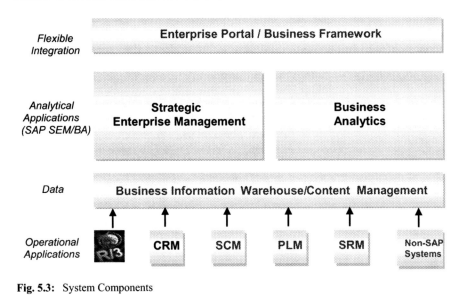

Fig. 5.3: System Components

Corporate and Business Unit Management with Strategic Enterprise Management

SAP SEM is used to determine, define, communicate, and implement strategies – either for an entire group of companies, an individual company in a group, or an organizational unit within a company (such as a business area or profit center).

The system facilitates the collection and evaluation of information from internal and external sources required for environmental and business analysis. It also provides functions for the subsequent identification, evaluation, and selection of alternative strategies. The selected strategy must be formulated, quantified, and described in relation to the existing strategies of the company. This is followed by operationalization, which converts the general requirements into concrete plans step-by-step down to the level of measures.

SAP SEM thus functions as a tool for coordinating the managers and employees involved in the planning and decision-making process. It also furthers communication with stakeholders. To be able to test whether the requirements were implemented and the anticipated effects realized, actual values for the measured variables must be collected, aggregated, and consolidated, and then presented in a form appropriate for the user (Performance Measurement and strategic feedback).

Process Control with Business Analytics

Business Analytics extends SAP SEM to include operational management tasks (that is, decisions intended to improve business processes). The goal is to combine process-specific data (including non-financial data) with aspects of accounting.

The focus is on situational, problem-oriented ad hoc analyses, which alert managers that a decision is needed, and that support the evaluation of alternative courses of action regarding their potential contribution to company strategy. Business Analytics thus forges a link between the management level and the operational level.

The term *analysis* should be understood here in its broadest sense. It includes modeling, simulating, planning, and evaluating defined subject areas. Such analysis is not limited to the firm itself, but can include cooperative scenarios with other firms (*Enterprise and Extraprise Controlling*). The main target groups are therefore middle and lower management as well as employees with staff functions, such as management accountants and internal consultants.

Operational Applications, Analytical Applications, SAP BW, and SAP Content Management

SAP Business Information Warehouse

Data integration – meaning the global availability and consistency of metadata and business data – is achieved by employing SAP BW in conjunction with SAP Content Management. The quantitative data for SAP SEM/BA resides in SAP BW, which consists of the components shown in figure 5.4.

The Administrator Workbench is the central administration tool of SAP BW for modeling, retrieving, and storing data. This tool monitors and controls the overall process – from the extraction of data from source systems to data storage. It also enables data loading processes to be scheduled, triggered, and monitored. SAP BW can integrate data from completely different sources, such as from one or more SAP R/3 Systems or other ERP software. This integration is realized through Business Application Programming Interfaces (BAPIs). External contents such as benchmarking data are used as well.

The SAP BW server consists of a staging engine which handles the data transfer from the source systems, plus the Metadata Manager, the Data Manager, and the memory areas (master data, metadata repository, Persistent Staging Area (PSA), Operational Data Store (ODS), and InfoCubes) for management of metadata and business data.

The master data repository holds the master data, while the metadata repository contains metadata that describe all data structures within SAP BW. The PSA is essentially an "inbox" in SAP BW where data is cleaned up and transformed by transfer rules before reaching the ODS. An ODS object contains cleaned-up transaction data.

Fig. 5.4: Components of SAP BW   © SAP AG

The central objects on which reports and analyses in SAP BW are based are called *InfoCubes*. An InfoCube describes a self-contained dataset for a particular business area, such as profitability analysis. InfoCubes in turn consist of InfoObjects. InfoObjects are evaluation criteria that SAP refers to as characteristics, as well as key figures. Characteristics are used to separate key figures for analysis. Examples of characteristics are products, customers, regions, months, distribution channels, and versions. Key figures are values or quantities such as turnover, invoice amount, purchase order quantity, warehouse stock, or lead time.

SAP BW also provides a separate tool for reporting called the *Business Explorer* (BW BEx), which is linked through an API to the OLAP processor that executes queries. Presentation software from other manufacturers can be used through the standardized OLE-DB-for-OLAP interface (ODBO interface). The Business Explorer can also be accessed from SEM-CPM.

SAP Content Management

SAP Content Management is SAP's document management system. In SAP SEM/
BA it handles unstructured, nonquantitative data such as text or graphics.

Logical View of Integration

Operational applications such as mySAP CRM involve individual functions or
business processes and represent the events in databases. If necessary, the system
can supply data for analyses as early as the planning phase, such as valuations or
account determination. This data is transferred into the data warehouse on a
periodic basis.

As described in section 4.4, analytical applications are used for comprehensive
control of individual areas such as sales or risk management. They execute read
and write operations directly on the data warehouse. Hence, a conflict arises with
the data warehouse which is designed for read access. To resolve this conflict,
analytical application systems normally have separate data marts.

If analysis results should be available centrally, they can be transferred periodical-
ly into a company-wide data warehouse. In some cases the results of analytical
application systems must be accessible to operational systems, such as when new
master data, budget requirements, or transfer prices are established.

Such data flows into the operational applications and from there returns to the
company-wide data warehouse. Since this increases the overall complexity, an
analytical application system needs functions that are used in the data warehouse
and in the operational systems as well, such as valuation and apportionment
methods. Appropriate implementation enables metadata, master data, and methods
to be utilized together with the data warehouse and the operational systems (Sinzig
2001b).

Both time-triggered connections (extractors, retractors) and transaction-based real-
time connections (middleware, bus systems) are available as implementation
concepts for data exchange in application system networks.

Extractors select data from operational systems and format it for transfer into a
data warehouse. Retractors, on the other hand, select data from a data warehouse
and transfer it back into the operational systems. Figure 5.5 clarifies these processes.

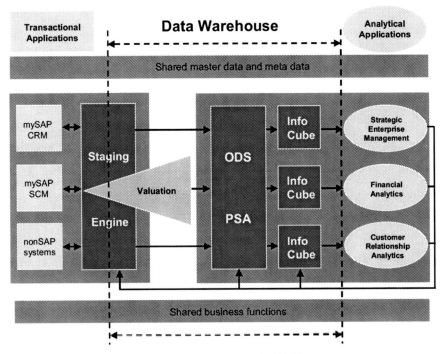

Fig. 5.5: Enterprise-wide Application Architecture (Sinzig 2001b)

Technological View of Integration

SAP SEM/BA uses SAP BW for storage and administration of data. The system includes both predefined applications and analytical tools that create such applications, such as the planning workbench (see section 5.2.1). An advantage of analytical tools is that they facilitate cross-functional integration between applications and enable a uniform look and feel. SAP SEM/BA provides the complete Business Content of SAP BW (queries, InfoObjects, InfoSources, InfoCubes, and so on). This content includes key figures on operational processes, such as in production or accounts receivable.

Function Integration with the mySAP Enterprise Portal and SAP Business Framework Architecture

Function integration between system components is achieved with the mySAP Enterprise Portal and SAP Business Framework Architecture. The Business Framework Architecture can encompass both heterogeneous subsystems and data sources within a local network, as well as systems linked together through the Internet (see figure 5.6).

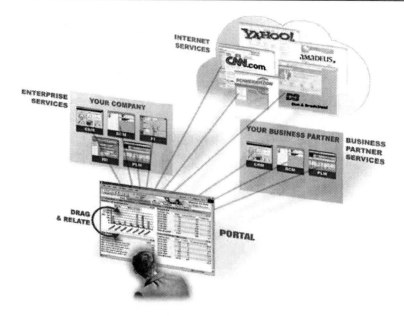

Fig. 5.6: mySAP Enterprise Portal   © SAP AG

SAP SEM/BA is based on an open architecture, making it a simple matter to integrate products of other software vendors, such as CRM software or an HR system. A number of different user interfaces are available, such as SAPGUI, a Web Browser, or external software (such as Microsoft Excel), all of which are integrated into individually configured portals.

5.2   Strategic Enterprise Management

SAP SEM consists of the five components shown in figure 5.2. These components cover the following business functions:

- **Business Planning and Simulation (SEM-BPS)**
  - Integrated planning applications
  - Modeling planning structures
  - Generic planning functions
  - User interfaces for planning
  - Coordination of planning processes

- **Business Consolidation (SEM-BCS)**
  - Consolidation based on legal requirements
    (German Commercial Code, US GAAP, IAS, etc.)
  - Consolidation for management

- **Corporate Performance Monitor (SEM-CPM)**
  Strategy Management
  - Balanced Scorecard
  - Risk management
  - Value Driver Trees
  Performance Measurement
  - Management Cockpit
  - Measure Builder
  - Benchmarking

- **Stakeholder Relationship Management (SEM-SRM)**
  - Management of master data and contacts
  - Stakeholder Portals
  - Bidirectional, active communication

- **Business Information Collection (SEM-BIC)**
  - Specification of research requests
  - Selection and requests with external sources of information
  - Editing and linking internal and external
    facts

These functions are described in detail below.

5.2.1   SEM Business Planning and Simulation (SEM-BPS)

5.2.1.1   General Aspects of Implementation

The SEM-BPS component is employed to plan areas of responsibility. These plans are linked to the processes in those areas. This has the following implications:

1. Data and processes must be integrated between strategic and operational planning on the one hand, and between planning and the actual business processes on the other.

2. It must be possible to run simulations independently of actual structures.

3. Planning must be possible both in complex, decentralized organizations and for small, simply structured units.

4. The appropriate business methods must be provided.

5. Planning within a self-contained structure of subplans must be supported.

To fulfill these requirements, SEM-BPS first of all provides complete planning applications. Examples are the Capital Market Interpreter for simulating shareholder value and the functions for planning the cash flow, balance sheet, profit and loss statement (P+L), investments, and cost centers. These applications can be combined with each other, and are continued in Business Analytics (see section 5.3) in planning the processes in responsibility areas (examples: sales planning, campaign planning, sales and operations planning, project planning). The individual plans are also partially linked to operational applications. For example, the results of cost center planning can be transferred back into SAP R/3 CO. The plans as a whole are based on a system of business classification.

Secondly, customized planning applications can be created with the planning workbench, which is useful in cases where the standard applications are not suitable. The workbench enables new planning applications to be defined to meet the requirements of a particular data, navigation, or interface paradigm.

Thirdly, individually programmed planning applications are possible using the services of this workbench through an API. Starting points are usually special planning functions to which the relevant data is assigned and that are processed with an individual interface. Figure 5.7 is a schematic representation of the relationships and approaches of planning based on OLAP data structures (such as in SEM-BPS and Business Analytics) on the one hand, and planning based on operational data structures (such as with SAP R/3) on the other.

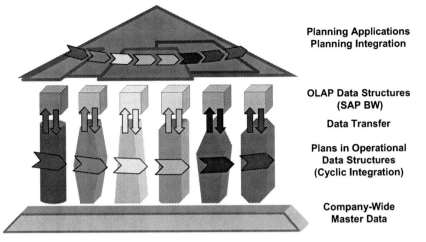

Planning Applications
Planning Integration

OLAP Data Structures
(SAP BW)

Data Transfer

Plans in Operational
Data Structures
(Cyclic Integration)

Company-Wide
Master Data

Fig. 5.7: Planning in Operational Data Structures and OLAP Data Structures   © SAP AG

SAP SEM/BA and therefore the planning features are implemented on SAP BW as analytical applications. The planning approach therefore differs from that of SAP R/3. The planning applications available in SAP R/3 (such as cost center planning, profit planning, project planning, or HR planning) are based on the data structures of the operational applications. This is true for both master data and transaction data. The operational applications are characterized by heterogeneous data models, and so the planning applications use this approach as well. The plans are integrated with each other through a cyclic process.

SAP BW represents a platform for a data model based on the principles of OLAP. Programs in SAP BW called *extractors* are essentially transformation functions that move the master data and transaction data from the operational world into the OLAP world. This process removes the transactional elements from the data structures, reducing their complexity. General planning functions are available on these OLAP data structures (copying, projections, distribution, and so on).

This enables more unified methodologies to be used than with planning applications based on operational data structures. The planning applications of SAP SEM/BA can also reference data models that represent multiple operational applications (such as Activity-Based Management linked to cost center accounting, Activity-Based Costing, and profitability analysis). This allows for accessing the input parameters of different operational systems, for example. It also facilitates the integration of plans, whether as a simulation or data update.

It is possible to use both actual and plan data from the operational systems as a basis for the SAP-SEM/BA planning systems. The plan data of the modeled world can be fed back into the operational systems. There are two reasons for doing this:

(1) The data may be used for more sophisticated purposes. For example, a budget approved during the investment planning process is assigned to a project and broken down into work packages.

(2) The data serves for operational business processes. For example, a transfer price for cost center activities calculated on the basis of plan price iteration can be used to valuate operations in production orders, or a purchasing transaction prevented from exceeding the purchasing budget assigned to a cost center (transaction-based availability check).

It is not possible to transfer plan values from the OLAP world to the operational applications on a 1:1 basis. This requires the definition of scenarios (closed-loop scenarios), such as investment fund allocation or personnel and cost planning.

5.2.1.2   Integrated Planning Applications

The integrated planning applications of SEM-BPS are designed to solve standard tasks in strategic planning with little configuration effort. A planning application can provide Business Content for a defined domain in the form of preconfigured SAP BW InfoCubes, suitable extractors from SAP R/3, special interfaces with input help, processing functions, and retractors (if necessary). If required by the business problem, a planning application provides special functions, special flow control, or special interfaces. Configuration through customizing settings is possible to some extent. The standard solutions may also serve as a starting point for planning applications created for an individual company. The planning applications are partially isolated from each other. However, they are able to exchange data among themselves (such as the cost center plan and the profit plan).

Figure 5.8 shows an overview of some of the planning applications currently available in SEM-BPS. Additional applications are continually being developed.

The focal point of the systematics is integrated annual financial statement planning, which includes subplans such as the profit plan, the cost center plan, and the investment plan. The following describes some of the existing planning applications in more detail. Cost center planning will be described in chapter 5.3.1 (Financial Analytics), sales planning as the basis of profit planning in chapter 5.3.2 (CRM Analytics).

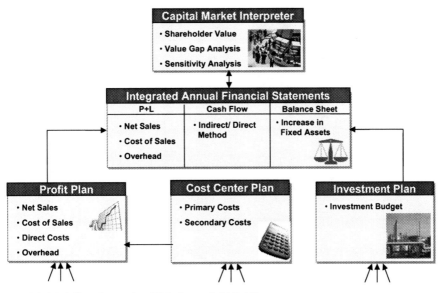

Fig. 5.8: Modeling of Associated Subplans   © SAP AG

Capital Market Interpreter

The Capital Market Interpreter enables forecasts of external financial analysts to be included in strategic planning and compared with the company's value based on internal planning data. This makes it possible to calculate "value gaps" showing the degree to which the company is over- or undervalued. On the basis of the actual business trend, the Capital Market Interpreter also determines whether the strategy is moving the company toward the desired external valuation. This tool is therefore an important element in strategy valuation and strategic control.

The valuation method currently used is based on the concept of shareholder value. The procedure starts from the seven classical generic value drivers by Rappaport (see section 2.2). A cash flow series can be defined from the trend over the years and the company's value determined using a DCF calculation (see figure 5.9).

The Capital Market Interpreter enables users to vary the value driver parameters in simulations, run various scenarios and save them. Sensitivity analysis, a function for calculating the influence of individual drivers and displaying the results as a graphic (see figure 5.10), completes the functionality.

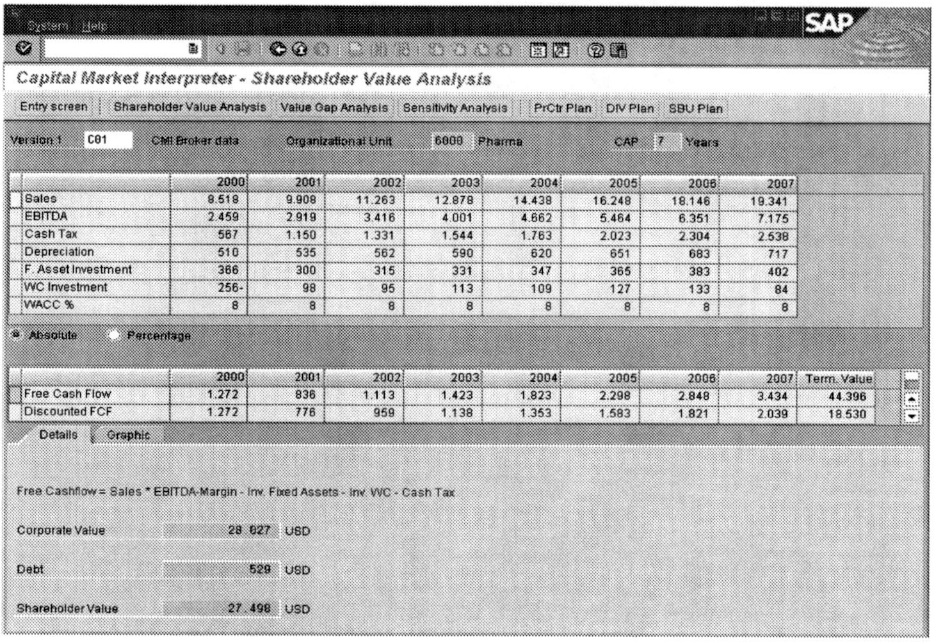

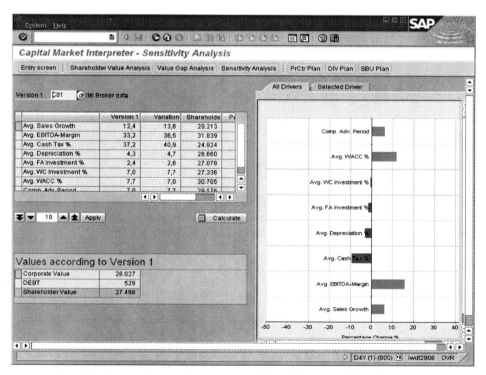

Fig. 5.9: Internal Calculation of Shareholder Value   © SAP AG

Fig. 5.10: Graphic Display of the Influence of Value Drivers   © SAP AG

Integrated Balance Sheet, P&L, and Cash Flow Planning

This planning application enables the effects on key figures for the year-end closing to be simulated and a final budget compiled based on detailed requirements such as for sales, costs, and investments.

The InfoCube on which planning is based contains general time characteristics (fiscal year and period) plus the plan version, the planning item, and the profit center and company as characteristics for the accounting unit. There are also characteristics that are used only to further differentiate particular income statement and balance sheet items, such as the country, the functional area, or the asset depreciation range. Key figures exist for value and quantity changes and for balance sheet items for the ending inventories.

This data model as well as the associated planning layouts and functions enable scenarios such as planning the sales revenues, cost of sales, overhead, working capital, and investments in a business area for a period of three years. The effects of the planned values on the balance sheet, income statement, and statement of cash flows can be seen (see figure 5.11). The system allows for depreciation and discounting effects.

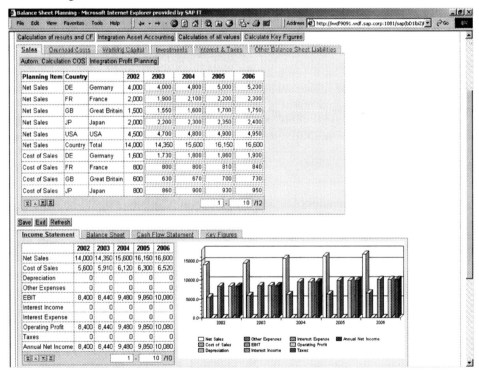

Fig. 5.11: Balance Sheet, P&L, and Cash Flow Planning with SEM-BPS   © SAP AG

The cash flow can be determined by either the direct method or the indirect method. As part of accounting, balance sheet planning uses the local currency or group currency, while liquidity planning – which controls the financial supply chain – uses the transaction currency which is translated into group currency in consolidation.

The following special planning functions are available in connection with balance sheet, P&L, and cash flow planning:

a) Depreciation

This function includes the calculation of asset depreciation rates and planning such rates based on the requirements of double-entry bookkeeping. Users can choose to have posting records generated only for the income statement or for balance sheet accounts as well. Posting records only for the income statement can be useful for example when analyzing investment plans that consider just the expense and no linkage to the balance sheet is desired. When posting records are produced both for the income statement and the balance sheet, a posting to an expense account and a posting to fixed assets are generated (depreciation is debited and assets are credited). The following depreciation methods are available: straight-line, sum-of-the-years, and declining-balance (book value method).

b) Accumulate Balances

The SAP BW key figures are either cumulative (such as sales revenues or quantity sold) or non-cumulative (such as the number of employees or the warehouse stock). The measures defined as non-cumulative values form a group together with additional data fields containing inventory changes (goods receipts and goods issues). To enable non-cumulative values to be planned, all key figures belonging to such a group are adjusted. The accumulate balances function supports this adjustment by determining values for missing data when inventories are updated. Either the ending inventory or the inventory change (based on the period) is calculated.

c) Account Determination/Offsetting Entry

This function assures that the balance sheet is balanced for planned data as well. Account determination enables posting to accounts in accordance with the principles of double-entry bookkeeping. To balance the debit and credit items, the system generates an offsetting posting for each entry. The offsetting account can be specified directly or defined in the customizing parameters.

d) Time Lag

With the time lag function, the delay between two business transactions that belong together can be planned. It is frequently the case that transactions are not completed before the end of the fiscal period. For example, it is possible to account for the fact that a payment, which increases the cash on hand, is received only after some time has gone by. This enables the system to handle extended processes such as required payment dates or the payment behavior of individual customers or customers in a particular region.

e) Account-Based Currency Translation and Rounding

In contrast to balance sheets, which are normally created for a specific key date, the income statement is posted period by period. Multinational companies whose subsidiaries prepare their financial statements in different currencies have special requirements regarding currency translation and the rounding of currency amounts. The balance sheet items are translated into group currency using the current exchange rate, while the items in the income statement are translated at an average exchange rate. This process can result in differences, which must be recorded in a separate account. The function for account-based currency translation meets this requirement.

In addition, rounding errors can result in differences between the balance sheet and the income statement. To enable these differences to be reported in a separate account, SEM-BPS supplies rounding methods that have the same functionality as the corresponding functions in the SAP R/3 system.

Capital Investment Planning

SEM-BPS supplies two applications within capital investment planning. The one is preinvestment analysis for individual investments and investment programs, while the other is structured entry of capital requirements by organizational unit. The second alternative is used to plan investment budgets. SEM-BPS enables group-wide planning and reconciliation of the investment volume across systems.

Capital investment planning is horizontally integrated with adjacent planning applications. Its results can flow into balance sheet planning as current-year acquisitions in the asset portfolio, and into profit planning as a change in profitability due to the investment.

The valuation of appropriation requests and alternatives is of particular signify-cance for the approval process. For this purpose, SEM-BPS supplies methods of static and dynamic preinvestment analysis. Payment balances, net present values, and internal interest rates can be calculated and undergo sensitivity analysis regarding the model parameters.

An additional key function is vertical integration of the planning process among the organizational units in the hierarchy. To enable group-wide, cross-system capital investment planning, the strategic requirements at corporate level must harmonize with the operational requirements of the local organizational units (such as individual companies, plants, and plant sections). This vertical integration is achieved in SEM-BPS through functions for bottom-up planning and top-down budgeting. They are supplemented by functions for vertical integration across systems.

Using SAP BW technology, the data of the current investment measures from SAP R/3 IM is collected, saved in the local SAP BW for reporting purposes, translated into group currency, and integrated into the data model for SEM-BPS capital investment planning. The plan and actual data from the operational systems are then available for comparison and copying functions in SEM-BPS.

By means of retractors, the plan values for the budget are transferred in the other direction from central capital investment planning in SEM-BPS directly into the different SAP R/3 systems in the local currencies. The plan values in SEM-BPS can be compared with the values in SAP R/3 IM at any time. This ensures a high level of transparency of the investment process from strategic planning to operational support. Figure 5.12 shows the interrelationships.

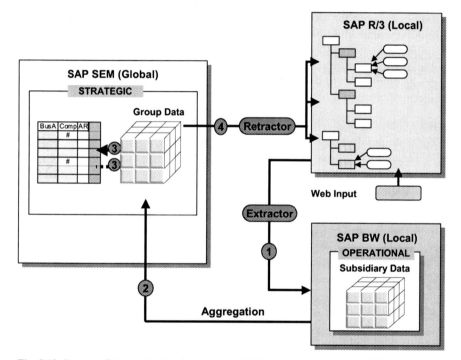

Fig. 5.12: Process of Approving, Implementing, and Monitoring Investments   © SAP AG

Dynamic Simulation with Powersim Studio

To simulate dynamic processes in the company and derive planning measures from such simulations, SEM-BPS features an interface to Powersim Studio® software from Powersim® Software AS. Powersim Studio uses the System Dynamics method (see section 3.3.3) to define complex business scenarios for investigating how the model behaves over time under varying conditions and with different parameters. The program has a special user interface that enables models to be developed using diagrams (see figure 5.13).

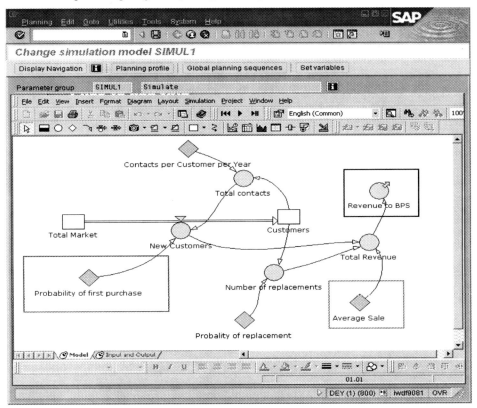

Fig. 5.13: A Simulation Model in Powersim Studio   © SAP AG

The link between the simulation model and the data and structures of SEM-BPS is established by a dataset object, which is a technical element of the simulation model. The purpose of the dataset object is to map the units, characteristics, and key figures of SEM-BPS to the corresponding objects in Powersim Studio. It also reads and writes master data and transaction data to and from the planning package.

5.2.1.3   Modeling Planning Structures

The basis for all planning activities is the modeling of planning structures. Modeling must reflect the multiple interdependencies between subplans in a complex organization. The planning workbench provides functions for OLAP-based multidimensional modeling. These functions establish which areas of the company, at which levels, and which objects will be planned.

Planning Area

In the planning area, the modeler selects from the contents of the SAP BW InfoCubes those characteristics (planning dimensions) that are relevant as classification criteria for the business domains. Such characteristics can be products, customers, regions, distribution channels, cost centers, time, and so on.

Planning Level

The planning level is the second level of the planning architecture. It determines the degree of aggregation or the granularity for the characteristics selected in the planning area – for example, whether divisions, product groups, or individual products are planned. In mixed top-down/bottom-up planning, the group is planned at division level while at the same time the plant managers enter their data at product level in another version.

Planning Package

The planning package is at the lowest level of the planning architecture. Here the user specifies the objects to be planned (such as the countries Germany, France, Great Britain, and United States or the distribution channels retail, wholesale, and Internet), defining a current selection in the dataset.

It is evident that the solution chosen by SAP improves the structuring and coordination of the activities for multidimensional planning in complex organizations. The following example illustrates this:

Example

Suppose you want to plan your sales. The board of directors has set targets for the sales quantities of the individual divisions for next year. These values have to be broken down into product groups and individual products in the same way as the actual data of the prior year, and revised by the division managers. The basis for this is a SAP BW InfoCube that contains the characteristics division, product group, product, version, and year as well as the key figures sales quantity and turnover. In SEM-BPS, the modeler creates a planning area for this InfoCube. A planning level is defined for the targets set by the board. The use of two plan versions keeps this data separate from the plan revised by the division managers.

Their work requires an additional planning level with the characteristics division, product group, version, year, and the key figures sales quantity as well as turnover. The version and year are entered in the selection conditions of the planning level. In addition, a planning package is created for each division manager in which he goes through the values for the individual product groups in his division.

5.2.1.4   Generic Planning Functions

Planning functions that are independent of a business context are referred to by SAP as generic planning functions. Such functions include:

Copy: The copy function is used to transfer plan or actual data from one characteristic value to another (such as from one plan version to another, one time period to another, or one planning object to another). When the copy function is executed, the user can choose to overwrite existing data or supplement existing data with the new plan data.

Repost: Reposting deletes the data records and gives the original values a new key. For example, after a reorganization in which cost center 5011 was changed to cost center 8715, the reposting function can be used to transfer the budget to the new organizational unit.

Distribute: This function breaks down annual data to the period level, or distributes it within organizational structures. The sum of the plan values remains constant during this process. For example, the annual sales volume can be distributed evenly across the individual periods of the fiscal year or based on the seasonal variation of the prior year.

Revaluate: This function can be used to increase or decrease the plan data by a certain percentage. Entire plans or individual characteristic values can be revaluated. A user may want to have the sales figures increased by 10% for France and 15% for the United Kingdom, for example. These filter techniques are available for all planning functions.

Forecast: The planning workbench provides a number of forecasting methods for establishing time series. Before a forecast starts, the planner must specify which model (see section 3.3.2) the system should use to calculate the forecast data. The selection depends on how much is known about the past trend of the time series. The "automatic model selection" feature suggests some appropriate models. The user can accept them or specify his own method instead.

Delete: This function removes selected data records from the planning package. For example, the user can remove simulation versions that are no longer needed or products that are no longer on the market.

Formulas and FOrmula eXtensions): If users want to change key figure values in planning in a way not possible with other planning functions such as revaluation, reposting, or forecasting, they can create their own formulas. The planning workbench provides a number of mathematical functions for this purpose, particularly in the area of financial mathematics. Formula extensions (FOrmula eXtensions (FOX)) go a step beyond this. In addition to the formula operators, they enable arithmetic operations to be made dependent on conditions, run through loops, and issue messages. This functionality approaches that of exit functions (see below) for calling self-contained Advanced Business Application Programming (ABAP®)programs. Formula extensions are, however, significantly less complex than ABAP instructions.

Exit function: Exit functions are employed when all other possibilities provided by the planning workbench for generating or changing plan data are insufficient to meet requirements. They provide comprehensive control over every detail in the calculation of plan data. The exit functions are written in the form of ABAP programs.

Currency translation: The currency translation function is needed when key figures, such as turnover or accounts receivable, are planned in different currencies. Translation into a single group currency enables the plan data to be compared and aggregated. The exchange rate can be the current exchange rate, an average exchange rate, a standard exchange rate, or an historical exchange rate.

Unit conversion: This function is used to convert quantity-based key figure data into another unit. This type of conversion is required in cases where key figures such as warehouse stock are planned for subsidiaries that use different units (for example, fuel supplies may be expressed in liters or barrels, weight in kilograms or pounds, machine running time in seconds, minutes, or other units). Converting the different values into a common unit enables quantities to be accurately compared.

Planning sequences: A planning sequence is a list of planning functions for a particular task, which is processed step by step. Planning sequences are used to execute recurrent, complex planning tasks as efficiently as possible. For example, suppose you want to plan the turnover in the pharmaceuticals division for a group of subsidiaries at the beginning of each quarter. A planning sequence simplifies this process, because the different planning functions such as copying, revaluation, or distribution supply results that are used as input in each of the subsequent functions. Planning sequences can also be run as a background job and released for processing with the SAP Computing Center Management System. This enables processes with a high data volume that place heavy demands on system resources to be run at times of low system utilization (such as at night or on weekends). Another benefit is that planning tasks may be repeated at periodic intervals, such as monthly sales forecasting based on the updated actual data.

Planning documents and comments: This function enables access to qualitative information on the characteristics and key figures of a plan. Comments are supported for all elements of the plan down to individual cells. Examples are annotations for figures (such as references to economic growth forecasts or market indicators), graphic visualization of plan data in presentation slides, or providing a planning handbook.

5.2.1.5   *User Interfaces for Planning*

Accessibility for all decision makers and employees is achieved through the use of different user interfaces that are adapted to the various user roles.

Web Interfaces

Web interfaces are appropriate for simple planning tasks. They may be implemented within a company or beyond company boundaries, such as between customers and suppliers. SEM-BPS provides a tool called the Web Interface Builder that generates Web pages automatically from the layout definitions of the SEM system (see figure 5.14).

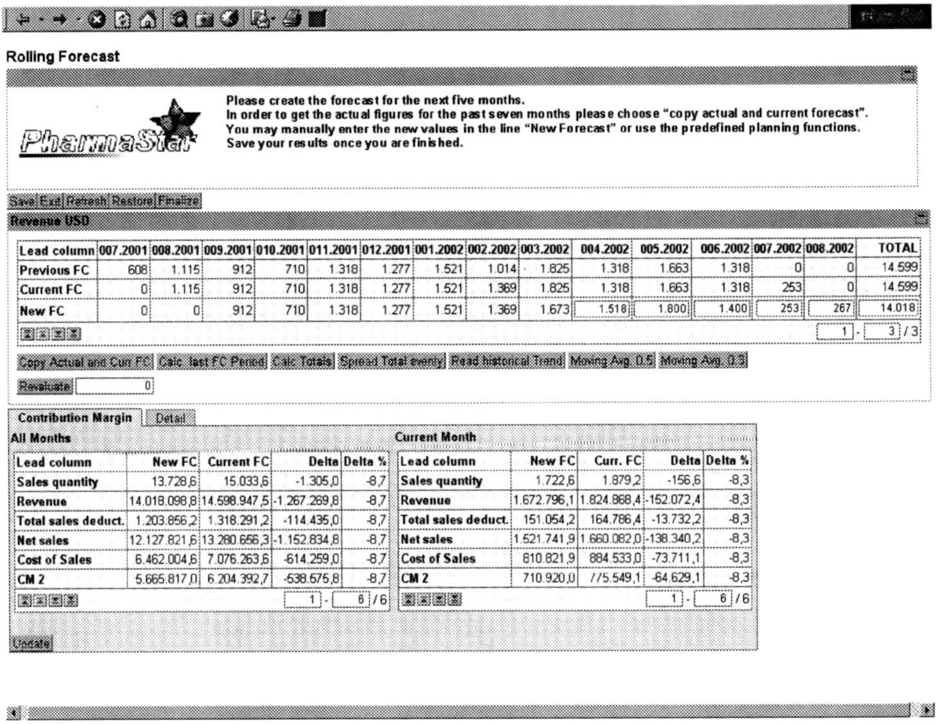

Rolling Forecast

Please create the forecast for the next five months.
In order to get the actual figures for the past seven months please choose "copy actual and current forecast".
You may manually enter the new values in the line "New Forecast" or use the predefined planning functions.
Save your results once you are finished.

Save Exit Refresh Restore Finalize

Revenue USD

Lead column	007.2001	008.2001	009.2001	010.2001	011.2001	012.2001	001.2002	002.2002	003.2002	004.2002	005.2002	006.2002	007.2002	008.2002	TOTAL
Previous FC	608	1.115	912	710	1.318	1.277	1.521	1.014	1.825	1.318	1.663	1.318	0	0	14.599
Current FC	0	1.115	912	710	1.318	1.277	1.521	1.369	1.825	1.318	1.663	1.318	253	0	14.599
New FC	0	0	912	710	1.318	1.277	1.521	1.369	1.673	1.518	1.800	1.400	253	267	14.018

1 - 3 / 3

Copy Actual and Curr FC | Calc. last FC Period | Calc. Totals | Spread Total evenly | Read historical Trend | Moving Avg. 0,5 | Moving Avg. 0,3

Reevaluate 0

Contribution Margin | Detail

All Months

Lead column	New FC	Current FC	Delta	Delta %
Sales quantity	13.728,6	15.033,6	-1.305,0	-8,7
Revenue	14.018.098,8	14.598.947,5	-1.267.269,8	-8,7
Total sales deduct.	1.203.856,2	1.318.291,2	-114.435,0	-8,7
Net sales	12.127.821,6	13.280.656,3	-1.152.834,8	-8,7
Cost of Sales	6.462.004,6	7.076.263,6	-614.259,0	-8,7
CM 2	5.665.817,0	6.204.392,7	-538.575,8	-8,7

1 - 6 / 6

Current Month

Lead column	New FC	Curr. FC	Delta	Delta %
Sales quantity	1.722,6	1.879,2	-156,6	-8,3
Revenue	1.672.796,1	1.824.868,4	-152.072,4	-8,3
Total sales deduct.	151.054,2	164.786,4	-13.732,2	-8,3
Net sales	1.521.741,9	1.660.082,0	-138.340,2	-8,3
Cost of Sales	810.821,9	884.533,0	-73.711,1	-8,3
CM 2	710.920,0	775.549,1	-64.629,1	-8,3

1 - 6 / 6

Update

Fig. 5.14: Web Interface   © SAP AG

Integrated Microsoft Excel Interface

Microsoft Excel is the de facto standard in cost accounting departments the world over. Being a purely local application, however, Excel cannot assure data consistency between different subplans and plan versions, as is frequently demonstrated in practice. Nevertheless, the user acceptance factor means that integration of Microsoft Excel into the SAP solution should be regarded as a near necessity. This is achieved by means of Excel-In-Place technology. Planning layouts are created and edited under the Microsoft Excel interface, and stored centrally in SAP SEM/BA. The planning functions and data are located in SAP SEM/BA. SEM-BPS provides cost managers with the Excel functions with which they are familiar, but there are no longer any scattered files – a significant advantage compared to other solutions (see figure 5.15).

Execute Target Setting CFO

Copy Actual to Plan | Release to Salesmanagers | Release to Financial Statement

USA | England | Canada | South Africa | Germany

| Country | USA |
| Currency | USD |

	Budget 2003	Actual 2002	Delta abs.	Delta %
Revenue in US$	20.000.000	15.377.040	4.622.960	30,1
% Net Sales / Revenue	40,0	86,2	-46,2	-53,6
% Net Revenue / Net Sales	20,0	88,3	-68,3	-77,3
% CM 2 / Net Revenue	77,0	76,9	0,1	0,1
Promotions in US$	3.240.000	3.240.000	0	0,0
Total Overheads in US$	2.520.000	2.520.000	0	0,0

	Budget 2003	Actual 2002	Delta abs.	Delta %
Revenue	20.000.000	15.377.040	4.622.960	30,1
Total sales deduct.	12.000.000	2.120.126	9.879.874	466,0
Net sales	8.000.000	13.256.911	-5.256.914	-39,7
Total dir. costs sls	6.400.000	1.555.200	4.844.800	311,5
Net revenue	1.600.000	11.701.714	-10.101.714	-86,3
Cost of sales	368.000	2.699.568	-2.331.568	-86,4
CM 2	1.232.000	9.002.146	-7.770.146	-86,3
Promotion	3.240.000	3.240.000	0	0,0
TotalOverhd	2.520.000	2.520.000	0	0,0
Operating profit or loss	-4.528.000	3.242.146	-7.770.146	-239,7

Fig. 5.15: Interface with Microsoft Excel In-Place Technology   © SAP AG

SAP Standard Interface

A third option is the SAP standard interface SAPGUI. In this context, it is used mainly for list-based data entry (see figure 5.16).

Enter plan data

Display navigation | Planning Profiles | Global planning sequences | Set Variables

Company	SAP3	BEM UK
Fiscal year variant	K4	Calendar year, 4 spec. periods
Version	BP1	BP1
Currency	USD	American Dollar

Lead column	2001	Unit	2002	Unit	2003	Unit	2004	Unit	2005	Unit
Net Sales	14.000.000,00	USD	14.000.000,00	USD	14.000.000,00	USD	14.000.000,00	USD	14.000.000,00	USD
Cost of Sales	5.600.000,00	USD	5.600.000,00	USD	5.600.000,00	USD	5.600.000,00	USD	5.600.000,00	USD
Depreciation	100.000,00	USD	90.000,00	USD	110.000,00	USD			95.000,00	USD
Other Expenses	480.000,00	USD	480.000,00	USD	480.000,00	UED	480.000,00	USD	480.000,00	USD
EBIT	7.920.000,00	USD	7.920.000,00	USD	7.920.000,00	USD	7.920.000,00	USD	7.920.000,00	USD
Interest Income	0,00	USD	0,00	USD	0,00	USD	0,00	USD	0,00	USD
Interest Expense	0,00	USD	0,00	USD	0,00	USD	0,00	USD	0,00	USD
Operating Profit	7.920.000,00	USD	7.920.000,00	USD	7.920.000,00	USD	7.920.000,00	USD	7.920.000,00	USD
Taxes	0,00	USD	0,00	USD	0,00	USD	0,00	USD	0,00	USD
Annual Net Income	7.920.000,00	USD	7.920.000,00	USD	7.920.000,00	USD	7.920.000,00	USD	7.920.000,00	USD

Fig. 5.16: SAP Standard Interface   © SAP AG

In addition, planning folders combine business-related planning interfaces, planning data, and planning functions into a unified view, giving the impression of a self-contained application.

5.2.1.6 Organization and Coordination of Planning

The Status and Tracking System of SEM-BPS is a type of workflow management system for monitoring the planning processes. In this system, the relationships between the employees involved in planning are registered on the basis of the organizational structure of the company. Each hierarchy node represents an employee responsible for a particular subtask.

The system logs what are called planning sessions, which are iterative runs of tasks for creating subplans such as profit planning or balance sheet planning. Processors see their own planning layouts, reports, and completion dates. They can monitor their lower-level units and control the planning process. With this function, SEM-BPS also documents approximation cycles – for example, those between requirement notifications and resource utilization or between sales forecasts and sales targets. A task within a planning session can have different statuses: *new, for approval, rejected, approved,* and so on (see figure 5.17).

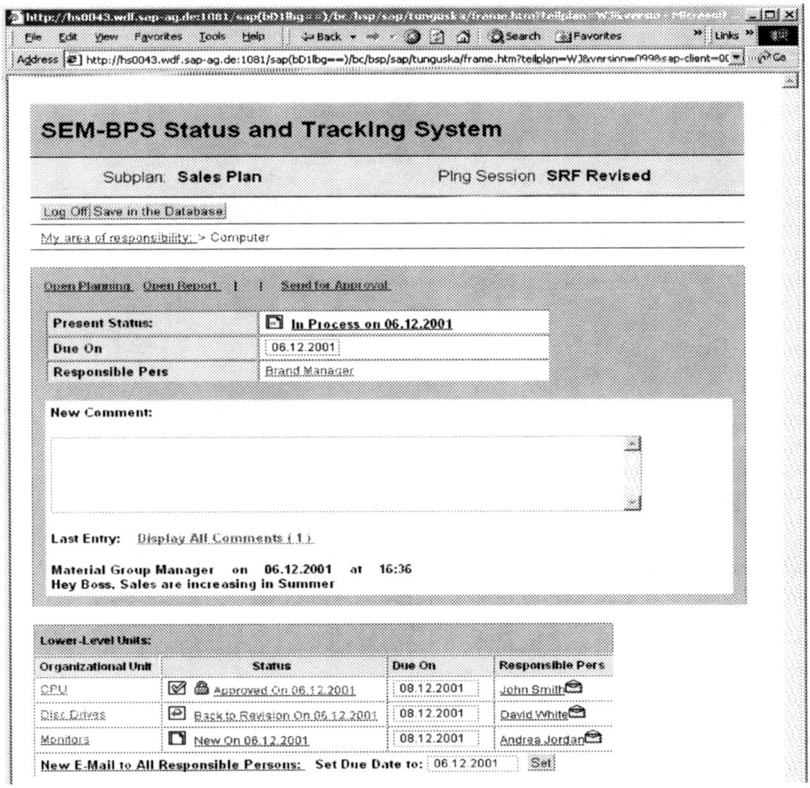

Fig. 5.17: SEM-BPS Status and Tracking System   © SAP AG

Status management also includes an automatic notification system. Employees are informed by e-mail when deadlines are approaching or new actions become necessary.

Example of Rolling Forecast

Textile Corp. executes a rolling planning process each month. As soon as the actual figures for the current month are available, automatic exception reporting in SAP BW sends an e-mail to the sales managers of the product groups, informing them about variances between actual and plan. Based on the data of the previous forecast, the managers now determine the revenues for the next periods in a new plan version. SEM-BPS provides the following alternative methods for this purpose:

1. *Update of the trend with an automatic planning function*

2. *Entry of the total value at fiscal year end and automatic distribution to the forecast periods*

3. *Calculation of the moving average based on the past, and projection into the forecast periods*

4. *Dynamic simulation with Powersim, in which market behavior (such as procurement of new customers or substitute investment of existing customers) is taken into account*

The planning workbench provides sales managers with all the information and functions they need to use these methods.

When simulation is complete, the sales manager stores the result in the system and sets the status of the planning task in the Status and Tracking System to completed. The administrator is notified automatically and then distributes all new plan data at the customer/product level using reference values. At the same time, the system calculates the contribution margins. On this basis, the administrator starts a new bottom-up planning session for all product managers with an e-mail generated by the system containing a link to the planner's individual planning workbench.

5.2.2   SEM Business Consolidation (SEM-BCS)

The SEM-BCS component includes functions for preparing external consolidated financial statements as well as internal management information.

For statutory consolidation (company/business area consolidation), the reported financial data of a group's consolidation units are collected to create aggregated financial statements. This data consists of key figures from individual financial statements or information for consolidation processes such as consolidation of investments or elimination of interunit profit and loss (see section 3.3.4). The following steps are required for statutory consolidation:

1. Standardization of reported financial data to conform to accounting and valuation policies of the group

2. Translation into the currency of the consolidation group

3. Elimination of effects resulting from the exchange of goods and services and crossholdings between the consolidation units

Consolidation for internal requirements (such as profit center consolidation) serves the purpose of controlling enterprise areas. Consolidation tasks remove the effects of the exchange of goods and services between these segments, such as internal business volume. SEM-BCS enables these consolidation tasks to be automated to a great extent.

5.2.2.1   Modeling Consolidation Structures

Consolidation builds on models of corporate group structures. SAP differentiates between what it calls *consolidation groups* and *consolidation units*, the latter of which are the smallest elements of the group structure capable of being consolidated. Such units may be subsidiaries, business areas, or profit centers.

Consolidation groups are used to combine consolidation units. The master record of a consolidation unit contains information such as the name, language key, correspondence data, local currency key, and reason for inclusion. It also provides control data: the level of detail (financial data type), translation method, tax rate, data transfer method, and so on. The following data transfer methods are available:

1. Periodic extracts from financial accounting

2. Online data entry in the SAP system

3. Offline data entry based on Microsoft Access

4. Flexible upload from non-SAP systems

SEM-BCS provides a range of both predefined and custom reporting criteria such as profit centers, products, customer groups, and regions. It is possible to define what are called flexible and parallel hierarchies for these criteria, as well as for consolidation units, consolidation groups, and individual items such as sales revenue or contribution margin.

Flexible hierarchies are based on the time period and version. They can easily be administered by users. *Parallel* hierarchies give users the option of structuring the consolidation units of a consolidation type (in business area consolidation, for example) by various criteria. For instance, a user might want to structure consolidation units in one hierarchy by subsidiary, and in another hierarchy by segment.

This type of maintenance requires little effort, as it can be accomplished simply by dragging and dropping elements in the hierarchy with the mouse (see figure 5.18). In simple situations (e.g. management consolidation with intercompany elimination), the consolidated results are automatically available in reporting based on the new group structure. In more complex situations (consolidation based on legal requirements with consolidation of investments, for instance), additional consolidation entries are necessary, which however are made automatically by the consolidation monitor. This feature is particularly beneficial for companies whose equity holdings frequently change due to acquisitions, divestitures, and reorganizations.

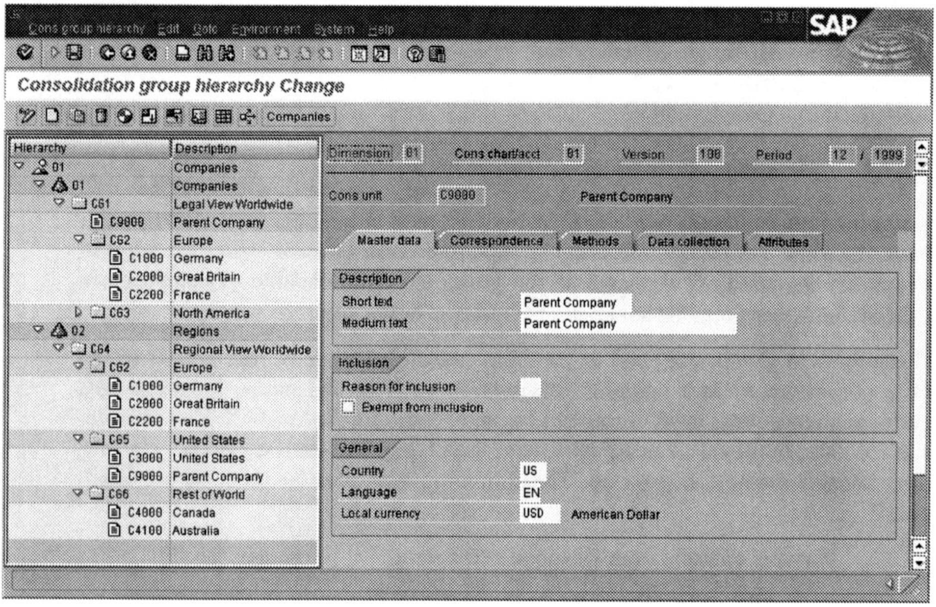

Fig. 5.18: Master Data Maintenance for Consolidation Structures   © SAP AG

Using the *financial statement item*, SEM-BCS enables analysis of shareholders' equity by origin, purpose, level of ownership, and availability, as well as other tasks. For the appropriation of retained earnings, therefore, the system takes into account information on prior year retained earnings, the distribution of dividends, and transfers to and deductions from appropriations. SEM-BCS enables the creation of individual, systematically composed consolidation charts of accounts. Their structure is based on external and/or internal requirements. For example, there are different consolidation charts of accounts for the financial statements compiled to meet different statutory requirements (such as US GAAP, IAS, or the German Commercial Code in connection with the 4th/7th EU directive) and other charts of accounts for the internal requirements of contribution margin accounting. This enables parallel financial statements to be prepared automatically to a great extent.

Furthermore, a number of different consolidation *versions* are available, which permit alternative consolidations for simulations or planning in addition to aggregation of actual data. These consolidation versions are a combination of what are called special versions, such as a data entry version, tax rate version, or currency translation version. The version concept was designed to avoid redundancies.

5.2.2.2 Collecting and Preparing Reported Financial Data

The data to be consolidated are entered and prepared with the data monitor, which controls the tasks, shows their current status, and ensures consistency (see figure 5.19).

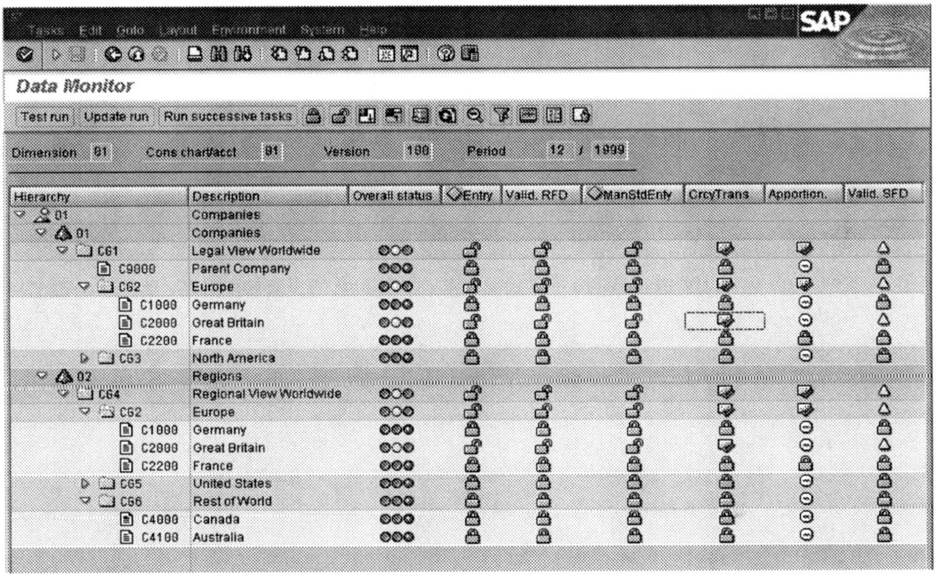

Fig. 5.19: Status of Data Collection   © SAP AG

The monitor shows the hierarchy of organizational units in the vertical direction and the overall status as well as the current status of the individual tasks in the horizontal direction. A traffic light symbol indicates the overall status of each organizational unit (see table 5.1).

Color	Meaning
Red	Error
Yellow	Open
Green	Complete

Table 5.1: Legend for Overall Status

The status of the individual tasks is indicated by the symbols shown in figure 5.20.

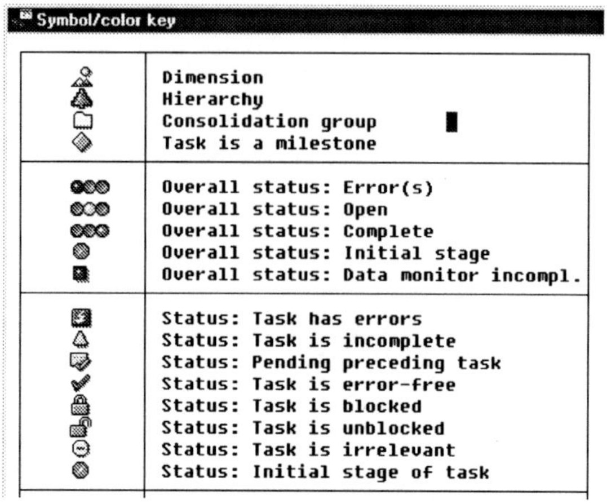

Symbol/color key

⚥	Dimension
♨	Hierarchy
☐	Consolidation group ▮
◇	Task is a milestone
⊕⊗⊗	Overall status: Error(s)
⊗⊕⊗	Overall status: Open
⊗⊗⊕	Overall status: Complete
⊙	Overall status: Initial stage
▪	Overall status: Data monitor incompl.
☒	Status: Task has errors
△	Status: Task is incomplete
☑	Status: Pending preceding task
✔	Status: Task is error-free
🔒	Status: Task is blocked
🔓	Status: Task is unblocked
⊝	Status: Task is irrelevant
⊗	Status: Initial stage of task

Fig. 5.20: Status Symbols for Individual Tasks   © SAP AG

The data monitor also has a detailed view for each of the functions mentioned (see figure 5.21).

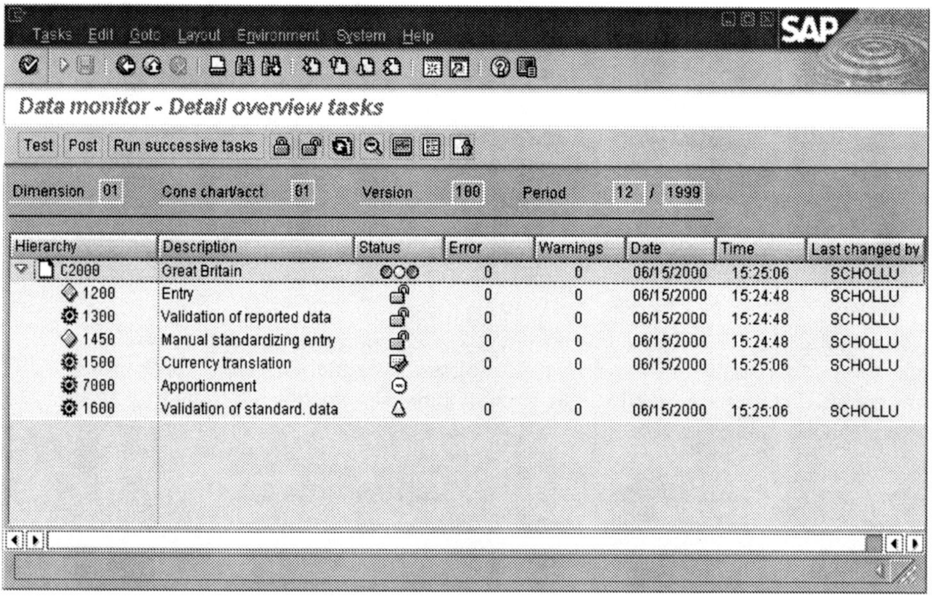

Tasks Edit Goto Layout Environment System Help

Data monitor - Detail overview tasks

Test | Post | Run successive tasks

| Dimension | 01 | Cons chart/acct | 01 | Version | 100 | Period | 12 / 1999 |

Hierarchy	Description	Status	Error	Warnings	Date	Time	Last changed by
▽ ☐ C2000	Great Britain	⊗⊗⊕	0	0	06/15/2000	15:25:06	SCHOLLU
◇ 1200	Entry	🔓	0	0	06/15/2000	15:24:48	SCHOLLU
⚙ 1300	Validation of reported data	🔓	0	0	06/15/2000	15:24:48	SCHOLLU
◇ 1450	Manual standardizing entry	🔓	0	0	06/15/2000	15:24:48	SCHOLLU
⚙ 1500	Currency translation	☑	0	0	06/15/2000	15:25:06	SCHOLLU
⚙ 7000	Apportionment	⊝					
⚙ 1600	Validation of standard. data	△	0	0	06/15/2000	15:25:06	SCHOLLU

Fig. 5.21: Data Monitor – Detail View   © SAP AG

Consolidation begins by carrying forward the data of the prior year. Since this is an integrated system, most of the data can be collected automatically. There are interfaces to SAP BW and to the SAP R/3 components Financial Accounting (FI)

and Profit Center Accounting, PCA). These components record additional account assignments, such as transaction type, trading partner, currency, or acquisition year in their documents and/or totals and feed them to SEM-BCS at the time of data transfer.

Additional financial data on trade within the group, on ownership relationships, assets, and equity balances are needed for the elimination of interunit profit and loss as well as consolidation of investments. Some of this information can be determined by SEM-BCS itself, while other information must be collected.

It is also possible to enter reported financial data and additional financial data online. As with SEM-BPS, SAP provides a Web user interface and a Microsoft Excel solution for this purpose in addition to the SAPGUI. This combines the functions of SEM-BCS with the spreadsheet functions of Microsoft, whereby the application logic is located in the SAP system. Microsoft Excel is used chiefly to provide a graphically formatted presentation (see figure 5.22).

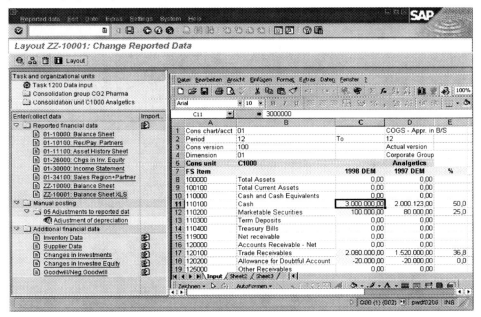

Fig. 5.22: Manual Maintenance of Reported Financial Data with Microsoft Excel © SAP AG

In cases where a consolidation unit does not use SAP software, SEM-BCS provides the option of importing reported financial data and additional financial data from non-SAP systems with the flexible upload feature. To enable this type of transfer, information on the required data format is entered in the master data record of the consolidation unit or consolidation group. A corresponding file normally consists of header and data lines, plus hierarchy information.

The upload is followed by reclassifications, where the reported financial data is standardized manually or automatically. If the financial data is reported in different currencies, SEM-BCS translates them into the currency of the consolidation group. The SEM component provides a number of methods for this purpose, as well as functions for reporting currency translation differences on separate items.

The last task in the data monitor is validation, in which the system checks the consistency of the data according to rules that the user defines individually. The data monitor thus prevents subsequent consolidation steps from being executed until the data is free of errors.

The functions provided by SEM-BCS for decentralized data entry and preparation add up to an overall time savings that results in higher-quality data and reduced workloads for group headquarters. The Web interface provides the additional advantage of making the functions of SEM-BCS available from any PC with Internet access – no installation of additional programs is necessary.

5.2.2.3   *Consolidation of the Financial Data*

Actual consolidation takes place in SEM-BCS using the consolidation monitor (see figure 5.23).

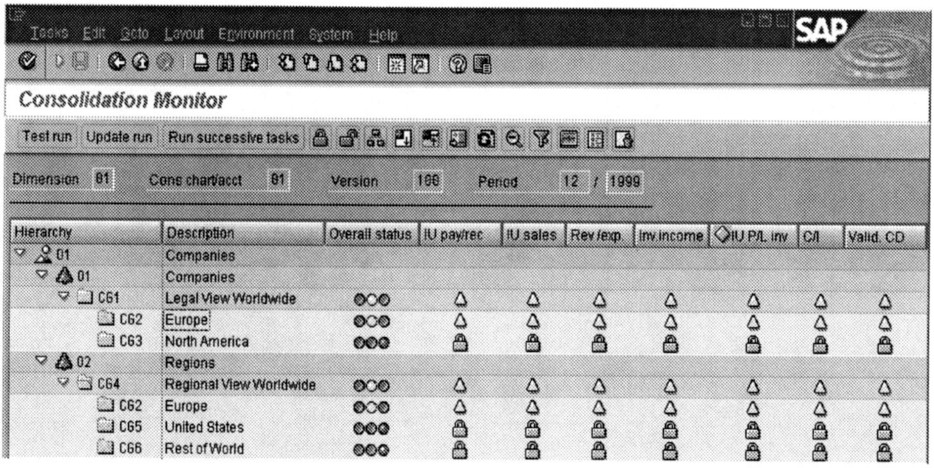

Fig. 5.23: Consolidation Monitor   © SAP AG

The layout of the consolidation monitor is similar to that of the data monitor, but it operates at the level of consolidation groups and has only a few restrictions regarding the sequence of the consolidation tasks. The degree of posting automation is very high. The monitor covers the following consolidation tasks:

1. Elimination of interunit payables and receivables

2. Elimination of interunit revenue and expense

3. Elimination of investment income, elimination of provisions, and so on

4. Elimination of interunit profit and loss in inventory
5. Reclassification (distribution, balancing, value adjustment, and so on)
6. Consolidation of investments based on different methods
7. Apportionment with the minimum or the product procedure
8. Automatic additional postings when hierarchies are changed

5.2.2.4 Consolidation Reports

SAP supplies a number of variants for reporting the consolidated data and consolidation audit trails of both monitors based on different criteria as individual specialized reports or standard reports.

These reports provide information on consolidation units, ownership, invested equity, and fair value adjustments. They differentiate the data by document type, subitem, and so on. Journal entry reports can be generated to disclose the value changes in the reported financial data resulting from consolidation postings. The system provides detailed views for information in the notes to the financial statements or for internal requirements, such as a statement of stockholders' equity or a breakdown of sales revenue by region.

The transaction data is available in SAP BW and in all SAP SEM/BA components, such as in the Balanced Scorecard (see section 5.2.3.1) or the Management Cockpit (see section 5.2.3.5), where it can be accessed through alternative user interfaces.

Example

The board of directors of a European group of companies wants to list its shares on the New York Stock Exchange (NYSE). This will provide exposure to the United States, enlarge its market share, enhance the internationalization of its stockholder structure, and enable the group to use its own stock as acquisition currency in takeovers.

Internal management is to be based on uniform data made up of all subgroups, legal entities, and segments. This decision has far-reaching consequences both for financial reporting of the group's subsidiaries and for the consolidation process.

Since the group currently prepares its financial statements in accordance with the German Commercial Code, the US GAAP financial statements are prepared in a parallel version using a second consolidation chart of accounts. The valuation and structure for the German Commercial Code are retained after the changeover to US GAAP but reduced in extent. This is because the parent company of the group must continue to prepare its own financial statements in accordance with German Commercial Code, a process which requires consolidation due to the group's complex internal structure. The subsidiaries extend their accounting to meet the reporting and valuation requirements of US GAAP in addition to local requirements. They also ensure that all critical components of the balance sheet and the income statement are reported by segments or even business areas. This information serves the purposes of managing the firm and is also the basis of segment reporting for US GAAP in accordance with the management approach. In order to eliminate intersegment relationships, the partner business area – or at least the partner segment – must be known in addition to the business area that reports the data. The multidimensional consolidation database contains additional information on regions, customer groups, products, and so on.

This integrated approach not only ensures consistency between internal and external reporting but also accelerates the entire reporting process since data only needs to be reported and processed once, eliminating the need for time-consuming reconciliation work. Group headquarters is developing new consolidation methods for nearly all consolidation tasks. In currency translation, the annual net income in group currency is no longer determined through translation of the local year-end value using the year-end exchange rate but by accumulation of the local values per period, each translated with period-based exchange rates.

A decisive factor in accelerating the preparation of financial statements is the SEM-BCS functionality for parallel processing of consolidation tasks. All subsidiaries of the group use the central consolidation database, more than 1,000 users report their data in parallel, validate them against the group validation rules, post standardizing entries, and translate currencies. After the conclusion of this first phase, responsibility is handed over from the legal entities to the business areas and segments, who are now responsible for all eliminations. In accordance with the matrix organization of legal entity and management unit, the financial statements can be evaluated as desired in both directions consistently. After successful changeover from German Commercial Code to US GAAP, the prerequisites for being listed on the New York Stock Exchange are met.

5.2.3   SEM Corporate Performance Monitor (SEM-CPM)

The SEM-CPM component is divided into two areas: Strategy Management and Performance Measurement.

Strategy Management focuses on the Balanced Scorecard. The system also provides modules and business content for value-based enterprise management, particularly value driver management. This area includes tools for risk management with functions for risk controlling as well as for cataloging and valuating risks. It thus fulfills the criteria required by the German law on controlling and transparency in corporations (KonTraG) (see section 2.5).

Performance Measurement includes the Measure Builder for defining and managing complex measures, and the Management Cockpit.

5.2.3.1 Balanced Scorecard

When a company sets up a Balanced Scorecard with SAP SEM, it first creates a list of scorecard elements (strategies, perspectives, objectives, and measures). These elements can be used in any number of scorecards. This particularly applies to strategies since they usually remain valid over relatively long periods of time. Initiatives are a special case because elements of this type are not defined globally but always in connection with a particular scorecard. To construct a scorecard, the user chooses the relevant elements from the list and links them together. A customizable cause-effect chain enables the interactions between the individual parts of a scorecard to be visualized in what is generally called a strategy map.

Various design environments are available for implementing a scorecard. Experienced users normally work with the standard functions in the SAPGUI. For inexperienced users, the BSC Wizard is available which guides the user step by step through all activities needed to set up a scorecard. Users can choose between express mode, in which certain parameters are predefined, and standard mode in which all settings are optional. The BSC Wizard runs in a Web browser.

Strategy Maps

Strategy maps provide an overview of the overall strategy of a business unit. They define and help visualize the causal relationships between the objectives in a scorecard. The system also shows the current status of the objectives. The screen is divided horizontally into the perspectives of the scorecard and vertically into the different strategies (see figure 5.24). The objectives appear with their current status symbol as oval objects.

Connecting lines between the objectives can be drawn with the mouse. There are *m:n* relationships possible between the objectives, meaning that a given objective may influence many others and in turn be influenced. It is also possible to display links that extend across the boundaries of perspectives and strategies, such as a connection between becoming a trusted advisor and reducing delivery times. This would establish a connection between the financial and customer perspectives, and between the strategies for encouraging innovation and those for improving customer management.

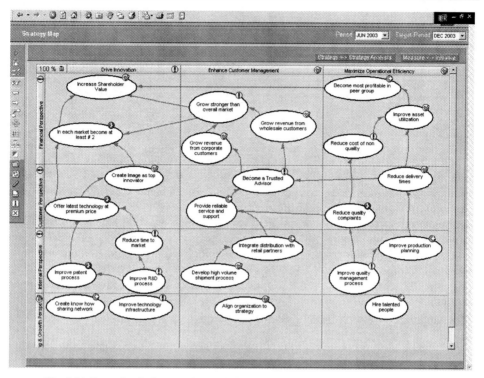

Fig. 5.24: Example of a Strategy Map   © SAP AG

A strategy can be analyzed interactively by selecting it in the strategy map. The left side of figure 5.25 shows one with the objectives spread across the four perspectives. The objectives are linked to each other through a cause-effect chain. The status is indicated by symbols and is set either by the person in charge or automatically by the system from the plan-actual comparison. The other columns show a score representing the overall status of the objective, the values of the assigned measures, and the responsible manager. The actual values of the measures are also used for status control purposes. Next to this appear optional plan and standard values. It is also possible to add additional columns for multiyear plan values and forecasts. Assessments and comments are accessed at the touch of a button. In the same view, the measures may be replaced by the initiatives assigned to the objectives.

BSC - PC4YOU Group
Strategy Map — Period: JUN 2003 — Target Period: DEC 2003

Strategy Perspective — Financial Perspective, Customer Perspective, Internal Perspective, Learning & Growth Perspective

Strategy map objectives: Drive Innovation · Increase Shareholder Value · In each market become at least # 2 · Create image as top innovator · Offer latest technology at premium price · Reduce time to market · Improve patent process · Improve R&D process · Create know how sharing network · Improve technology infrastructure

Objective / Measure	Trend	Actual	Plan	Target
Increase Shareholder Value				
Economic Value Added	↓	262,52 EUR	291,70 EUR	332,86 EL
Total Shareholder Return over 1 Year	↑	11,10 %	12,00 %	12,00
Discounted Cash Flow	→	14.161,68 EUR	12.102,08 EUR	14.755,16 EL
In each market become at least # 2				
Market Rank Hardware	↓	3,0 P	1,0 P	1,0
Relative Market Share H/W	→	78,0 %	100,0 %	100,0
Market Rank Software	→	2,0 P	1,0 P	1,0
Relative Market Share SW	↑	88,0 %	100,0 %	100,0
Offer latest technology at premium price				
Price Premium vs. Competition	↘	6,0 %	8,0 %	8,0
Create image as top innovator				
Survey Result: Customers Agreeing	↓	83,2 %	90,0 %	90,0
Reduce time to market				
Improve patent process				
No. of New Patents	↓	26,0 PC	30,0 PC	30,0 F
Time to Patent Approval	↓	3,5 YR	3,0 YR	3,0 Y
Improve R&D process				
Improve technology infrastructure				
Downtime of Mission Critical Systems	→	1,120 %	1,000 %	1,000
Percentage of completion SCM Project	↓	71,0 %	75,0 %	100,0
Percentage of completion CRM Project	↓	41,0 %	48,0 %	100,0
Create know how sharing network				

Fig. 5.25: Analysis of Strategy Maps © SAP AG

Strategy Templates

SAP supplies strategy templates as Business Content for the Balanced Scorecard. They consist of predefined strategies, perspectives, objectives, and measures, as well as a cause-effect chain for each strategy. Each individual object from these classes (around 60 objectives and 150 measures) contains a comprehensive verbal definition. SAP worked together with partners to design templates for four different strategies that carry the designations *innovation*, *customer intimacy*, *process optimization*, and *regulation of industry*. The first three strategies are each divided into a focus and a baseline version, while the fourth exists only as a baseline strategy (see figure 5.26).

A *focus* strategy concentrates on the areas in which a company's superior performance sets it apart from its competitors. The *baseline* strategies describe all other activities of strategic importance where the company does not significantly differ from the competition. Individual strategy maps can be put together from a combination of focus and baseline strategies.

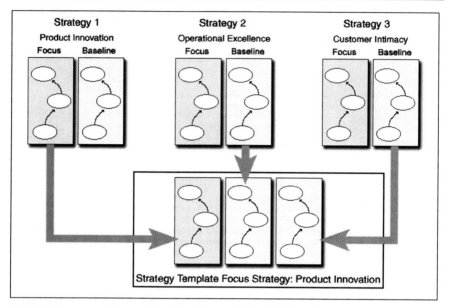

Fig. 5.26: Designing a Strategy Map from Focus and Baseline Strategies

Users can view the contents of the strategy templates in an environment preconfigured for them and activate entire strategy maps or selected elements. The
objects then become available in the scorecard design and are ready to be linked to
new or existing scorecards.

Detail Views for Balanced Scorecard Analyses

In addition to transparent formulation of strategies, the Balanced Scorecard in
SAP SEM provides an extensive range of predefined analysis paths. A number of
different overviews and detail views are available. For example, users see definitions, the current status, assessments, time series, and external documents for individual objectives, measures, and initiatives. The values of the status scale, which
are used to valuate objectives, measures, and initiatives, range from unsatisfactory
to excellent and can be set by the user or derived by the system automatically on
the basis of formulas for threshold values. Users are also able to call up SAP BW
reports or planning layouts from SEM-BPS directly.

Perspective View

This view provides a quick overview of the perspectives of a scorecard and the
objectives, measures, and initiatives it contains. Users select scorecard elements to
be displayed here. For example, in figure 5.27 the scorecard element *objectives*
has been selected. Users also restrict the analysis time period. From the perspective view, users may go directly to additional views (drilldown view, scorecard
comparison view, or detail views for the different scorecard elements).

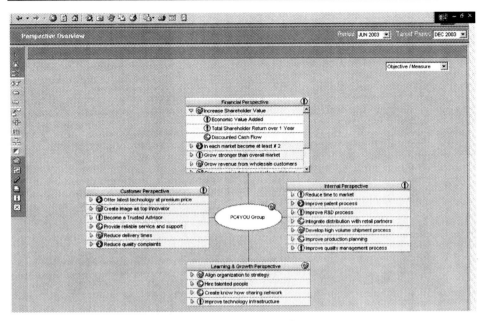

Fig. 5.27: Balanced Scorecard – Perspective View   © SAP AG

Drilldown View

While the perspective and detail views have a fixed arrangement of scorecard elements, in the drilldown view it is possible to navigate at will within the dimensions. This enables the user to follow the interdependencies within and between scorecards and access contents for organizational units that lie at deeper levels of the hierarchy.

Using any element as a starting point, the decision-maker receives a hierarchy graphic showing an overview of the links between the element and other components of the Balanced Scorecard (see figure 5.28). The status of each object is shown as a navigation aid. Detailed information is available at the touch of a button.

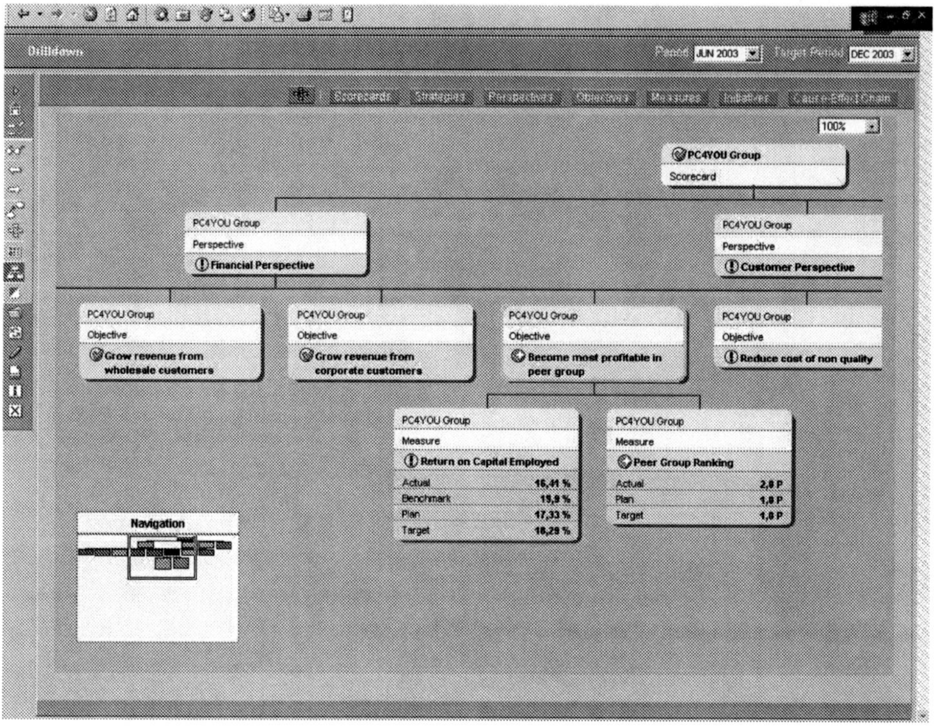

Fig. 5.28: Balanced Scorecard Drilldown   © SAP AG

Scorecard Comparison View

Scorecard comparisons show how different parts of the company are involved in implementing a strategy. These are either organizational units or – in a system of cascading scorecards (see section 3.1.6) – hierarchically structured areas.

The use of common objectives allows scorecards to be compared against each other. For further analyses, users are able to observe in detail how variables change over time. Grounds for suspicion may arise when the valuation of an objective varies greatly between the different scorecards.

Detail Views for Balanced Scorecard Elements

There is a different combination of useful details for each element of the Balanced Scorecard (strategies, perspectives, objectives, measures, and initiatives). The following detail information is available for each element:

1. Definition
2. Status and assigned score
3. Owner
4. Owner's assessment and comments from other people involved

5. Integration of planning layouts from the SEM-BPS component

6. Integration of data warehouse reports

7. Integration of documents from SAP Content Management

8. URL address field

Detail View of Objectives (Objective Analysis)

For a selected strategic objective, the system informs you about the exact definition of the objective and the owner. The example in figure 5.29 shows the objective *grow stronger than overall market* for which Mr. John Smith is responsible.

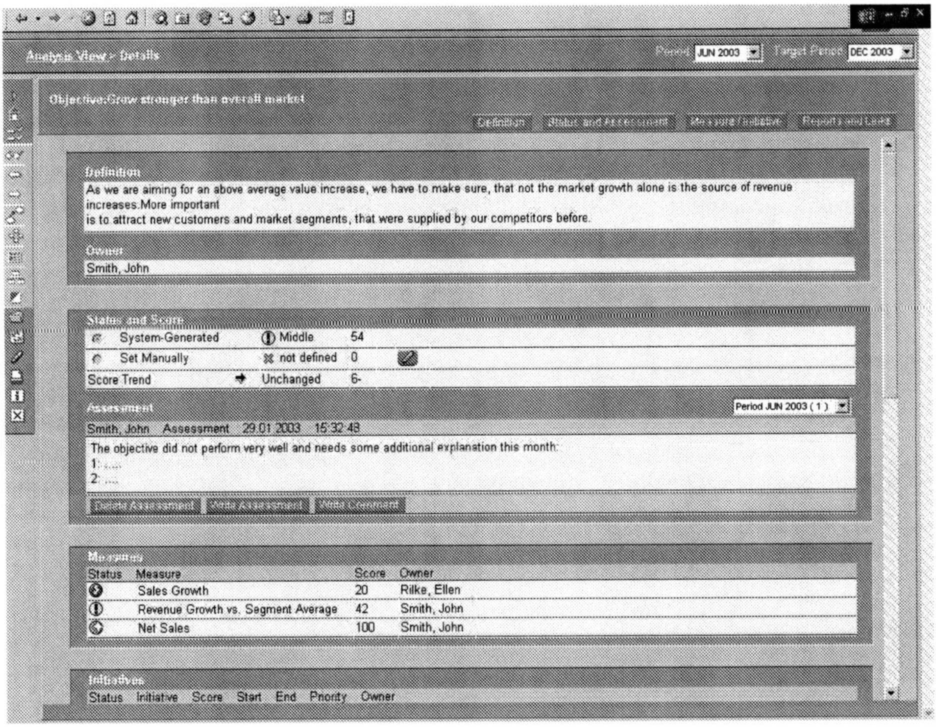

Fig. 5.29: Details of the Objectives   © SAP AG

The overall status (*good* in this example) is determined automatically on the basis of the substatuses of the measures, which quantify the degree to which the objective has been reached. In the example shown here, the measures include before-tax earnings, economic profit, and shareholder value added. Comments can be entered to explain how the measure has developed over time, or other details. An elegant feature is the ability to link the contributions to performance determined in the Balanced Scorecard with results-based remuneration systems as part of Management by Objectives (MbO) (see section 5.3.5). The system calculates the employee scores and sends them to the SAP R/3 HR system.

Detail View of Measures (Measure Analysis)

Individual measures can be the starting point for analyses as well. For this purpose, SAP SEM provides a number of alternatives for different analyses or display preferences. In this context, measure trees are a useful tool for visualizing the calculation of complex measures. Measure trees display formulas in SAP BW in the form of tree diagrams. Depending on which value fields have been selected for the measure, the diagram displays the actual version, plan version, or other versions. A zoom function and an overview map provide assistance in navigating within the tree structure. When the user selects a particular measure, the system switches to the detail view (see figure 5.30).

The detail view contains an exact definition of the measure, including a formula, status, and comments. For variables of value-based management, which companies frequently modify individually, this seemingly insignificant function provides a valuable means of efficient communication within management. This includes comments to which additional contributions can be added, enabling the resulting discussions to be moderated and followed similar to newsgroups in the Internet.

Tabular and graphic information showing how the measure has developed over time (see figure 5.31) are included as well. It is also possible to go into the SEM-BPS component and modify measures or assigned planning objects.

Direct access is provided to reports in SAP BW and to external or internal documents, for example in the Internet or the company intranet. Such documents are particularly helpful in interpreting the results by providing background information for analyzing variances, such as market forecasts or labor market reports.

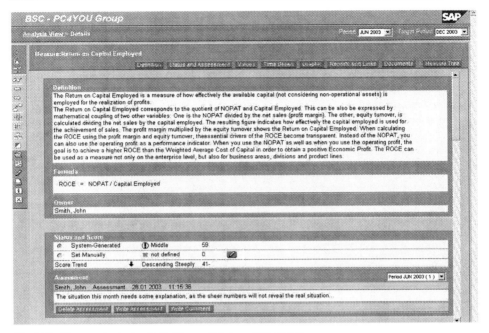

Fig. 5.30: Measure Analysis - Definition and Status   © SAP AG

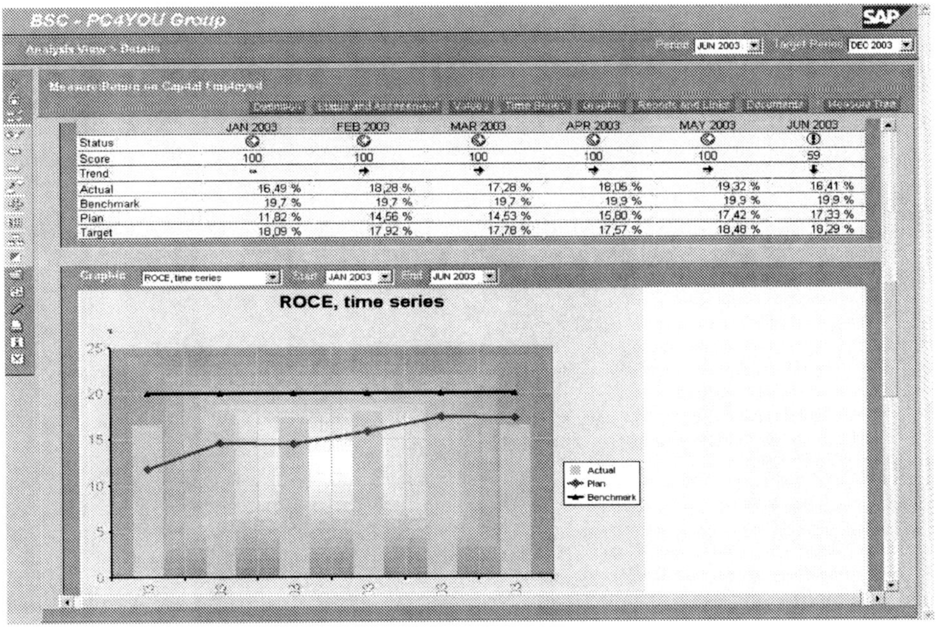

Fig. 5.31: Measure Analysis – Time Series   © SAP AG

Detail View of Tasks (Initiative Analysis)

The detail view of initiatives (see figure 5.32) contains additional information on the personnel and financial resources assigned. Milestones can be defined and monitored here as well. As with all other scorecard elements, documents and data warehouse reports can be assigned to the initiatives to make them available for use in detailed analyses.

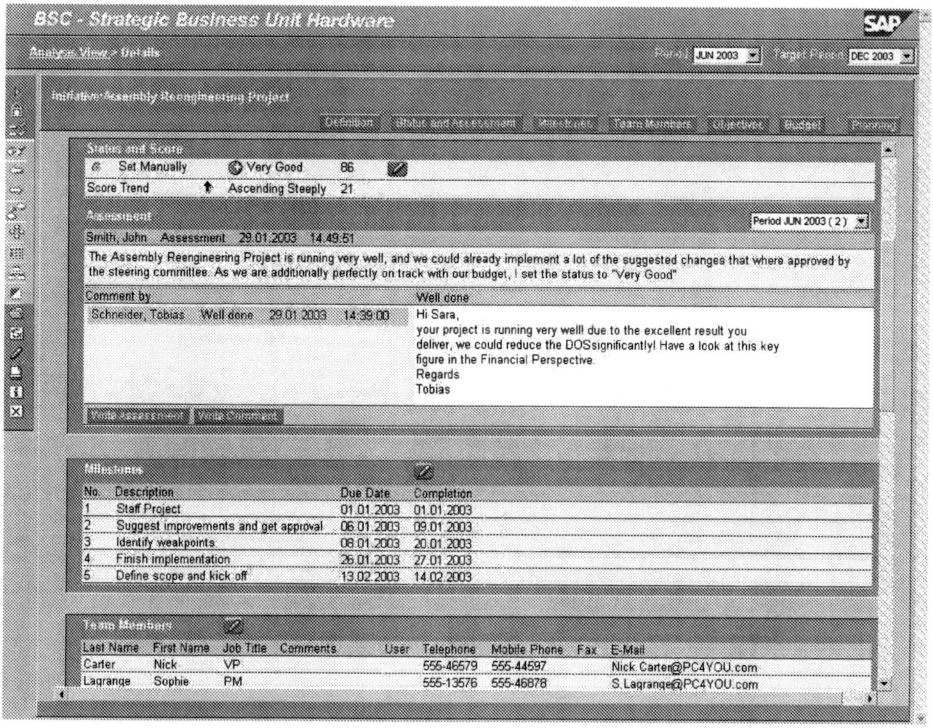

Fig. 5.32: Task Analysis   © SAP AG

5.2.3.2   *Value Driver Management*

Value Driver Trees are a tool for value-based management. They help to visualize and interpret the influence of operational value drivers on strategically relevant measures. A given element in a Value Driver Tree may influence other variables and be influenced by them in turn. This means that a Value Driver Tree is not simply a hierarchy but a network in which the root node is corporate value, for example. The value drivers that directly influence the root node are attached to it. The linkages lead from generic value drivers such as that of the *shareholder value* approach to the business-specific value drivers (see section 2.2). Value Driver Trees therefore enable abstract variables to be traced back to concrete parameters that can be controlled by the company.

The SAP product is not based on a particular method, so users can create Value Driver Trees for any top-level measures. The relationships do not necessarily need to represent mathematical dependencies (quantitative relationships) but can be based on expertise or practical experience regarding assumptions about the effects of value drivers (qualitative relationships).

In addition to visualizing influences on measures and displaying planned and actual data, Value Driver Trees are also used for simulations and planning tasks. Quantitative relationships enable sensitivity analysis: when the settings for a value driver are changed, the system immediately recalculates the tree and shows the effects on the top-level measure. Qualitative linkages indicate the direction in which measures influence particular KPIs. Converting these into derivative quantitative variables enables the strength of the effect to be determined. Figure 5.33 shows part of a Value Driver Tree with the root node *economic profit*.

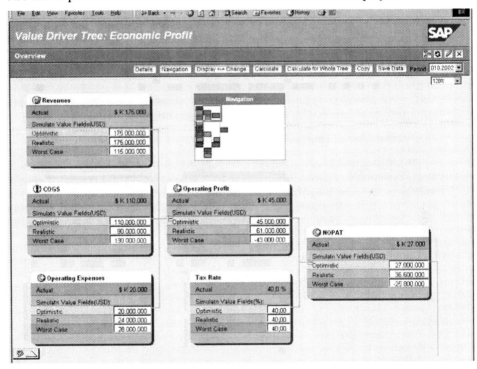

Fig. 5.33: Value Driver Tree for Economic Profit   © SAP AG

Parts of the tree can be magnified with the zoom function. The planned and actual value is shown on each node. When the user touches an element with the mouse, the system displays the definition of the measure from the Measure Builder on which it is based (see section 5.2.3.4). For better understanding and to assist in interpreting the dependency relationships, the system provides the option of switching between the display variants *X influences Y* and *X is influenced by Y*. A navigation tree (shown at the top center of figure 5.33) and a search function enable elements and relationships to be examined in more detail. The detail view also shows the development of measures over time for each value driver.

As with the objects in the Balanced Scorecard, detailed information on each value driver can be accessed by double-clicking:

1. Definition
2. Owner
3. Integration of data warehouse reports
4. Integration of documents from SAP Content Management
5. URL address field

5.2.3.3   Risk Management

SAP SEM provides a number of risk management functions for identifying, valuating, and handing risks as described under section 2.5. The basic requirement is that a target system exists, for example in the form of a Balanced Scorecard. SAP SEM provides a structured view of the effects of the defined risks on this target system and enables users to reach decisions on suitable countermeasures as well as monitor the implementation of such measures. It also assists in combining risk management tasks with value-based management.

Integration of Risk Management and Value-Based Management

Value-based management and risk management are integrated by means of a target system (see figure 5.34). The central elements linking the two areas are the measures. In value-based management, the measures are used to determine the extent to which objectives are reached within the Balanced Scorecard, while in risk management they are used to investigate how particular risks affect the measures.

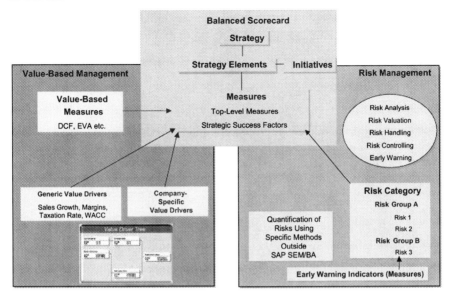

Fig. 5.34: Integration of Risk Management and Value-Based Management

Risk Identification

The Risk Builder provides detailed descriptions of the risks that a company has identified and defined in a risk catalog. Moreover, it assigns appropriate early warning indicators (see figure 5.35).

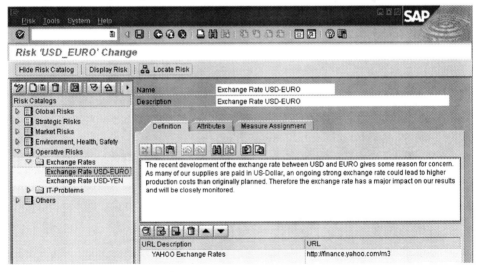

Fig. 5.35: Risk Builder   © SAP AG

The Risk Builder structures risks into a hierarchy. The highest level of the hierarchy is that of the risk categories. Below the risk categories are risk groups, while the lowest level is that of individual risks. Search and filter functions enable existing risks to be found quickly, helping to prevent them from being entered more than once.

Risk Valuation

The next step is to valuate the recognized dangers. The company defines any number of value fields to describe the risk situation. The amount of loss may be expressed by values such as the absolute change in the measures affected. *Expectation value of variance*, *best-case variance*, and *worst-case variance* are the value fields most frequently encountered in practice (see section 2.5).

BSC - Risk: PC4YOU Group									SAP
Risk View					Risk Value Field Expectation	Period JUN 2003	Target Period DEC 2003		
Perspective / Objective / Measure / Risk									Define Filter
jective / Measure / Risk	Risk Status	Risk Score	Actual	Plan	Target	Score	Trend	Expectation
Increase Shareholder Value						71	→	
✓ Economic Value Added			262,52 EUR	291,70 EUR	332,86 EUR	73	↓	
① Total Shareholder Return over 1 Year			11,10 %	12,00 %	12,00 %	40	↑	
✓ Discounted Cash Flow			14.161,68 EUR	12.102,08 EUR	14.755,16 EUR	100	→	
In each market become at least #2						20	→	
① Market Rank Hardware			3,0 P	1,0 P	1,0 P	40	↓	
● Relative Market Share HW			78,0 %	100,0 %	100,0 %	20	→	
✓ Market Rank Software			2,0 P	1,0 P	1,0 P	70	→	
① Relative Market Share SW			88,0 %	100,0 %	100,0 %	50	↑	
Grow stronger than overall market	🔵	25				51	→	
● Sales Growth			10,00 %	15,00 %	15,00 %	20	→	
① Revenue Growth vs. Segment Average			95,0 %	105,0 %	105,0 %	42	↘	
✓ Net Sales	🔵	26	5.087,97 EUR	4.958,94 EUR	10.175,20 EUR	90	→	8.795,20 EUR
Corrected value								200,00 EUR
Effects of Lower-Level Scorecards								-530,00 EUR
Political instability in Z								-500,00 EUR
New Competitor entering the market								-250,00 EUR
Failed Product Introduction								-300,00 EUR
Grow revenue from wholesale customers						66	↗	
① Revenue Growth Wholesale Customers			25,50 %	28,00 %	28,00 %	52	→	
✓ Revenues from Wholesale Customers			2.084,30 EUR	2.194,00 EUR	5.485,00 EUR	80	▬	
Grow revenue from corporate customers						62	↑	
① Revenue Growth Corporate Customers			19,50 %	22,00 %	22,00 %	44	↑	
✓ Revenues from Corporate Customers			2.284,56 EUR	2.404,80 EUR	6.012,00 EUR	80	▬	
Become most profitable in peer group						90	↘	
✓ Return on Capital Employed			16,41 %	17,33 %	18,29 %	80	↓	
✓ Peer Group Ranking			2,0 P	1,0 P	1,0 P	100	→	
Reduce cost of non quality	①	42				20	▬	
● Cost of Non Quality	①	42	23,99 EUR	18,00 EUR	36,00 EUR	20	▬	39,40 EUR
Corrected value								-2,00 EUR

Fig. 5.36: Analysis View of the Balanced Scorecard with Risks   © SAP AG

By combining risks with measures from the Balanced Scorecard, a risk status can be determined for each affected measure and for the higher-level objects such as objectives, perspectives, or strategies. The risk status is computed by comparing the original target value of a measure at the target time point (the last period of the current fiscal year, for example) against the value arrived at based on the expectation values or the best-case and worst-case data (see figure 5.36).

From the analysis views of the Balanced Scorecard, it is possible to directly access the details of a measure's risk situation (see figure 5.37). An authorized user can also change the data displayed there.

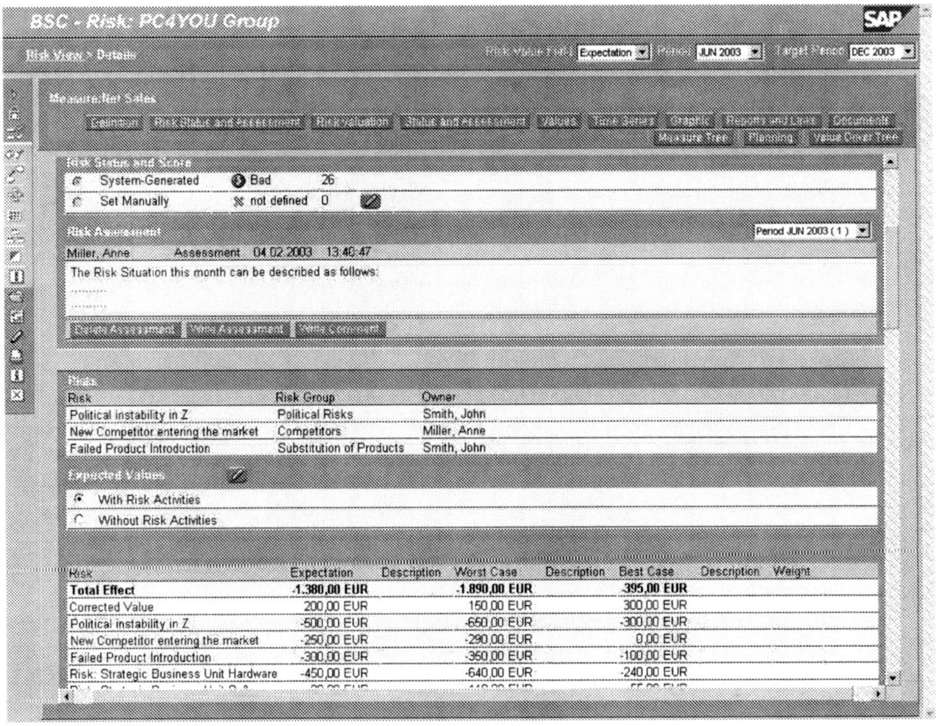

Fig. 5.37: Details of the Risk Situation of a Measure   © SAP AG

5.2.3.4   *Measure Builder*

The Measure Builder is a tool for defining complex measures to valuate the company's performance and for setting up comprehensive measure systems such as for value-based concepts like EVA, EP, or CFROI (see section 2.2). The Measure Builder frees the user from technical limitations when creating a measure system since it is not dependent on the availability of transaction data. This makes it a tool that is tailored to business analysts rather than system administrators.

Measure catalogs are the elements at the highest level of a measure system. For example, some users may find it useful to have a catalog for measures from each functional area of the company (finances, logistics, personnel, and so on). The Measure Builder structures the measures into hierarchically connected groups within the catalog. The lowest level consists of individual measures.

The Measure Builder contains functions for transferring metadata (definitions and formulas) into the measure catalog and for transferring benchmark values directly into the InfoCube of SAP BW. In both cases, the procedure is based on an XML file.

The Measure Builder includes the SEM measure catalog which contains a large number of predefined measures. Users copy these measures into their own catalogs or reference them through formulas (see figure 5.38).

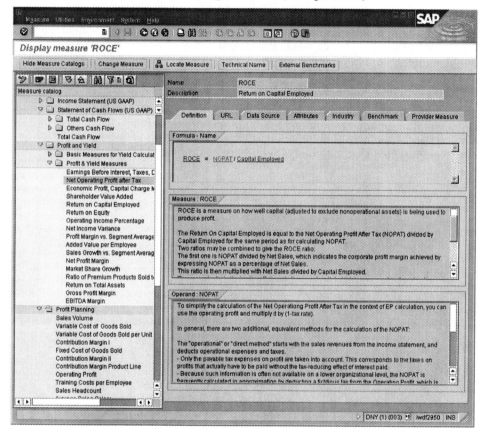

Fig. 5.38: Predefined Measures from Financials   © SAP AG

The definition of a measure includes a formula that places the measure in a mathematical relationship with other measures, and a description with information such as an explanation of the business significance of the measure, the intended usage, or sources.

Each measure has an attribute record containing information such as whether there are any industry-specific aspects, which units of measurement apply, and the future trend for the measure that is to be regarded as positive. You may use this type of information as search and filter criteria in the measure catalog.

Under the data source, the measures defined from a content point of view can be assigned to one or more technical key figures from SAP BW. The key figures defined in the available InfoCubes are displayed on the right-hand side of the screen for this purpose (see figure 5.39).

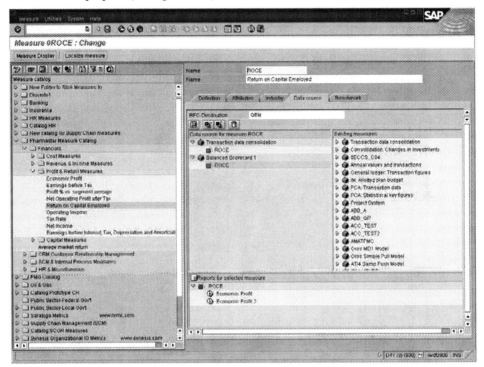

Fig. 5.39: Assignment of Data Sources   © SAP AG

In Performance Measurement, the assignment of benchmarking data is of particular significance. This data is entered here directly or loaded into SAP BW online from benchmark providers such as market research institutes or industrial federations.

To select and display benchmark data in the Measure Builder, the user specifies attributes including the validity period, industry or country, external data provider, and benchmark companies (see figure 5.40). The benchmark values can be either "best in class" or average values for an industry or region.

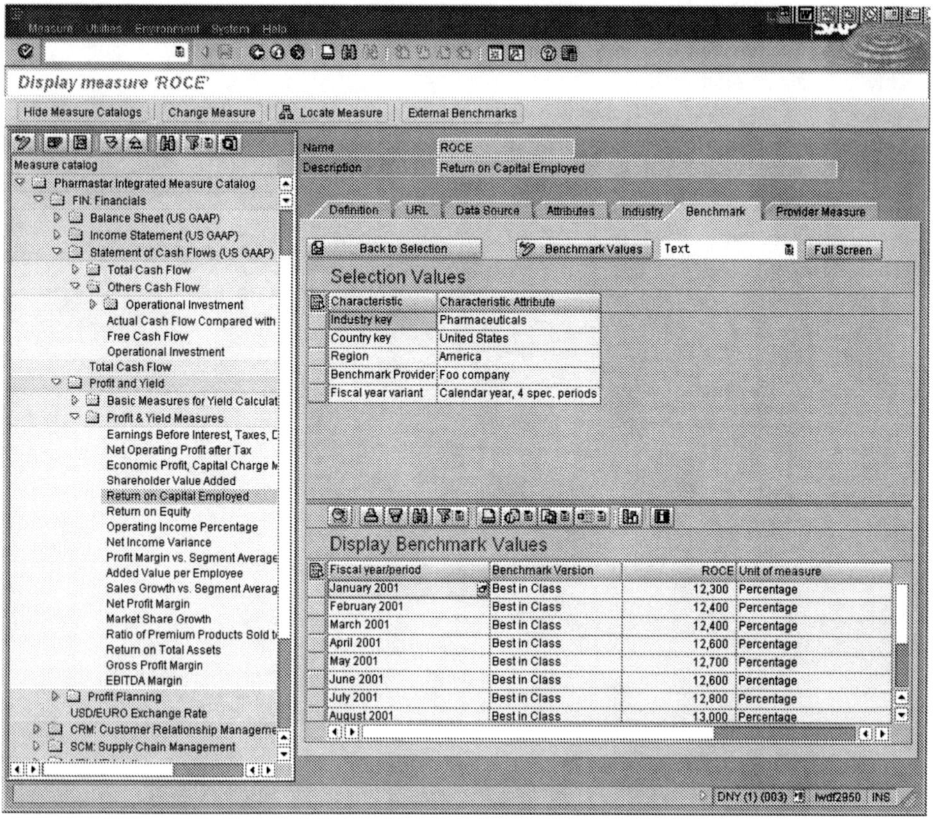

Fig. 5.40: Selected Benchmark Values   © SAP AG

5.2.3.5   Management Cockpit

The Management Cockpit in SAP SEM/BA is tailored to the information needs of upper management. The design goals were an intuitive interface and a special layout and graphic presentation of information that is easily understood.

The graphic displays resemble the instruments in an airplane cockpit and enable managers to recognize the company's overall situation and weaknesses at a glance. This design is based on research conducted by neurosurgeon Patrick Georges (Georges 1999) on the capacity of the human brain to process information. The goal is to focus communication among the members of the management team and increase cohesion.

To structure information, the Management Cockpit is divided into walls, views, and frames. Each of the walls is divided into views, which in turn consist of frames (see figures 5.41 to 5.43).

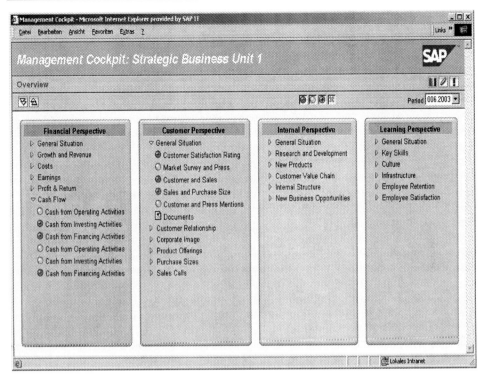

Fig. 5.41: Walls in a Management Cockpit   © SAP AG

Users are free to arrange the individual objects as they want. The SAP SEM Management Cockpit also enables the frames, views, and walls that have been configured in one cockpit to be used in other cockpits.

The main feature of the interface is simple and intuitive navigation. Traffic light symbols help users to recognize problem areas quickly. For example, a decision-maker could start from the overview of the walls (figure 5.41), switch to an outline of the views for a selected wall (Financial Perspective in this example) as shown in figure 5.42, and then access an overview of the graphics in the General Situation view (see figure 5.43).

Enlarging individual frames displays the measures on which the frame is based. A very useful feature is the capability of running dynamic drilldowns during meetings. If more detailed information is needed, data warehouse reports or documents can be accessed directly from the Management Cockpit.

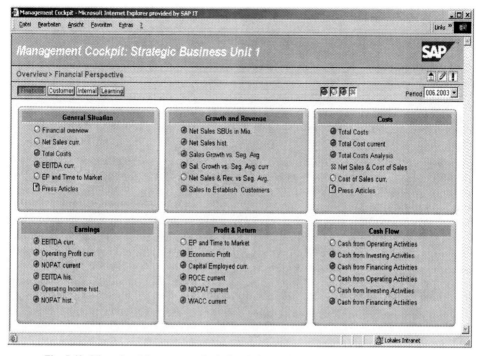

Fig. 5.42: Views in a Management Cockpit   © SAP AG

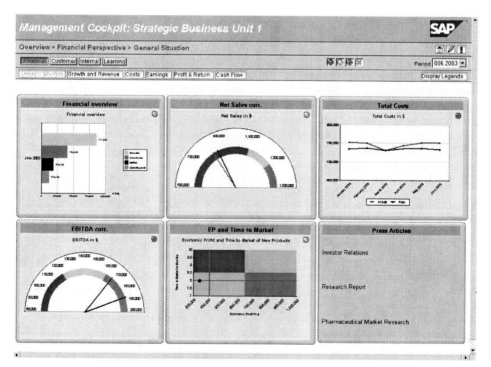

Fig. 5.43: The Frames in a View   © SAP AG

Example

The management team of an automobile manufacturer is worried about the declining sales of one of its models. This particular model is one of the company's mainstays, but it is reaching the end of its lifecycle and will soon be replaced. Market share has deteriorated along with sales. The Management Cockpit shows these changes on the wall for customer, market, and competitor information. The marketing department believes that sales have declined because customers are waiting for the new model to appear. It is regarded as quite normal for sales of an existing model to weaken shortly before its replacement.

Another wall of the Management Cockpit displays the status of strategic projects. Unfortunately, severe technical problems have developed during production ramp-up for the replacement. These problems are so serious that a delay of several weeks is expected before production can begin. If no corrective action is taken, the launch date for the new model will have to be postponed, resulting in further deterioration of sales for the current car.

Although the key figures for sales revenue and contribution margin on the financial wall have not yet been visibly impaired, it is clear to all concerned managers that action must be taken.

The decision makers discuss the situation and decide to continue production of the current model longer than originally planned. Procurement of the materials necessary to continue production is organized. The responsible board member handles the production ramp-up of the new model himself, temporarily increasing personnel and technical resources for this purpose. To stimulate sales of the old model until production of its replacement is up to speed, the company comes up with a special version featuring improved equipment levels, a catchy name, and a low price. At the same time, the company starts an advertising campaign for the special version to revitalize sales as quickly as possible.

These measures result in changes in cost and quantity planning. In SEM-BPS, the planners adjust the affected subplans (such as those for sales, material costs, personnel costs, and marketing costs) and save them as a new plan version. By the next management meeting, the updated data for plan-actual and plan-plan comparisons will be available with the originally budgeted version.

The actions undertaken to accelerate production ramp-up for the new model and the advertising campaign for the current model are both added to the company's Balanced Scorecard as initiatives. Each initiative is under the supervision of a particular person. The workflow functionality of the Balanced Scorecard enables the supervisors to regularly check the progress of their projects and make their assessment available to the other members of the management team through the Balanced Scorecard and the Management Cockpit. As the effects of the actions are observed over time, it will be seen whether they are producing the intended result or whether further actions are necessary.

This example shows that the Management Cockpit is closely linked to the other SEM components and represents yet another important tool besides Value Driver Trees and the Balanced Scorecard for integrating strategic and operational management.

5.2.4   SEM Stakeholder Relationship Management (SEM-SRM)

Section 2.3 discussed the significance of various stakeholders for management. The SEM-SRM component meets the need for efficient communication and management of relationships with the different stakeholder groups.

SEM-SRM includes Stakeholder Contract Management, the Stakeholder Portal, and functions for active communication with individual stakeholder groups. It also offers functions for analyzing stakeholder data.

5.2.4.1   Stakeholder Contract Management

SEM-SRM is based on master data which classifies stakeholders and enables them to be supplied with customized information. Stakeholders are individual people, groups of people, or companies. Various interrelationships can exist between these parties (such as "is married to," "is a shareholder of", and so on). The information entered as master data falls into the following categories:

Address data: This data is used for managing the communication channels with the stakeholders. Such data might include postal addresses, telephone and fax numbers, e-mail addresses, Web sites, the names of contact persons, and visiting hours.

Relationship data: This information describes the relationship between the stakeholder and the company, such as whether the stakeholder belongs to an interest group, how much influence the stakeholder has on the company, a description of the stakeholder's expectations and consequent information requirements, and a history and status of contacts. Because SAP SEM keeps a record of all this information, questions are answered more quickly.

Investor data: SEM-SRM provides additional information on the type and extent of stock held by investors.

Stakeholder data is accessed in different ways (see figures 5.44 and 5.45):

1. Using the search function on different criteria (such as city, country, or number of shares) for such purposes as preparing a marketing campaign
2. Looking at the relationships that a stakeholder has with others
3. Selecting from a list of stakeholders whose data was last processed
4. Selecting from a list of favorites (*My Stakeholders*)
5. Description of predefined hierarchies (such as by stakeholder group, influence, and last name)
6. User-defined hierarchies

Some of this data is taken directly from other SAP systems (such as SAP R/3 HR for employee data or mySAP CRM for customer data). SEM-SRM also lets you import information from non-SAP systems. For example, Taylor Rafferty and other knowledge providers can supply facts on the shareholdings of institutional investors and major stockholders. Insights to be gained may include learning that a mutual fund weights competitors more heavily than your own company. The entries can also be entered manually. A stakeholder researcher, for example, could gather facts about prospects in the Internet. The information could also come directly from a potential customer who requests marketing material (such as an annual report, newsletter, or company literature).

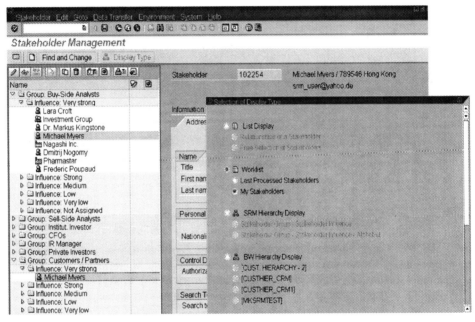

Fig. 5.44: Alternative Display of Stakeholder Contact Data   © SAP AG

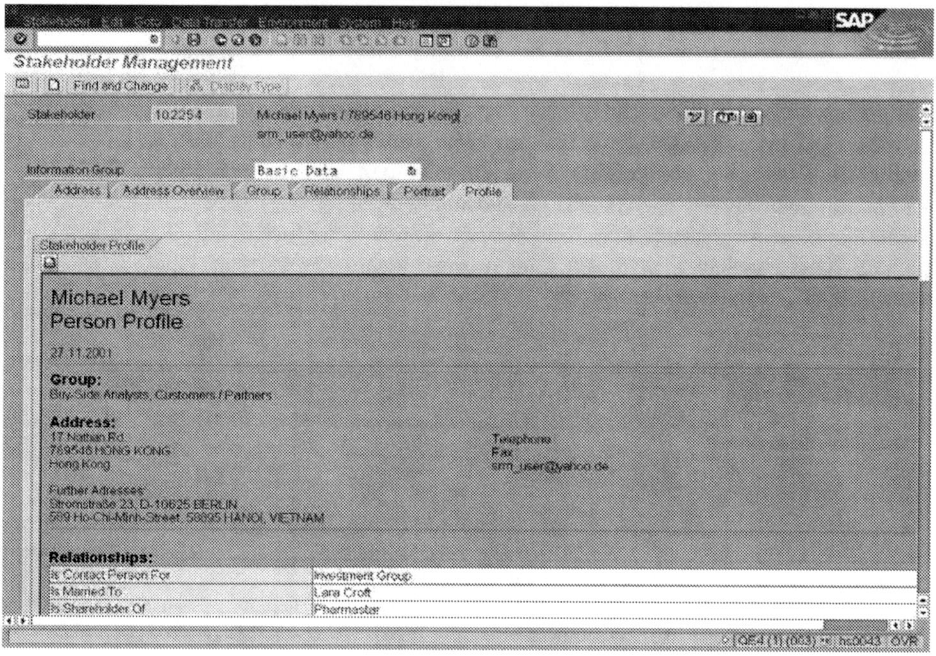

Fig. 5.45: Detail View of Stakeholder Data   © SAP AG

5.2.4.2   Stakeholder Portal

The Web-based Stakeholder Portal utilizes the "pull" principle, whereby a company gathers measures and news items and sorts them by different stakeholder groups. Interested parties can then download them at any time. The data basis is substantially the same as that of the other SEM components in the context of management information. Tools such as the Balanced Scorecard or the Management Cockpit (see figure 5.46) are thus available to stakeholders as well. An authorization concept prevents stakeholders from accessing sensitive information.

The Stakeholder Portal also provides interactive functions in addition to simply displaying data. For example, financial analysts can use the simulation functions of SEM-BPS (see section 5.2.1). In addition to internal data, it is possible to include items from external sources such as valuations by financial analysts or business and technology news.

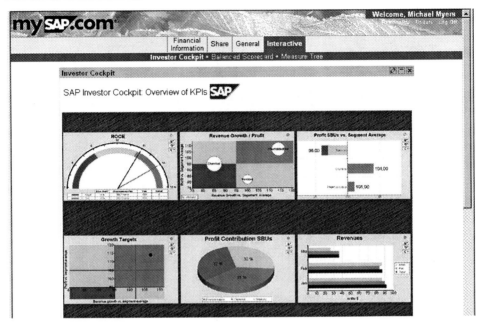

Fig. 5.46: Management Cockpit for Stakeholders © SAP AG

5.2.4.3 Stakeholder Communication System

While the Stakeholder Portal is a passive medium where stakeholders retrieve information on the company themselves, the Stakeholder Communication System is a bidirectional exchange medium between the company and prospects that actively supplies customized information.

The system provides the following functions for streamlining employees' daily work, such as in an investor relations department (see figure 5.47):

1. The system checks the sender of incoming e-mails. If the e-mail address does not yet exist in the database, it creates a new stakeholder data record. Otherwise it generates a new entry in the contact history.

2. A number of different channels are available for communication, such as standard letters, faxes, or e-mail.

3. Distribution lists can be generated from the stakeholder data.

4. Documents can be distributed automatically. If information is considered especially relevant for individual stakeholders, the company may want to send it to them even if they have not specifically requested it. An example of this would be sending all current and potential investors the electronic version of the annual report (or at least a message telling them that it is available on request).

A complement to this is Event Management. Using an electronic form (figure 5.48), you can enter data for an event such as a trade fair, a general meeting of stockholders, or a press conference. From the data entered in the form, the system automatically generates a Web site for the Stakeholder Portal (see above) and helps you send announcements to the target group.

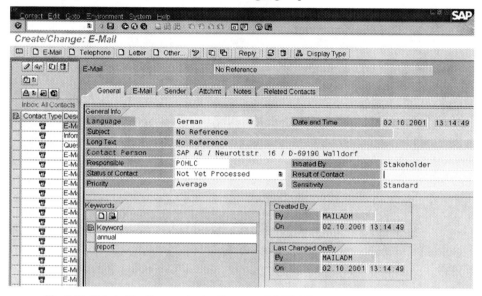

Fig. 5.47: Stakeholder Communication System   © SAP AG

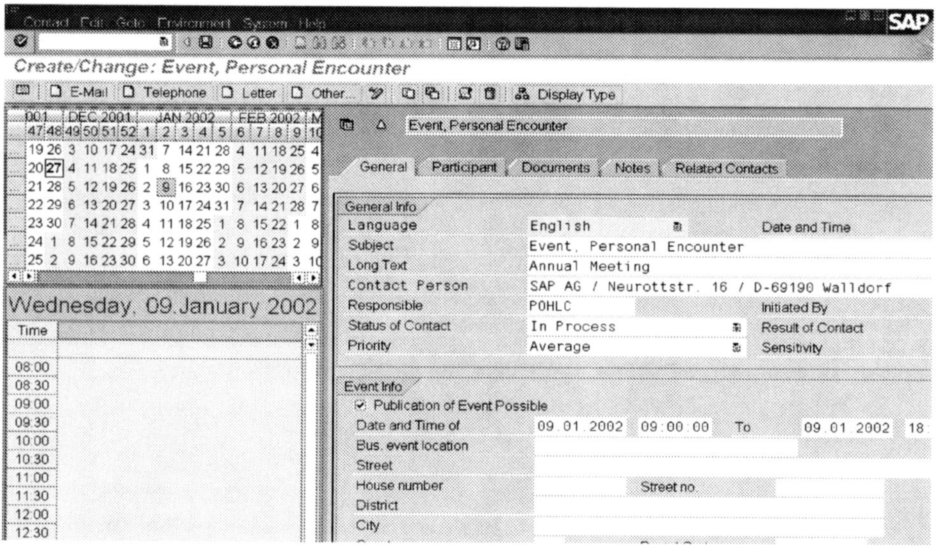

Fig. 5.48: Stakeholder Event Management   © SAP AG

Web Surveys

Web Survey technology lets you quickly and easily create electronic question-naires and evaluate them statistically. The interesting feature of this technology is that the input fields on the Web page are linked directly to the corresponding data fields of the SAP system, enabling addresses or other input to be matched up with data in the system (see figure 5.49).

This makes it possible to learn more about interest groups and to more accurately judge their expectations and information requirements when they request or subscribe to particular news categories and submit replies.

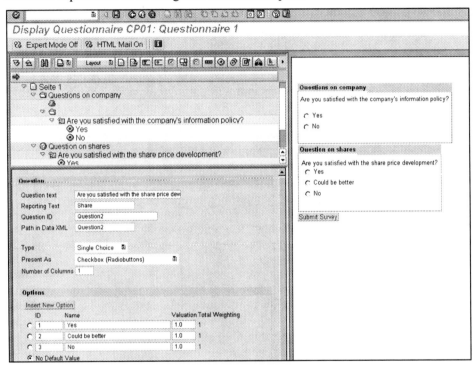

Fig. 5.49: Web Questionnaire for Information Request   © SAP AG

5.2.4.4   Document Management

Documents intended for stakeholders are managed by SEM-SRM using SAP Content Management. The files can be grouped by topics which users define themselves. This is a prerequisite for automatically sending out messages as described above.

For attachments, the system distinguishes between logical and physical docu-ments. For example, when you send out the logical quarterly report, the system searches for the file that matches the preferred language of the addressee.

5.2.4.5   Stakeholder Analysis

SEM-SRM provides functions for analyzing stakeholder data using a number of different reports. You can create your own reports or use the supplied standard reports, which are divided into the following categories (see table 5.2):

Category	Description
Stock Information	List of stakeholders that own shares (including the historical trend of the ownership)
Contacts	Time and type of contact with prospects
Information Requirements	Structured display of information requested by stakeholders
Stakeholder Expectations	Reports on the expectations of stakeholders

Table 5.2: Report Categories of Stakeholder Analysis

Example

Because of ongoing losses in its cellular telephone division, a consumer electronics manufacturer has decided to withdraw from this industry and concentrate on its core competencies in audio, video, and television equipment. This decision now needs to be communicated to the stakeholders affected by it. Different stakeholders, however, have different information needs:

1. *The financial analysts and investors are mainly interested in the effects on the company's goodwill.*

2. *Employees are most concerned about job security.*

3. *Customers want to know how long the company will supply spare parts.*

4. *Suppliers need information regarding the future purchasing volume as quickly as possible so that they can adjust their capacity planning accordingly.*

All these different types of information were taken into account for planning with SEM-BPS and are available as key figures in SAP BW or as documents in SAP Content Management. Using the communication system of SAP-SRM, the public relations department gathers the information appropriate for each stakeholder group and sends it out using distribution lists from Stakeholder Contact Management.

The financial analysts and investors can also interactively analyze the public plan values in an Investor Relations Portal. Views from the Management Cockpit and the Balanced Scorecard are available for this purpose.

5.2.5   Business Information Collection (SEM-BIC)

SEM-BIC gathers business information from internal and external sources, and assists in structuring and editing this information and linking it to internal data. This brings significant advantages in Stakeholder Relationship Management when searching for information on and for the different stakeholder groups. The facts and information researched with SEM-BIC are also used as a basis for planning and decision support in the other SEM components, where documents with qualitative background information can be accessed directly.

5.2.5.1 Information Request Builder

Research requests are entered in an electronic form (see figure 5.50).

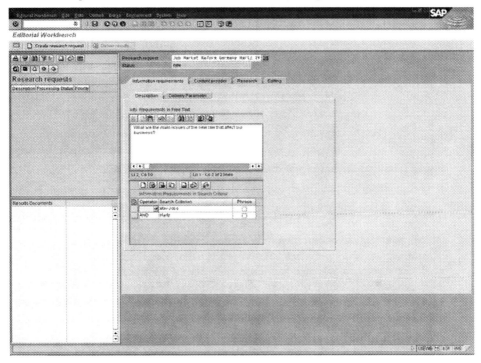

Fig. 5.50: Entry of a Research Request © SAP AG

The person submitting the request specifies what information is required, when and how often it is required, and in what form. The information can be accessed through SAP SEM (such as with the Balanced Scorecard and the Management Cockpit) or in planning, or it can be sent by e-mail.

5.2.5.2 Source Profile Builder

Before the actual research can be conducted, it must be decided which sources of information to use. This can be thought of as similar to the selection of raw material suppliers by a manufacturer. SEM-BIC provides the Source Profile Builder for this purpose, which is a kind of catalog of information sources such as Reuters or the Genios economic databases. In addition to identifying the sources of information, the system also stores access parameters so that external databases can be queried directly (see figure 5.51).

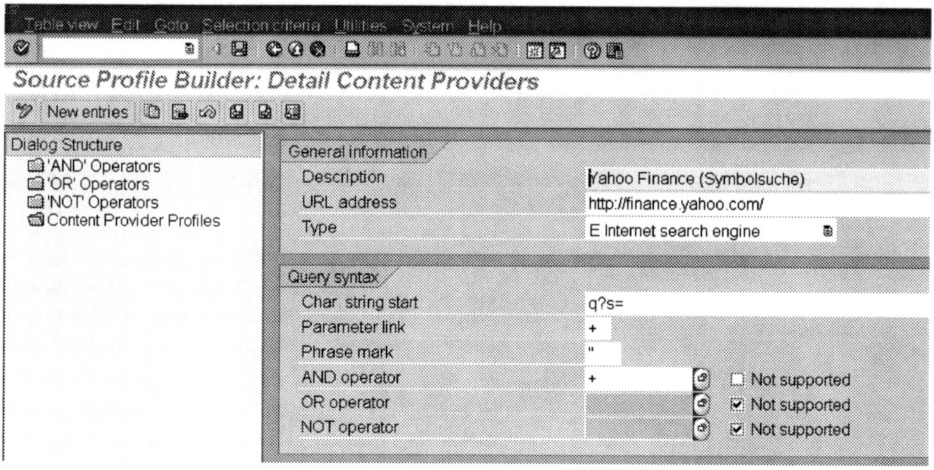

Fig. 5.51: Source Management with the Source Profile Builder   © SAP AG

5.2.5.3   *Editorial Workbench*

Actual research and editorial work is accomplished with the Editorial Workbench. The objective is to pick out relevant facts from the information sources and associate them with internal data. Potentially useful documents can be edited and formatted directly with Microsoft Word, Microsoft PowerPoint, Microsoft Excel, or with the text processing functions integrated in the SAP system. This feature enables market forecasts from different institutes to be compiled.

Users can then assign characteristics of the SAP BW InfoCubes to the results. The documents are stored in SAP Content Management (see section 5.1) with these characteristics, making the information available to all other SEM components.

Example

A pharmaceutical company decides to use SEM-BIC to observe competitors. An InfoCube is created for this purpose with the characteristics competitor, threat potential, region, product group, and time. Using the Information Request Builder, the assistant to the director enters a research request asking to be supplied with news about patents and clinical studies for all competitors that have a high threat potential. The news is to be delivered by e-mail.

A member of the market research department receives this research request in her worklist in the Editorial Workbench. For the source, the Source Profile Builder proposes two news agencies that have published reliable articles about pharmaceutical companies in the past. She accepts this proposal but also selects the option to receive an e-mail notification each time the press release section of the companies' Web sites are updated.

Each morning, she transfers the documents and sources sent to her into Microsoft Word with a simple mouse click. If necessary, she edits the contents for the director by deleting unimportant passages and highlighting critical information. She then sends this personalized newsletter by e-mail to the R&D director. She also assigns the news items to the characteristic values in SAP BW (the names of the competitors, the affected product groups, and so on). This enables all other SAP SEM/BA users to access this external information with the context of the internal data.

When you are planning with SEM-BPS, this enables you to see how individual competitors have reacted to your price increases or new product variants in the past. This information can be used for such purposes as parameters in a dynamic simulation model. The news is also available as background information in the Balanced Scorecard and the Management Cockpit as well as the BW Business Explorer, and can help explain events or developments such as why sales targets were not reached.

5.3   Business Analytics

Business Analytics controls the functions and processes in a company or one of its business units. The subdivisions within Business Analytics are based on cross-functional areas (see figure 5.2).

The following functions are supported by Business Analytics:

- *Financial Analytics*
  - Working Capital Management
  - Cost Management Analytics
    - *Group Costing*
    - *Activity-Based Costing*
  - Planning Applications
    - *Resource Planning*
    - *Cost Center Planning*

- *Customer Relationship Analytics*
  - Customer Analytics (customer value, customer potential, new customer acquisition, customer retention)
  - Marketing and Sales Analytics
  - Customer Service Analytics
  - Interaction Channel Analytics

- *Supply Chain Analytics*
  - Supply Chain Management
  - Supply Chain Benchmarking
  - Supply Chain Event Management
  - Supply Chain Optimization

- *Product Lifecycle Analytics*
  - Product Structuring
  - Concurrent Costing
  - Target Costing
  - Lifecycle Profitability Analytics
  - Product Change Analytics

- *Human Resources Analytics*
  - Personnel Planning
  - Employee Turnover Analytics
  - HR Benchmarking
  - HR Balanced Scorecard
  - Target Monitoring in Management by Objectives

These functions are described in detail below.

5.3.1   Financial Analytics

Financial Analytics includes classic management accounting tasks such as cost and revenue management, but also provides capabilities for analyzing and controlling measures to improve customer payment patterns, liquidity safeguarding, and working capital management. In contrast to operational cost management with systems such as SAP R/3 CO where the emphasis is on valuing business transactions, Financial Analytics focuses on modeling and simulating the quantity and value flows that are relevant to decision making.

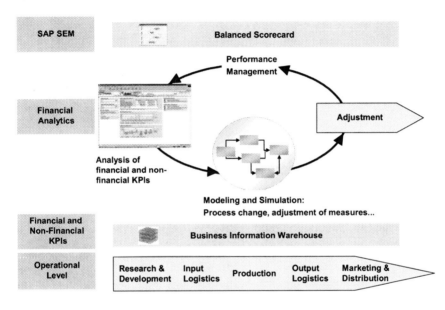

Fig. 5.52: Financial Analytics Architecture   © SAP AG

Figure 5.52 shows an overview of the architecture of Financial Analytics. The data comes from the business process transactions and is initially recorded in cost management as line items. From there it is formatted and transferred into SAP BW which provides additional non-financial and external data. Some of the applications that are part of Financial Analytics are discussed below.

Working Capital Management

Working capital is equal to current assets less short-term liabilities and provisions. The goal of Working Capital Management is to maintain liquidity – that is, to ensure that long-term capital is not acquired through short-term financing. The latter would be the case if the value of the working capital were negative. On the other hand, efforts are also undertaken to contribute as much as possible to the profitability of the company. Figure 5.53 gives an idea of the range of problems that can be handled by Financial Analytics.

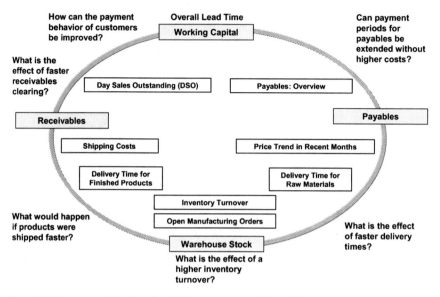

Fig. 5.53: Elements of Working Capital Management   © SAP AG

For liabilities, the goal is to find ways of extending payment deadlines without incurring additional costs. This may involve instruments for short-term financing such as special conditions for supplier credits. Financial Analytics provides assistance for this purpose with user-definable evaluations of open supplier items.

Another approach in Working Capital Management is to reduce capital tie-up and the prices of received goods, such as by reducing the safety stock or increasing inventory turnover. Financial Analytics provides methods for detailed analysis of price trends, inventories of raw materials, semifinished products, and finished products, as well as lead times and turnover.

For receivables, the problem is the exact opposite of that for payables: How can customers be encouraged to clear open items more quickly, accept higher interest rates for credits, or make down payments? The standard method in Financial Analytics for investigating the payment history is called *Day Sales Outstanding (DSO)* analysis. It calculates the number of days customers take to clear invoices by dividing the sum of the accounts receivable balances by the sales in a period (in this case one month) and multiplying by the number of days (DSO = Accounts Receivable Balance ÷ Period Sales x 30). Monitoring this figure enables the firm to spot critical trends in the speed with which invoices are cleared. Possible reactions include altering the cash discount rates for particular groups of customers or blocking credit memos in the transaction system for customers who are in arrears until payment has been received.

It can be seen that Working Capital Management is a typical example of a cross-functional control task. It includes analyses with several Business Analytics components: inventories of physical goods and transport activities are handled by SCM Analytics, while receivables management is handled by Financial Analytics, which offers DSO analysis (see above). In connection with CRM Analytics, the decision maker may also want to measure the effects of improvements in SCM on customer satisfaction and simulate the effects of different pricing structures.

Rather than each component narrowly focusing on its particular area, the idea is to reduce the cost and duration of cross-functional processes and improve the quality of results.

Cost Management Analytics

Cost allocations in operational systems are bound to certain mandatory accounting requirements, such as to supply information requested by external stakeholders (government agencies, banks, investors, and so on). Management decisions, however, require additional perspectives on cost information. Since Business Analytics is technically separate from the operational systems, it is possible to simulate a wide range of scenarios for cost allocation. The need for additional perspectives is clearly demonstrated by the critical aspect of customer profitability. From the point of view of external stakeholders, there is no need to allocate service costs, the costs of complaints, or the costs of purchase orders and sales orders down to the customer level. However, the customer focus encouraged by CRM should not entail economic disadvantages. Recognizing the profitable customers and assigning these overhead costs accurately is necessary to support decision making.

Financial Analytics provides functions for setting up networks with objects and links for simulation purposes and analyzing them as input/output models (Value Network Analyzer, VNA). This enables unification of Cost Element Accounting, Cost Center Accounting, and Cost Object Controlling. An object in the model represents all value-adding processes or products. Each object has a rule for the relationship between input and output (such as proportional or independent). Links represent the quantity flows between the sending and receiving objects. This has the advantage of providing users with a uniform presentation and calculation logic.

The following will describe two applications that are based on the VNA: group costing and Activity-Based Costing.

Group Costing

Companies often have separate operational systems for individual production sites. If supply relationships between these sites are so tightly intermeshed that they constitute an integrated system, the only logical approach is to cost the products in a higher-level analytical system. One often encounters networks where the individual sites are linked across multiple levels. For example, the first level may be a country-based production network, the second level an international network, while the third level is a global analytical application where products are costed from the perspective of the corporate group as a whole. This makes it necessary to eliminate intercompany profits. It is also important that the original cost structure be retained (direct costs and overhead costs, as well as fixed and variable costs). Figure 5.54 illustrates this. Columns 1, 2, 4, and 6 show the detailed breakdown of costs in group costing (column 7 shows the sum), while columns 3 and 5 show the cost breakdown in conventional costing systems.

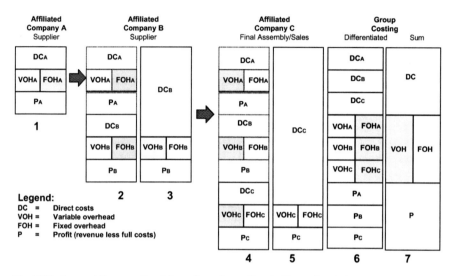

Fig. 5.54: Cost and Revenue Breakdown for a Group Supply Network   © SAP AG

The same thing applies when legally independent companies cooperate to produce a single product. For customer quotation costing or as a product cost estimate, data from different specialized operational systems are integrated into a unified analytical application which costs the product.

Analytical applications can also handle new types of costing approaches, such as simulations of entire plants. For example, it is possible to calculate the effects of changing the price of a raw material on the cost of goods manufactured of all finished products in a plant. The safety stocks of these raw materials and existing semifinished products are taken into account in such calculations.

To make local costing data available, solutions for group costing must be based on the following situation. The companies involved in the process chain of the group product usually have different classification systems (material numbers, costing elements, allocation bases, and so on) and different software systems. Among the most important but time-consuming preparatory tasks when group costing is implemented is to overcome these incompatibilities. The software solution for group costing is divided into different layers for this purpose.

1. The *data collection layer* consists of interfaces for the costing data from SAP systems and general XML interfaces with mapping mechanisms for data from non-SAP systems.

2. The *data cleansing layer* is where preparation and harmonization of the data take place. The data transfer is first checked syntactically, then the data can be completed with derivation rules. To unify the data semantically, all classification elements are converted into a specified form. Logical validation of the data concludes this layer. The system compares the new values against data from previous periods and indicates any variances that are above predefined threshold values.

3. The *calculation layer* calculates the group cost of goods manufactured (Müller 1995, pp. 194-231).

The entire process is continuously monitored. The group cost of goods manufactured is then transferred to downstream applications such as the information system, consolidation, and planning. Together with the group revenues, the results flow into group profitability analysis (see figure 5.55).

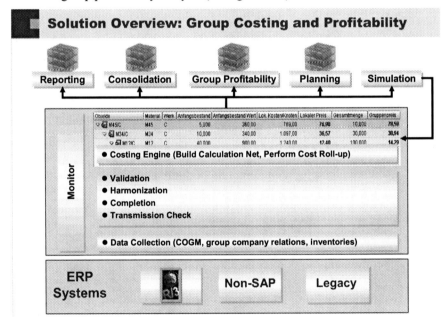

Fig. 5.55: Software Layers in Group Costing © SAP AG

Activity-Based Costing

In Activity-Based Costing, costs that are assigned to resources (such as cost centers) are allocated to cost objects (such as products) by means of processes. Figure 5.56 shows the value flow from the personnel area to the operational processes of a bank.

In this allocation model, products such as checking accounts, loans, and mortgages are regarded as cost objects, as are the customers. The costs of the bank branch that handles a certain customer are allocated to the cost objects using Activity-Based Costing. This allocation is based on simulations of order processing for the different products. For example, the bank may want to allocate the administrative costs for mortgages only to those customers who actually have a mortgage, rather than to all customers of the branch. A query in SAP BW returns the number of mortgages per customer group for costing. This is based on a three-level model consisting of the entities *resource, process,* and *cost object.* Costing is based on freely definable formulas that contain allocation methods such as assessment or direct/indirect activity allocations.

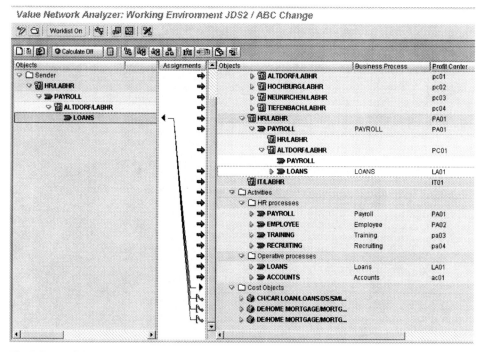

Fig. 5.56: Activity-Based Costing with the Value Network Analyzer   © SAP AG

The three-level allocation model is often unsatisfactory in practice because – as in this case – the branches themselves generate administrative costs at the bank's headquarters, such as for personnel administration and information technology.

These costs are charged to the branches and not to the cost objects. To be able to implement Activity-Based Costing in such situations, personnel processes such as payroll accounting, recruitment, or employee support can be modeled and the costs allocated based on key figures such as the number of employees in the branch or the number of new hires.

In addition to assigning actual costs through the costing network, the model also serves as a basis for simulations. For example, if the bank is thinking of setting up a new distribution channel, the effects on costs and capacities in the branches can be simulated. For simulation purposes it is important that all relevant factors are displayed on the same screen, so that when one parameter is changed, the decision maker can immediately see the effect on all other parameters.

Planning Applications

A key element of Business Analytics is planning. Financial Analytics supplies predefined planning applications that are based on the Planning Workbench of SEM-BPS. They can be used as delivered or modified to meet specific requirements. Resource planning and cost center planning are discussed below as examples.

Resource Planning

Before the actual planning cycle begins (in which the cost of goods manufactured is calculated in Cost Object Controlling, for example), the estimated resource consumption for the planning time period needs to be known. The objective is to be able to answer the following questions:

1. What resource quantities are required by the company?
2. How does a change in output quantity affect resource consumption?
3. What organizational units (plants, cost centers, or work centers) are being utilized too heavily or too lightly?
4. What effects do resource price changes have on the cost of goods manufactured?
5. What turnover is expected from the different suppliers?

These questions are answered in the form of scenarios with different output quantities, resource input quantities, and delivered prices. The results serve as a basis for decisions on material sourcing alternatives (in-house production or external procurement) and on the internal distribution of manufacturing orders, as well as for price negotiations with suppliers.

In resource planning, the materials at the lowest production level and the activities of the cost centers are combined into what is called a *flat itemization* for each end product or semifinished product. This itemization is extracted from the SAP R/3 system and transferred to SAP BW together with the prices for the individual resources. The data is then available for use in simulations. Planned output quantities are multiplied by the resource input quantities in the itemization to calculate the expected consumption. The costs for each resource and product are then obtained by multiplying the required quantities by the prices for the individual input factors.

Example

A manufacturer of chocolates wants to determine how different output quantities, milk prices (resource price), and milk proportions (resource input quantity) affect resource consumption and total cost for a particular flavor variant.

The flat itemization provides the input quantities for cacao powder, milk, sugar, and the activity "mixing" for each product. It also includes the prices for these resources. In a simulation, the output quantity for the different products (flavor variants) is changed. It is also possible to simulate changes in the resource proportions for a product. The effects of raw material price changes can be calculated for an individual product or product group. The results of the different scenarios can be saved for later reference, allowing best-case results to be compared with worst-case results.

Cost Center Planning

Cost center planning establishes activity relationships and assessment structures between cost centers. This data is used as a basis for allocating costs and quantities. Financial Analytics provides different methods for determining cost drivers, activity types, primary costs, and secondary costs (see figure 5.57).

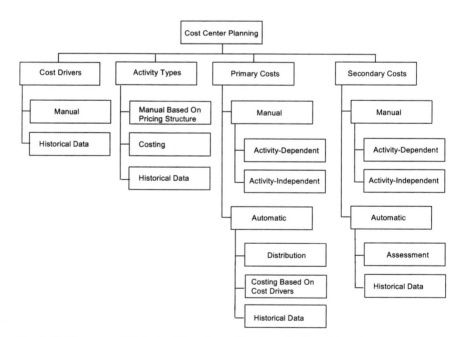

Fig. 5.57: Elements and Methods of Cost Center Planning with Financial Analytics   © SAP AG

The system provides the option of entering data manually or letting it determine the data automatically based on historical or other plan data.

Variables such as the number of new employees, IT services, or further training are planned in *cost driver planning*. The costs for a cost center are then calculated by valuating the cost drivers with predefined cost rates or prices. An example of cost driver planning is shown in figure 5.58.

Cost Center Planning

Save Exit

Primary Costs Activity Input

Resource Consumption

Select Cost Center Brewery(SEM0001200) Refresh

Cost Element	Stat. key figure	Unit of measure	1. 2002	2. 2002	3. 2002	4. 2002	5. 2002	6. 200
Wages and Salaries	Number of Employees: Manager	PC	2.00	2.00	2.00	2.00	2.00	2.0
Wages and Salaries	Number of Employees: Senior	PC	10.00	10.00	10.00	11.00	11.00	11.0
Wages and Salaries	Number of Employees: Junior	PC	15.00	15.00	15.00	15.00	15.00	15.0
IT Costs	Number of PC's	PC	26.00	26.00	26.00	26.00	26.00	26.0
Barrels 5 l	Number of Barrels 5 l	PC	5,000.00	5,000.00	5,100.00	5,150.00	5,100.00	5,000.0
Barrels 10 l	Number of Barrels 10 l	PC	2,000.00	1,980.00	2,000.00	2,050.00	2,070.00	2,100.0
Barrels 50 l	Number of Barrels 50 l	PC	1,000.00	1,000.00	1,020.00	1,050.00	1,070.00	1,100.0

Carry Forward Values Valuation

Primary Costs

Select Cost Center Brewery(SEM0001200)

Cost Element	1. 2002	2. 2002	3. 2002	4. 2002	5. 2002	6. 2002	7. 2002	8. 2002	9. 2002	10. 2002	11. 2002	12. 2002
Barrels 5 l	25,000.00	25,000.00	25,500.00	25,750.00	25,500.00	25,000.00	24,750.00	25,000.00	25,600.00	25,750.00	25,800.00	25,500.00
Barrels 10 l	14,000.00	13,860.00	14,000.00	14,350.00	14,490.00	14,700.00	14,350.00	14,000.00	13,790.00	14,140.00	14,070.00	14,000.00
Barrels 50 l	12,000.00	12,000.00	12,240.00	12,600.00	12,840.00	13,200.00	12,960.00	12,600.00	12,240.00	12,000.00	11,760.00	12,000.00
IT Costs	13,000.00	13,000.00	13,000.00	13,000.00	13,000.00	13,000.00	13,000.00	13,500.00	13,500.00	13,500.00	13,500.00	13,500.00
Wages and Salaries	125,000.00	125,000.00	125,000.00	130,000.00	130,000.00	130,000.00	130,000.00	134,000.00	134,000.00	134,000.00	134,000.00	134,000.00
Total	189,000.00	188,860.00	189,740.00	195,700.00	195,830.00	195,900.00	195,060.00	199,100.00	199,130.00	199,390.00	199,130.00	199,000.00

Fig. 5.58: Primary Cost Planning Based On Cost Drivers © SAP AG

The cost driver for personnel costs in this case is the number of employees in different positions (manager, senior, junior). The system calculates the personnel costs of the cost center for each period using formulas. An advantage of cost center planning is that the data of other subplans is used directly as input variables. This way, the plans at different hierarchy levels can be harmonized with each other.

The SAP term for the output of a cost center (such as a production hour or consulting hour) is *activity type*. One option for valuating internal activity types is to use external market prices or internal (manually set) prices. It is also possible to automatically calculate the costs by activity type or derive the costs from the data of previous periods.

Primary costs can be entered by the user for each cost element, either per unit of activity output or independent of the output. This direct method differs from indirect planning of primary costs with cost drivers. Automatic planning of primary costs provides a function for distributing costs. This function is particularly useful in cases where primary costs are first recorded on a collective cost center as an aggregate amount and then distributed to the individual cost centers.

Secondary costs can be planned in the form of activity input planning for other cost centers. Secondary costs are calculated by valuating the activity quantities. An automatic assessment function is also available in addition to this manual method of planning secondary costs. In cost center assessment, the costs of a cost center are allocated to other cost centers based on a key defined by the user.

Example

The cost center managers in a company budget the primary costs. Cost elements that can be planned only with great effort (such as energy costs) are first defined centrally and then distributed to the cost centers using keys. Corporate cost accounting reviews the results of this bottom-up planning process, and makes corrections if necessary based on top-down specifications. After several iterations, budgeting of the primary costs is completed. Next, selected primary costs are distributed based on keys such as the number of employees in the cost center receiving the costs. To prepare for planning the activity relationships, the planners set prices for individual internal activities. This valuates the planned requirements of individual cost centers and thus determines the secondary costs. This in turn enables the available capacity of a cost center to be adjusted to the planned requirements of other cost centers.

5.3.2   Customer Relationship Analytics

The purpose of CRM Analytics is to measure, predict, and plan all relevant aspects of customer relationships and to make decisions regarding alternative courses of action.

The first goal is to analyze the profitability aspects of customer-related processes such as order or complaint processing. The variables to be measured are closely associated with corporate strategy and are therefore to be found in the Balanced Scorecard as well.

One challenge is to identify behavior patterns and use them for forecasts (see section 3.3.2). Models that represent homogeneous customer segments, cross-selling potential, or churn behavior form an important basis for planning and controlling the areas of marketing, sales, and customer service.

The measures instituted in these areas provide benefits in the selection of target groups and in the design of campaigns, as well as in direct contact with customers. For instance, CRM Analytics can assist a call center employee to quickly judge the needs of the caller and select the appropriate call center script.

For this purpose, CRM Analytics supplies a knowledge base (Customer Information Platform) that enables the relevant aspects of customer relationships from different sources to be combined and structured. A number of different analysis methods operate on this data (see figure 5.59).

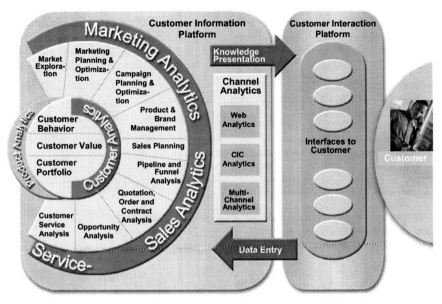

Fig. 5.59: Spectrum of Customer-Based Analyses in CRM Analytics   © SAP AG

Market Exploration concerns itself with the rules and current developments on certain markets. *Marketing* and *Campaign Planning & Optimization* are designed to improve the success of sales promotions and advertising campaigns. *Product & Brand Management* deals with the profitability of products, product groups, and brands. The classic sales planning functions are found under the term *Sales Planning*. One of the foundations of this area is *Pipeline and Funnel Analysis*, which determines which potential buyers can be made into prospects and finally into customers. Detailed analysis of documents such as bids, quotations, and contracts is the subject of *Quotation, Order and Contract Analysis*. *Opportunity Analysis* plays a role mainly in B2B environments. It attempts to systematically discover untapped sources of revenue. For example, a PC retailer might estimate a company's need for new computers, monitors, and printers over the next few years based on the number of employees. Customer service activities, especially complaint processing, are the subject of *Customer Service Analysis*. The analyses focus on the following areas:

1. Customers (Customer Analytics)
2. Marketing (Marketing Analytics)
3. Sales (Sales Analytics)
4. Customer service (Service Analytics)
5. Interaction channels (Channel Analytics)

The tools in the area of *Customer Analytics* help lead to a better understanding of customer requirements, customer behavior, and customer value. The functions of *Marketing, Sales*, and *Service Analytics* supply the information needed to increase the efficiency and effectiveness of the processes in these areas. *Channel Analytics* answers questions concerning interaction and communication channels such as the Internet, a point of sale (Customer Interaction Center (CIC)), or field service.

As shown in figure 5.60, this analytical knowledge is integrated into the operational CRM system (called the *Customer Interaction Platform* here) and is available for improving the transaction processes.

Acquisition of New Customers

The acquisition of new customers involves finding answers to the following questions:

1. Which new customers have the potential to become key customers in the future?
2. What distinguishes them from other customers?
3. What types of offers would most interest them?
4. What would a corresponding advertising campaign or promotional event cost?

The market analysis tool in CRM Analytics helps find the most profitable potential customers and supplies information on how such customers can best be approached. This tool is based on data from Dun & Bradstreet and other providers of external market data.

Customer Lifetime Value Analysis is one possible way of estimating the value of a potential customer and using it in marketing decisions. Cluster analysis (see section 4.3) helps identify the profiles of particularly profitable customer segments. When potential buyers have the same or similar characteristics, increased efforts are undertaken to gain them as customers.

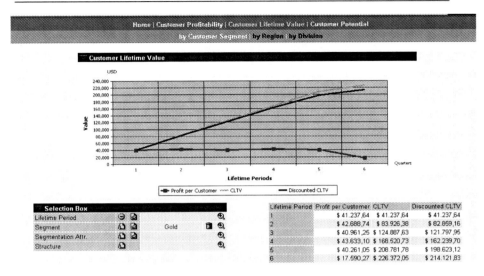

Fig. 5.60: Customer Lifetime Value © SAP AG

Figure 5.60 shows the relationship between profit of the periods and the Customer Lifetime Value (CLTV). The profitability of a customer segment is plotted along the time axis. In contrast to conventional periodic analysis, the units of the time axis are not calendar periods but the duration of the customer relationship (lifetime periods). This means that the CLTV increases continuously the longer the customer is retained. The period profit of a customer segment is based on the beginning of the customer relationship, and takes into account the churn rate observed in that customer segment in the past. The CLTV can serve as a guide for deciding how much to invest in an acquisition or retention (see below) campaign for a buyer in a particular customer segment.

Making the Most of Customer Potential Through Cross-Selling

Another goal of CRM is to recognize and take advantage of cross-selling potential. This is achieved through functions for analyzing buying patterns. Associative analysis is the most important data mining tool used in evaluating shopping carts and customer behavior to reveal cross-selling patterns.

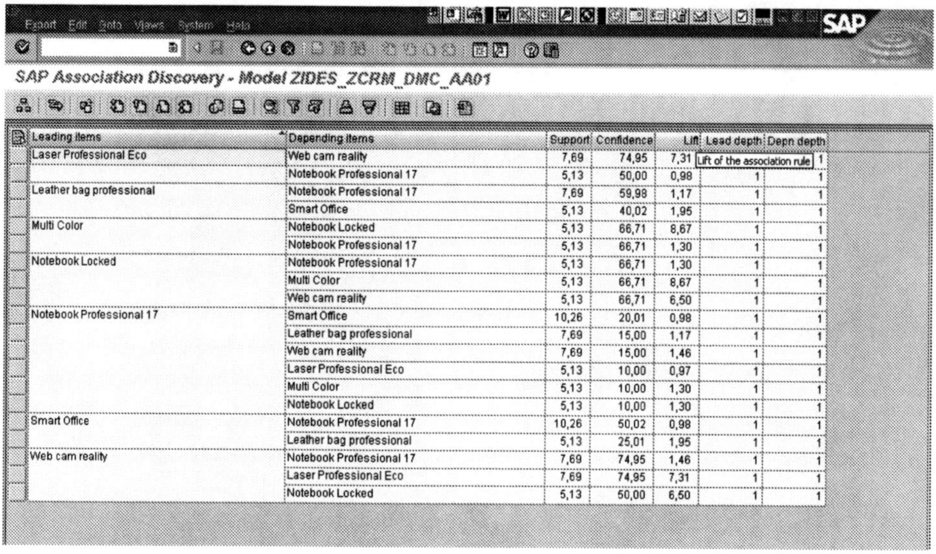

Leading items	Depending items	Support	Confidence	Lift	Lead depth	Depn depth
Laser Professional Eco	Web cam reality	7,69	74,95	7,31	Lift of the association rule	1
	Notebook Professional 17	5,13	50,00	0,98	1	1
Leather bag professional	Notebook Professional 17	7,69	59,98	1,17	1	1
	Smart Office	5,13	40,02	1,95	1	1
Multi Color	Notebook Locked	5,13	66,71	8,67	1	1
	Notebook Professional 17	5,13	66,71	1,30	1	1
Notebook Locked	Notebook Professional 17	5,13	66,71	1,30	1	1
	Multi Color	5,13	66,71	8,67	1	1
	Web cam reality	5,13	66,71	6,50	1	1
Notebook Professional 17	Smart Office	10,26	20,01	0,98	1	1
	Leather bag professional	7,69	15,00	1,17	1	1
	Web cam reality	7,69	15,00	1,46	1	1
	Laser Professional Eco	5,13	10,00	0,97	1	1
	Multi Color	5,13	10,00	1,30	1	1
	Notebook Locked	5,13	10,00	1,30	1	1
Smart Office	Notebook Professional 17	10,26	50,02	0,98	1	1
	Leather bag professional	5,13	25,01	1,95	1	1
Web cam reality	Notebook Professional 17	7,69	74,95	1,46	1	1
	Laser Professional Eco	7,69	74,95	7,31	1	1
	Notebook Locked	5,13	50,00	6,50	1	1

Fig. 5.61: Associative Analysis with CRM Analytics © SAP AG

As shown in figure 5.61, the sales data is analyzed for factors such as dependencies between products in a shopping cart. Associative analysis determines the probability with which two products will be sold together, or the probability that if product A is sold, product B will be sold as well.

The combinations of products or product groups determined in this way can serve as the basis for advertising campaigns or new product offerings (as part of bundling or Category Management).

Cross-selling analysis can be applied to different customer segments (target groups) or individual customers, enabling different buying patters to be taken into account. Analysis based on geographical areas is also possible.

Retaining the Best Customers

Sometimes just a slight increase in the average duration of customer relationships improves business results significantly. In addition to CLTV, useful methods of determining which customers are worth keeping include systematic analysis of customer profitability, customer potential (see also RFM analysis, section 3.2.5), and the customer portfolio (see figure 5.62).

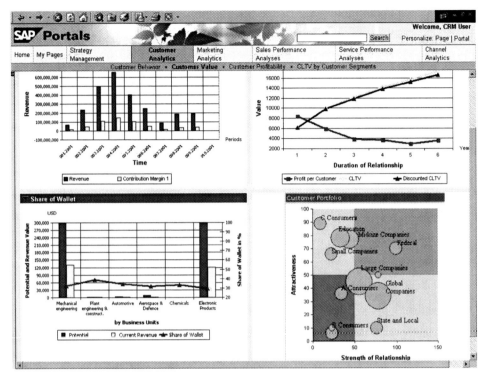

Fig. 5.62: Methods of Analyzing Customer Value © SAP AG

These customers should be examined more closely, especially when there is a danger that they will churn in large numbers. In addition to conventional survey methods, tools such as decision trees (see figure 5.63) enable customer profiles to be better understood. This knowledge can then be utilized in marketing and sales.

Decision trees are based on customer behavior observed in the past and establish the influence of various characteristics (such as the customer's age, gender, hobbies, living situation, and income level) on a dependent variable such as the probability with which the customer will react to an offer.

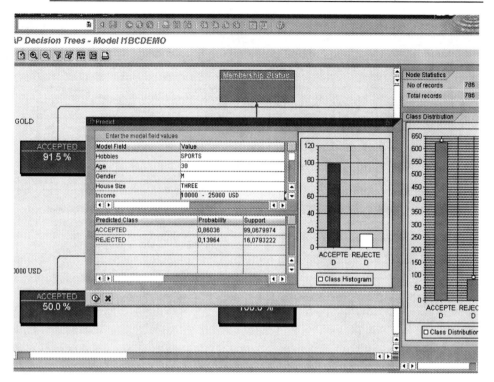

Fig. 5.63: Example of a Decision Tree   © SAP AG

Sales Planning and Forecasting

In addition to the strongly customer-focused areas just presented, CRM Analytics provides functions for sales planning and forecasting and for permanent variance analysis. In addition to typical sales key figures such as sales quantities or revenues, here the analysis is oriented toward predictive information on open sales orders and other factors that affect future revenues.

Since people in the sales area typically use planning functions only for particular deadlines or events, SAP made a special effort to ensure that the planning interface is intuitive and can easily be adapted to different users. This applies both to the type of planning interface and to the contents (that is, the dimensions – product hierarchies, customer hierarchies, regions, and so on – or typical CRM terms such as territory) and key figures.

The planner receives a selection list of the relevant planning objects (see figure 5.64). Guided by individually arranged tabs, the planner can successively fine-tune an automatically generated planning proposal.

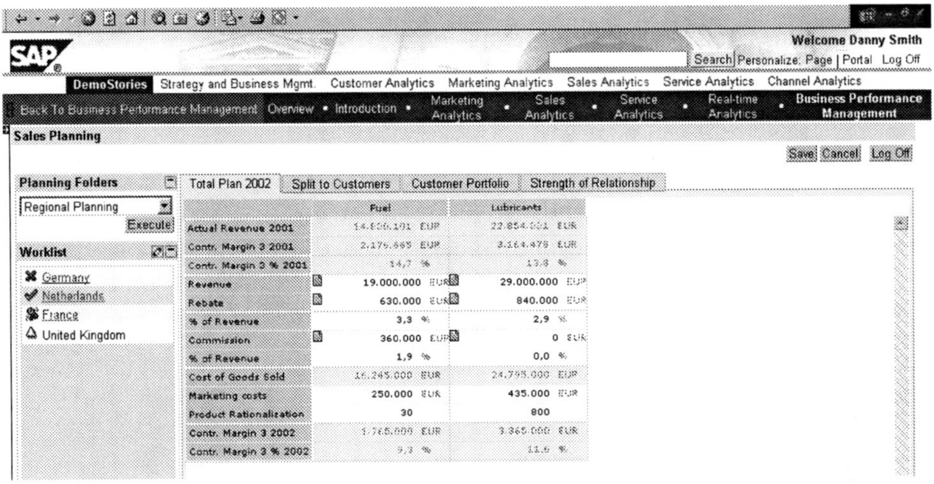

Fig 5.64: Sales Planning in the Portal

Sales planning and forecasting as well as additional planning applications in sales, such as for promotions, campaigns, or opportunities, are integrated with SAP SEM/BA. This also applies to financial, profit, and balance sheet planning, ensuring company-wide coordination.

5.3.3 Supply Chain Analytics

The rise of Internet-based Business-to-Business (B2B) and Business-to-Consumer (B2C) commerce has accelerated business processes between companies. This in turn has resulted in the need to keep all partners in the supply chain up to date regarding the profitability of the network or of the individual elements and connections within it.

While supply networks of this type have positive synergistic effects, they also harbor the danger that problems such as delays or incorrect deliveries in one area can quickly impact other areas.

There is a need to recognize local deviations from plan as quickly as possible, to estimate their effects on the overall network, and to implement suitable measures. This requires a central information component that takes all criteria into account (including inventories, times, quantities, and costs). SCM Analytics provides the following functions for this purpose:

Supply Chain Performance Management

Supply Chain Performance Management involves defining, selecting, and measuring KPIs, which enables integrated monitoring of supply chain performance. Analyzing the KPIs shows what parts of the supply chain are not performing well so that changes can be made to improve processes and resource consumption.

Purchasing costs, for example, are an appropriate measure of the efficiency of procurement processes. These costs can be lowered by measures such as evaluating suppliers to identify the source with the best value in different situations.

SCM Analytics continually monitors the supply chain's KPIs at both the strategic and operational levels, and automatically generates warning messages when discrepancies are detected. Since the measured variables are also part of the Balanced Scorecard (see figure 5.65), locally defined requirements can be brought into alignment with company targets.

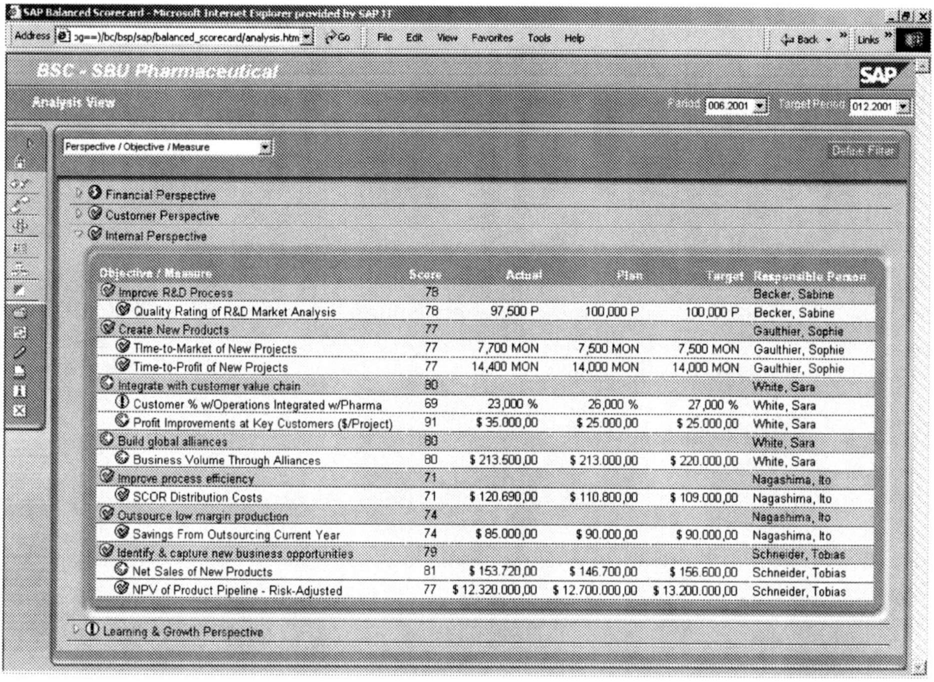

Fig. 5.65: Measures for Supply Chain Management in the Balanced Scorecard   © SAP AG

SCM Analytics includes a measure catalog, which is based on the Supply-Chain Operations Reference Model (SCOR model) developed by the Supply Chain Council (SCC) (see figure 5.66). The SCC is a non-profit organization composed of member companies from different industries and regions. The SCOR model consists of a comprehensive description of nearly all processes encountered in actual supply chains, as well as proposals for measures of process efficiency. The central areas are purchasing (*Source*), production (*Make*), shipping (*Deliver*), and product returns to suppliers or from customers (*Return*), which themselves contain subprocesses for different environments such as mass production or engineer-to-order. The model focuses on planning both individual process elements as well as the entire process chain.

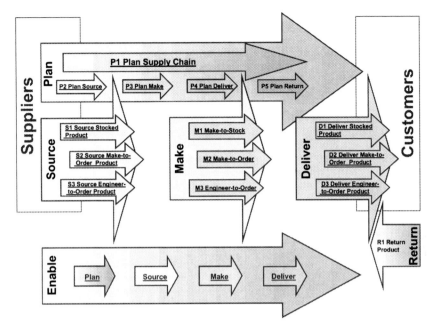

Fig. 5.66: SCOR Model (Supply Chain Council 2002)   © SAP AG

Benchmarking in the Supply Chain Environment

Continuous benchmarking provides indicators that point to areas where supply chain performance could be improved (see section 3.1.2). One frequent problem in supply chain environments is a lack of comparable data. For example, it is difficult to directly compare lead times for transport processes when the different companies have different transportation connections and use public road systems of varying quality. Exact descriptions of the objects being compared are therefore needed. Another problem lies in the lack of standard definitions of measures.

The SCOR model provides valuable support in resolving this problem. Benchmarking projects based on this model are widespread in the United States, and are gaining acceptance in Europe as well. In response to this development, the most important and frequently used SCOR measures were determined by a survey among SAP customers and added to the SAP measure catalog (see section 5.2.3.4). Examples of such measures include forecasting accuracy, production lead time, and "cash-to-cash" lead time.

In addition, SAP BW supplies predefined business content for some of the SCOR measures, which easily enables the values of the measures to be determined from the mySAP SCM system. It is also possible to exchange benchmark data with a provider in XML format and use the Measure Builder to either save data directly in SAP BW or extract data from SAP BW and send it to benchmark providers for purposes such as a contribution to a study.

Supply Chain Event Management

Supply Chain Event Management (SCEM) can be understood as an intermediary constituent between process monitoring and process improvement. Based on Supply Chain Performance Management (see above), SCEM can significantly decrease the time needed to react to disruptions and can automatically compile proposals for solving problems. SCM Analytics provides the following functions for this purpose:

Monitor: The monitor continuously supplies information on what are called *supply chain objects* and *supply chain events*. Supply chain objects can be real or abstract: they include physical products, batches, pallets, or truckloads, but also purchase orders and transport requests. Supply chain events might be a late delivery or an accident of a truck.

Notification: A notification component transmits messages to employees whenever a decision is required.

Simulation: The system simulates the economic effects of measures or even makes recommendations. It does this by valuating the new situation in the direction of material flow toward the customer (downstream) as well as in the opposite direction toward the supplier (upstream). The basis for such valuations can be missed orders, contractual penalties, or the added costs of overtime incurred as a result of the disruption (Mertens/Griese 2002).

Supply Chain Optimization

The functions for improving the supply chain (Supply Chain Process Optimization) serve to enhance processes with the goal of meeting both local and company-wide standards. The system supports building up a comprehensive integrated overview containing both logistical and economic criteria (such as costs and revenues). This component includes the following areas:

Planning: The Supply Chain Network Design contains functions for increasing the efficiency of logistics networks that reflect sales and cost structures. Demand and Supply Planning enables prediction and planning of requirements on the basis of sales data, marketing campaigns, and causal factors. In the construction industry, for example, causal factors are the number of building loan contracts and building permits (see also the information on indicator forecasting in section 3.3.2). In the area of production planning, mySAP SCM provides methods for rationalizing production processes while taking into account material and capacity restrictions. Cost and revenue planning furnishes information on the economics of logistical processes.

Activity-Based Management: The methods of Activity-Based Management assist in judging the efficiency of production and logistical processes. Since Activity-

Based Costing allocates the overhead costs in production and logistics to activities rather than simply to units of output, measures such as customer or product profitability can be investigated in more detail than is possible with traditional absorption costing.

A tool in SCM Analytics for modeling processes and value chains can link logistics processes to KPI and thus also to a Balanced Scorecard or resources. SAP is also developing ready-made process models as Business Content that are likewise based on the SCOR model.

5.3.4 Product Lifecycle Analytics

Operational management is concerned with product-related questions such as the following:
1. What is the target cost of a new product?
2. Does the new product fit into the existing product range?
3. What would it cost to modify an existing product?
4. How would this modification affect service costs?

Many companies use simple spreadsheet programs to answer these questions. However, this results in the problems described in section 1.1 regarding data storage, integration, and multiple user access. PLM Analytics focuses on the entire lifecycle of a product from the original product idea to recycling.

Concurrent Costing and Product Structuring with Integrated Product and Process Models

Cost-benefit analysis is beneficial even in the early phases of product develop-ment. Concurrent costing aims at calculating the accumulated costs after each step of product design. It thus contributes to cost controlling in a number of ways. It can lower fixed costs by helping you select the best production methods, and it increases profitability because its fast yet rigorous cost estimates enable you to recognize quotations that would result in a loss.

At the same time, this early phase of product development exercises a critical influence on product costs, which are then gradually incurred across the lifecycle (see figure 5.67). The differing trends of defined and realized costs is called the innovation window.

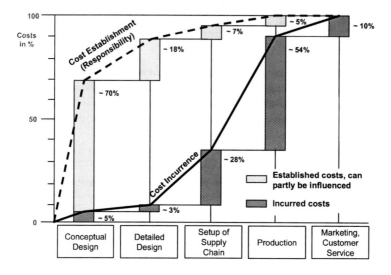

Fig. 5.67: Timeline of Cost Definition and Determination (Ehrlenspiel 2000, p. 12)

Since concurrent costing is employed at a time when no exact master data yet exist, it is based on reference data such as the costs of similar development projects in the past, or the costs of existing components and assemblies that are used in the new product directly or in only lightly modified form.

PLM Analytics can therefore indicate at a very early stage how the product characteristics affect the cost of goods manufactured. As the new product takes on more concrete shape, the data used for costing becomes more exact. PLM Analytics can simulate the cost degression effects of higher unit quantities from factors such as price reductions in procurement, better utilization of fixed-cost resources, and learning effects in production.

Development of a new product normally begins with a set of design specifications that are gradually transferred to the product structure. A product structure can be thought of as a rough bill of material in the early stages of design that contains different variants of components. This process is based on the master data models in Integrated Product and Engineering (IPPE) in the mySAP PLM operational system.

The link to PLM Analytics is established in controlling when a configured product structure from mySAP PLM is loaded. This structure can then be valuated, costed, and simulated. Figure 5.68 illustrates an example of concurrent costing in the system. The elements of the product structure are shown here in the lower-left part of the screen (the example is of different materials in a worklist). Information such as cost data and documents describing the attributes of the components can be accessed.

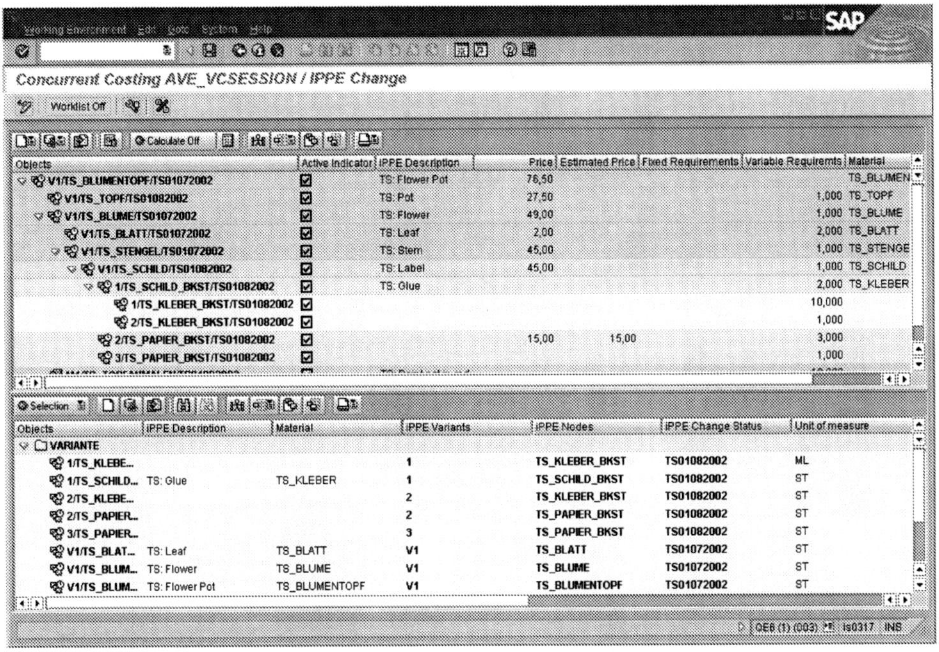

Fig. 5.68: Concurrent Costing   © SAP AG

Target Costing

The task of the development engineers is to convert customer requirements into products while simultaneously keeping costs within the limits defined by the market. In target costing (see section 3.2.1), market prices are broken down into maximum costs for the individual components.

As in many designs there are components that cannot be replaced, this process is semiautomatic: First, the user assigns fix amounts to such components. Then the system updates automatically the "budget" for all other parts.

Comparing the current total cost against the specified maximum cost provides a measure of how closely the target has been reached. This *early warning system* enables cost accountants to recognize problems during the early design phases.

Lifecycle Profitability Analytics

The calculated costs are used in planning the lifecycle for the new product. Together with the pre-production and follow-up costs – as well as prices, quantities, revenues, and sales deductions – they constitute an important factor in estimating the profitability. All products in a company's portfolio can thus be evaluated and compared with each other based on objective criteria. In addition to the dimensions *market growth* and *market share* from BCG Portfolio Analysis, any other dimensions are possible as well (Hähne/Schmitz/Vetter 2001). A

Lifecycle Profitability Analytics application can be set up with SEM-BPS (see figure 5.69).

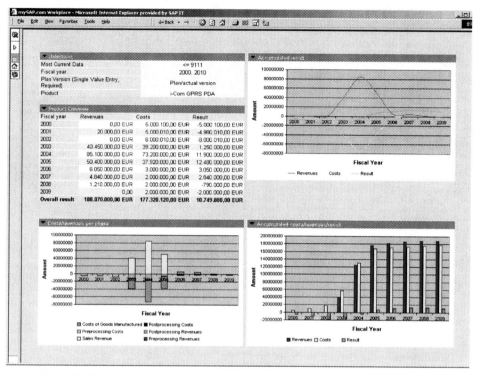

Fig. 5.69: PLM Analytics – Lifecycle Profitability Analytics   © SAP AG

Analysis of Product Modifications

Once a product has been developed, further modifications require not only engineering effort but also have effects on work scheduling and will incur costs. Any proposed modification must thus be evaluated to determine how it influences the product's contribution margin.

An accurate assessment of changes is usually only possible by considering all costs across the entire lifecycle of the product. It is therefore necessary to track the direct costs of modifications to the design and work scheduling and their influence on unit costs. Consequently, the data basis of Lifecycle Profitability Analytics includes the planned output quantities as well as the service costs (which could be lower after the design modification).

5.3.5   Human Resources Analytics

HR Analytics is SAP's workforce planning and control system, and is based on the operational system mySAP HR. This area is particularly important for companies whose employees are a decisive success factor. Companies can analyze their workforce, evaluate different personnel policies with regard to how well they support the company's goals, and monitor the implementation of decisions.

Personnel Planning

Data located in the transaction system mySAP HR and maintained in Organizational Management is available in SAP SEM/BA as well. This data forms the basis for personnel and cost planning. Starting from the organizational structure, workforce requirements may be planned using the key figures *employees* or *full-time equivalents* for positions (such as junior consultant or senior consultant). It is possible to transfer these measures and their associated personnel costs as summarized data from personnel cost planning of mySAP HR.

In SAP SEM/BA, personnel planning alters both the number of employees and the average wage and salary level, and determines the effect on overall personnel costs. The costs of the work center (such as for a PC) can be included.

HR BW Web Cockpits

SAP BW supplies two Web Cockpits for the area of Human Resources: *Headcount Overview* (see figure 5.70) and *Overtime/Illness Overview*.

The Web Cockpit *Headcount Overview* contains a number of reports called Web reports that are graphically integrated into a single cockpit which can be used for SAP Portals. Among other information, the reports include figures on the number of employees joining and leaving the company. It is possible to navigate within the cockpit to the different reports. By clicking on the graphics in the cockpit, the decision maker can access analyses in which detailed information is organized by organizational unit. For example, you can break down the headcount overview by cost center or employee subgroup (such as permanent employees, temporary personnel, and placement students) or compare the current headcount to that of previous months.

Similar navigation functions are available in the *Overtime/Illness Overview* cockpit, which has reports on illness rates or the costs of absence times.

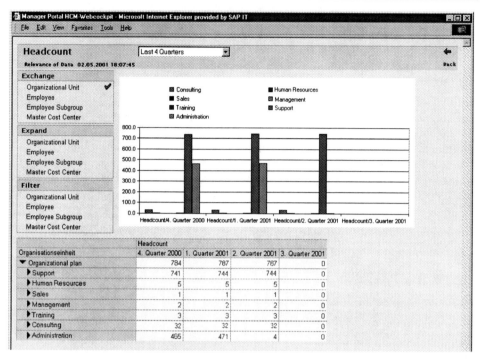

Fig. 5.70: Web Cockpit – Headcount   © SAP AG

Employee Turnover Analysis

Another area in HR Analytics provides functions for detailed analysis of employee turnover with key figures on the turnover rate, the number of employees leaving and joining the company, the average length of service, initial training costs, and recruitment costs. Employee Turnover Analysis gives answers to questions such as the following:

1. How high is the turnover rate?

2. Which employees leave?

3. Are there particular organizational units, employee groups, or age groups where the problems are concentrated?

4. What reasons are given for leaving? How frequent are these reasons?

5. Do those who leave have many years of service, or do they tend to be relatively new?

6. What is the average length of service?

7. How long do open positions remain unfilled?

8. What costs are incurred when employees leave (costs for training, orientation, moving, and so on)?

Figure 5.71 shows an example of fluctuation analysis by cause.

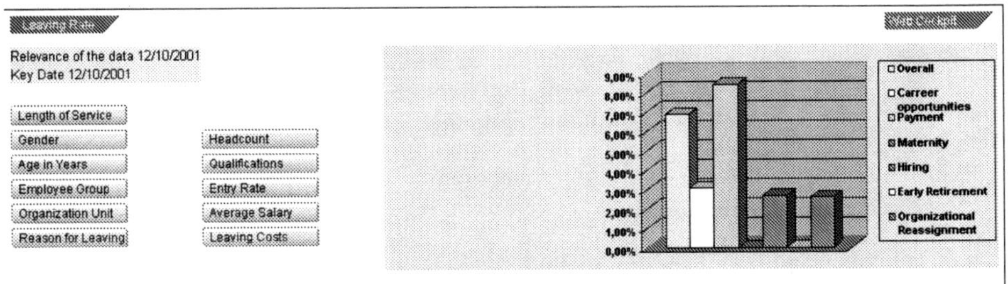

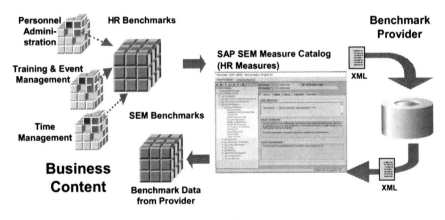

Relevance of the data 12/10/2001
Key Date 12/10/2001

Reason for Leaving	Number of leavers 2001	Leaving rate 2001
Overall result IDES Co.	14	6,88% ●
Carreer oppurtunities	2	3,08%
Payment	10	8,41% ●
Maternity	0	0,00%
Hiring	1	2,88%
Early Retirement	0	0,00%
Organizational Reassignment	1	2,61%

Fig. 5.71: Fluctuation Analysis   © SAP AG

HR Benchmarking

HR Benchmarking is a particularly good example of SAP's new strategy for developing planning and control systems, since content is offered in addition to programs (see figure 5.72).

Fig. 5.72: HR Benchmarking Scenario   © SAP AG

The measure catalog supplied with SAP SEM provides the business definitions for around one hundred measures frequently used in Human Resources. For participation in a benchmarking study, definitions can be imported from the benchmark provider through the *SAP Service Marketplace*. The current internal values of the measures are taken from the InfoCube *HR Benchmarks* which contains data such as the headcount, the turnover rate, and the illness rate. This set of data is transferred over an XML interface to the benchmark provider, who then returns the results of the comparison back over the same interface. This data can be saved in another InfoCube in summarized form and used for custom analyses.

HR Balanced Scorecard

Human resources departments can adapt their HR strategy to harmonize with company strategy using Balanced Scorecards. For this purpose, SAP has identified thirteen examples of critical success factors or strategic objectives such as increasing employee satisfaction or reducing unplanned absences. These strategic objectives were assigned to four perspectives (see figure 5.73 and section 3.1.6).

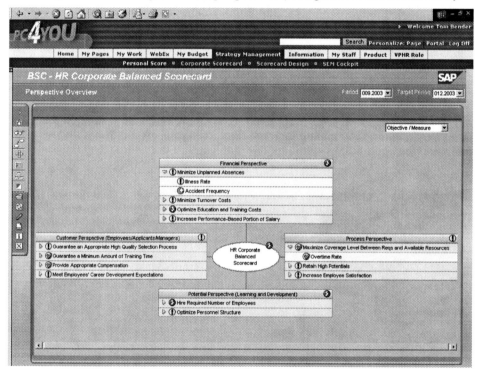

Fig. 5.73: Perspective View of HR Balanced Scorecard   © SAP AG

This example is based on a fictitious company whose human resources department is having great difficulty finding skilled workers and is incurring extremely high costs in its recruitment efforts. Each of the strategic objectives includes examples of instructions (initiatives) as well as HR key figures that are used to measure the degree to which the objectives have been realized (such as for the illness rate). A cause-effect chain was constructed to illustrate the interdependencies between the strategic objectives (see figure 5.74).

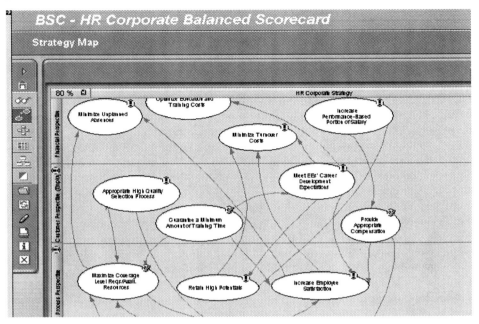

Fig. 5.74: Cause-Effect Chains in the HR Balanced Scorecard © SAP AG

Management by Objectives

Employee objectives are stored in the SAP R/3 component *Objectives and Appraisals* in mySAP HR and are based on the strategic objectives of the employee's department as defined in a Balanced Scorecard. This capability has been realized through the integration of mySAP HR and SAP SEM/BA.

1. The employees involved in the objective setting and appraisal process can access their Balanced Scorecard with a simple mouse click.

2. The strategic objectives relevant to the employee (such as "double our market share in South America") can be added to the employee's objectives for information purposes.

3. A performance overview containing selected elements from the Balanced Scorecards can be created in SAP SEM/BA for each employee. The rows contain elements such as the objectives of the employee, his team, his area, and the entire company, while the columns show the scores, weighting factors, and the product of the two. The contents of the performance overview can be added to the objective.

This gives employees the opportunity to see how their personal targets relate to the goals of their department and area, as well as to the overall company objectives.

6 Case Studies

6.1 Empresas Polar

Company Profile

Empresas Polar is the largest private-sector corporation in Venezuela, with annual sales of more than US $2.7 billion. The company, founded in 1941 as a brewery, focuses on the manufacture and distribution of consumer goods such as beer, soft drinks (the main products include Pepsi-Cola, 7UP, mineral water, and fruit juices), foods including corn, rice, wheat, semolina, noodles, wheat germ oil, margarine, mayonnaise, cheese, sauces (catsup, mustard, soy sauce, vinegar), snacks and ice cream, as well as animal feed.

In addition, Empresas Polar has shares in other manufacturers, financial groups, and trading firms as well as oil and petrochemical companies. These shares are primarily in well-known, top-of-the-line, international companies such as BBVA - Banco Bilbao Vizcaya Argentaria (Spain), Mitsubishi (Japan), Koch Industries (USA), Casino (France), Snamprogetti (Italy), Owens Illinois (USA), PepsiCo (USA), and Pequiven (Venezuela).

Empresas Polar's products are the market leaders in almost all categories, reaching about 220,000 retailers in Venezuela. Deliveries are made from more than 200 distribution centers served by a fleet of over 4,500 vehicles. The group also exports certain products to the United States, Western Europe, and other countries.

Goals

Having had SAP R/3 in place for over five years, Empresas Polar carried out an internal reorganization. As a result, the need for a group-wide management information system became clear. The main requirements for this system were:

1. The system had to offer differing levels of aggregation in reporting to reflect different hierarchical levels in management, and information retrieval needed to be both related to functions and cross-functional.

2. It should be linked to the SAP R/3 system in all strategic business units.

3. The solution should help the whole group and each strategic business unit in implementing its mission statement.

To realize these goals, Empresas Polar started a project in October 1999, initiated by a member of the executive board. The project was staffed principally by managers of the functional areas, experts from the different business areas, a small group of consultants and a few employees from the IT department.

Solution

During this analysis, a total of 290 different key performance indicators (KPI), recognized as necessary for covering the needs of operational areas, were identified. The indicators were classified according to differing levels in the group. Of the 290 KPIs, 68 were considered strategic – that is, valid for all business areas and therefore needing to be monitored by top management.

These strategic KPIs have a significant influence on decision-making processes, from the highest strategic level down to the operational level, across all business areas and functional areas. The solution consists of three layers that make it possible to represent the various aggregation levels and consolidation levels (see figure 6.1).

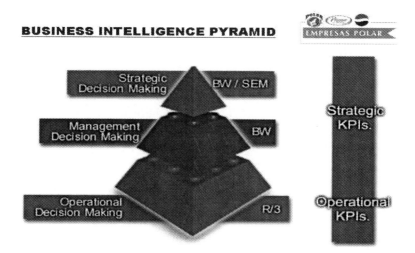

Fig. 6.1: The Business Intelligence Pyramid of Empresas Polar

The SAP R/3 system is the basis for the lowest layer. Most operational KPIs stem from this system and it also forms the backbone for processing transactions in all companies. A company-specific menu provides a uniform user interface that is available to every SAP R/3 user. At management level, the decision maker can use it to access all reports in his business area by function. The majority of queries are accompanied by drilldown functions that enable the user to view detailed trans-action data.

The second layer is oriented toward the needs of middle management and is based on SAP BW. The main users here normally need reports that relate directly to functions but also go across functional areas. The data originates for the most part in the SAP R/3 system. However, the SAP BW system is also connected to other information processing systems such as sales, and to external data sources such as market research institutes.

The top layer is built on SAP SEM. The focus is on the Management Cockpit, aimed at users in top management. The Management Cockpit standardizes graphic visualization of KPIs for the entire company. The contents are grouped in seven cockpits. The first four cockpits have a similar structure. They provide a picture of the overall situation in the corporation, as well as the situation in its three strategic business units. Each of the cockpits is divided into four walls (see section 5.2.3.5) that comprise 36 KPIs from Financials, Sales, Logistics, and Human Resources. They can be depicted using the various graphic types provided in the SAP SEM Management Cockpit. Moreover, the user can move from aggregated figures for the entire group to detailed information on each strategic business unit. Three additional cockpits were defined that relate to specific information for the Financials, Logistics and Human Resources functional areas. Each of these cockpits affords detailed information about a series of KPIs and other indicators related to these areas. In this way, managers of functional areas can measure performance in their areas on a global level. The data basis of SAP BW, and thus of SAP SEM, is updated regularly. Financial data is updated once a month, while production data are updated weekly and sales figures daily.

The implementation of SEM-BCS means that efficient tools are available for consolidation, as well as for aggregating key figures in many different ways – not just those dictated for statutory consolidation. Once consolidation structures were set up, the project team defined rules for automatic elimination of interunit profit and loss, groupings, and distribution of values to multiple profit centers. As soon as the annual financial statements are available in the SAP R/3 system, the consolidation process automatically begins in SEM-BCS. Using the consolidation monitor (see section 5.2.2.3), management accountants can continually monitor the current status of consolidation tasks in the subsidiaries.

The final data produced in SEM-BCS is stored in SAP BW, which then makes it available to all users at the middle and upper levels of the information system. Managers at these levels can then perform any number of varied analyses based on this data.

IT Infrastructure

At Empresas Polar, there are currently about 3,600 SAP R/3 users of two instances of the SAP R/3 system, running on two HP Superdome servers each with a total of 76 processors and 256 GB RAM. The SAP R/3 data basis containing data for three fiscal years is approximately 1.6 TB. Data protection is provided by a RAID system.

About 100 users work with SAP BW and SAP SEM (as of March 2003), and approximately 400 additional users are planned. The software runs with SAP APO on five HP N 4000 servers with a total of 28 processors and 50 GB RAM. SAP BW occupies about 400 GB of memory. As with all OLAP applications, response times vary considerably depending on the characteristics of the query and the data volume. The servers are linked via a fiber-optic network that functions independently of the control and user network. This facilitates rapid transfer of data between the operational system and the data warehouse system. SAP users are spread out over 45 locations.

Benefits

The development and implementation of the system has led to a large number of direct and indirect benefits for Empresas Polar. Some of the most important of these are highlighted here:

1. *Standardization of SAP R/3 within the whole corporation:* Since it was necessary to provide a homogeneous data basis, use of SAP R/3 modules was standardized throughout the organization. By eliminating legacy systems and making user interaction unnecessary in certain cases, it was possible to improve processes on the operational level and better the collection of detailed data.

2. *Reduction of time needed for year-end closing:* By using SEM-BCS, processes previously performed manually (and subject to frequent errors) were modified so that the time needed for creating financial statements for each strategic business unit was significantly reduced. Even the formal presentations made by the executive board can be obtained directly from the system, without any need for further adaptation.

3. *Elimination of inconsistencies:* Removing legacy systems and automating certain procedures also had the further benefit that conflicting versions of reports on the strategic business units or on the corporation as a whole were eliminated. This also solved the old problem of different departments having different values for the same key figures.

4. *Accelerated decision-making processes:* The benefits listed above led to additional advantages for middle management: they could devote more time and energy to operational tasks and less to verifying the quality of data. The ability to produce and present data more quickly also frees up time for actually analyzing the data – as a basis for making new decisions.

6.2   Henkel Surface Technologies

Company Profile

With sales of nearly 1.1 billion euros in fiscal year 2001 and over 4,000 employees, Henkel Surface Technologies (HST) is a worldwide leader in providing a broad spectrum of products, systems, and services to the metal finishing industry. These include pretreatment and finishing of metal and non-metal surfaces, as well as adhesives and sealants.

The company is headquartered in Düsseldorf, Germany. It serves mainly the automotive industry and its suppliers, along with other metal working and metal finishing operations. By the company's own account, the body of every second car produced worldwide receives a coating of zinc phosphate from HST before getting its first coat of paint.

In the last ten years, HST has acquired or founded around two dozen companies. The corporation is active in 63 countries, with 48 production plants (Browarzik 2002).

Goals

The starting situation was that around 60 affiliated companies around the globe delivered their planning figures for sales, turnover, and profit to group headquarters in their annual operating plan. Every August, the affiliated companies received close to two dozen Microsoft Excel spreadsheets, which they were to fill out and return by mid-September. Aside from the fact that they often did not adhere to this deadline, there were often numerous questions back and forth that led to exceptions being made, which in turn muddied the waters so that the overview was lost. There was also no direct comparison of plan values with actual values and data from prior years.

Entry and consolidation of plan data as well as preparing the data in chart and table form for planning meetings took up considerable time and required additional personnel in management accounting. A number of problems arose, for instance because users altered the Microsoft Excel spreadsheets from their original form and reported in mixed currencies. Every time planning data was changed, new reports and charts had to be created. "The whole process was too time-consuming. We needed to find a better solution," stated Dr. Raimund Browarzik, Global System Manager at HST.

The main goals that HST wanted to satisfy with the new solution were: simplifying the planning process, having all relevant information entered in one, globally uniform system, and improving the quality of the data. In addition, the following requirements were of central importance to them:

1. Rolling quarterly and monthly planning
2. Monthly plan/actual comparisons

3. Planning in local currencies of subsidiaries and in group currency (euros)

4. Bottom-up and top-down planning (country, affiliated company, industry segment and vice-versa)

5. Reporting according to IAS and US GAAP

6. Planning of hard and soft figures. Here soft figures are primarily external indicators, which are used as a basis for planning the hard, internal figures such as production quantities, costs, number of employees, and profits. All of this should be augmented by background texts and comments (see figure 6.2).

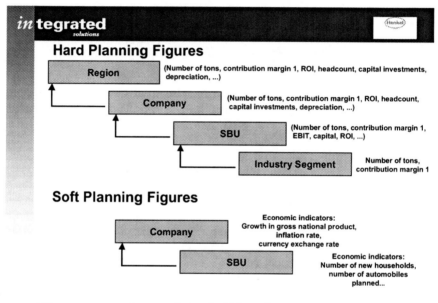

Fig. 6.2: Planning at HST (Browarzik 2002)

IT Infrastructure

HST and its affiliated companies have a heterogeneous system landscape in which a number of other systems are employed in addition to SAP R/3. As a consequence, the hardware configuration in group headquarters differs from that in the individual companies.

Solution

Considering this set of complex requirements, HST decided on SAP SEM. Their main focus was on the SEM-BPS component in conjunction with SAP BW. SEM-BIC was installed for integrating background texts and comments.

The project started in April 2001 and IDS Scheer AG, an SAP partner, was engaged for consulting and implementation assistance. The project team was made up of two specialists from the management accounting department at HST and five experts from IDS Scheer. IDS Scheer programmed interfaces for HST, aligned different data structures, and transposed the Microsoft Excel spreadsheets into a Web layout. Joachim Schirra, senior consultant and project leader on the IDS Scheer side, explains the approach: "Each user here and abroad should be able to work in the familiar Microsoft Excel environment in a standard browser with the new system. Therefore we copied all 23 Microsoft Excel planning sheets exactly from the originals." Through this effort, Microsoft Excel was combined with central data storage (see figure 6.3).

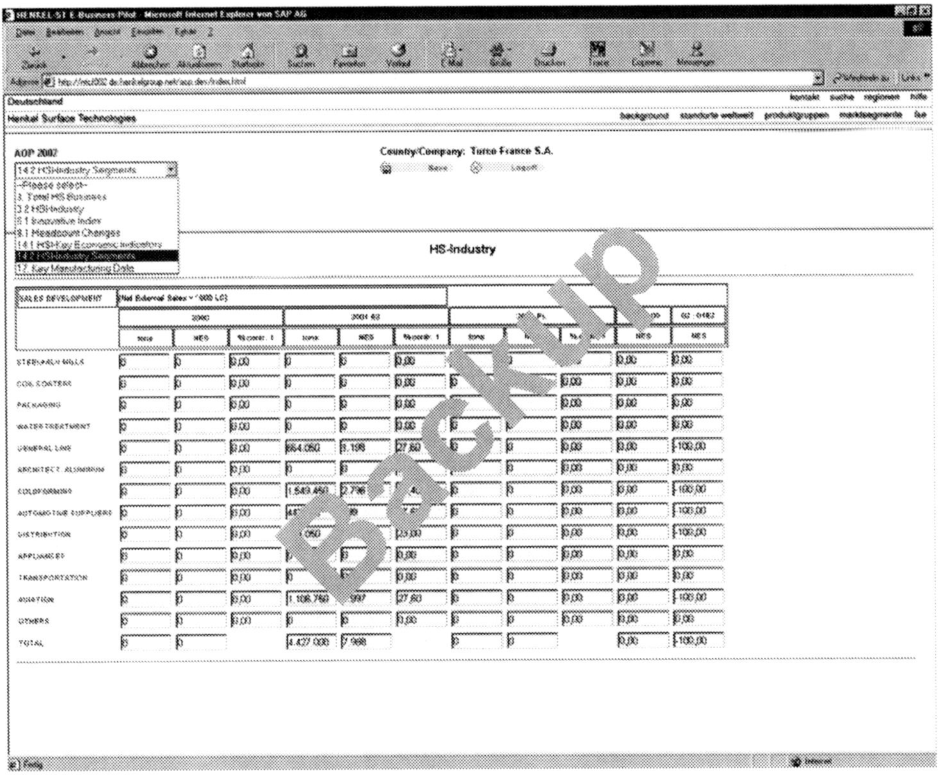

Fig 6.3: Planning Sheet (Browarzik 2002)

This procedure, and the related high performance capabilities of the system, not only ensured the acceptance of users worldwide but was also a primary factor in being able to put the project into effect within the short timeframe planned. The new planning system was ready to go live in August 2001, at the start of the planning phase for fiscal year 2002. IDS Scheer continued to support the system until the end of 2001, after which time it was taken over completely by HST employees.

Benefits

The 100 or so users at central headquarters and in affiliated companies now all work with a globally uniform system for sales and profit planning in their local currencies and in euros. Plan/actual comparisons can be easily made, and other reports are possible all the way down to the industry segment level. Developments over time are made transparent through the integration of historical data. The comments that users can enter about planning objects (such as region and industry segment) proved to be especially helpful. An additional benefit is that frequent structural changes in the group can be reflected in the system immediately.

The planning process was simplified and its efficiency was increased, since employees now invest considerably less time and energy in annual planning. HST also noted an improvement in the quality of the planning data, since incorrect entries could be detected earlier and with less difficulty.

Overall, HST was able to achieve consistent bottom-up planning. With little effort, they can also adjust this planning from the top down, for example by increasing sales predictions across the board by five percent.

6.3   Norwegian Defense

Company Profile

With approximately 19,000 employees in peacetime (not including conscripts), Norwegian Defense is one of the largest employers in Norway, consisting of an army, air force, navy, and logistics units. The annual budget is 30 billion Norwegian kroner ($4.4 billion).

A long-term structural crisis has led to significant reorganizations in recent times. One of the main reasons for this is that the organization was originally set up based on a cold war scenario and has had difficulty adapting to future military challenges. A number of incidents in the past few years demonstrated that the Norwegian military needs to be in a position to change its strategy at short notice. The main objective of the current reorganization is to establish a new structure that enhances the operational capabilities of the armed forces. This reorganization is based on a vision: "The right armed forces at the right time – to guarantee national security and fulfill international obligations."

Goals

At the beginning of the reorganization, Chief of Defense General Sigurd Frisvold looked around for a tool on which the impending changes in his organization could be based. After evaluating different methods, he decided to use the Balanced Scorecard. During the planning phase of the project, it quickly became clear that a management information system was needed as a basis for the scorecard processes.

One of the principal means for setting up the new and more efficient military organization is a large IT/reorganization project called GOLF. It was decided to use SAP R/3 as the basis and SAP SEM for realization of the Balanced Scorecard. The first SAP R/3 module will go live in 2004, but SAP SEM in conjunction with SAP BW has been in use since the beginning of 2002.

The reorganization will result in the following savings:

1. Reduction in the annual operating budget by more than two billion Norwegian kroner

2. Approximately 5,000 fewer employees in peacetime

3. The sale of around two million square meters of property and buildings

Solution

Norwegian Defense based its design and use of the Balanced Scorecard on the following five principles:

1. Conversion of the strategy into operational goals

2. Organizational structure based on the strategy

3. Motivation of all employees by conferring strategic responsibility

4. Strategy as a process of continuous adjustment

5. Implementation of changes at the highest level of management

The management teams at the top three management levels designed their scorecards using local project groups and external consultants. A scorecard consists of around 25 to 35 KPIs, some of which are typical key figures as used in almost all scorecards. When implementation is completed, SAP SEM will administer approximately 60 different scorecards.

In addition to supporting the Chief of Defense, the project team at the highest level serves to coordinate all other groups. It must be ensured that a common approach is taken and that resources are distributed as needed.

The scorecards with their KPI, initiatives, and strategic goals assessed monthly by those responsible for the strategic goals, who are usually members of the management team. The results of the assessments form the agenda for the monthly staff meetings. The focus is usually on a strategic goal or a group of goals. The key elements are those that have a critical status and that therefore require special attention by management.

A meeting takes place once a quarter to assess the strategy as a whole. Managers hold their own status meetings before attending the meetings at the highest level. This ensures that everyone is well informed about their own initiatives before important decisions are made that affect the entire unit.

Another beneficial side effect is that everyone uses the same data sources and KPI definitions. This means that decision makers no longer need to spend time discussing the origin of the data and the basic assumptions but can move right to the actual problems at hand.

IT Infrastructure

The IT infrastructure of Norwegian Defense consists of separate solutions for the army, navy, and air force, with some common sources of master data. The only system currently used in common is personnel administration, which is based on Oracle. For logistics and financials there are eight different systems, some of which have been in use since the early 1970s. This is one of the main challenges faced in implementing SAP SEM and SAP BW as the top-level management information system.

Therefore, the data warehouse paradigm and tools are used to define a common KPI and extract data from legacy systems. SAP BW serves as a data warehouse in connection with the PowerCenter ETL tool from Informatica. These application systems communicate with each other across BAPI interfaces. In addition to scorecards, SAP Business Explorer is the OLAP tool most frequently used by top management.

Due to the relatively complex task of automatically calculating KPIs on the basis of nonintegrated legacy systems, SAP SEM BPS is used to get critical information directly from the people responsible for the KPIs. This enables the information to flow into the different scorecards.

To a certain extent, scorecards in SAP SEM are implemented by local project groups using the new BSC Wizard (see 5.2.3.1). This reduces the need for a central "design center" but complicates the system transports needed for SAP solutions. Nevertheless, this approach is the subject of permanent evaluation to ensure that the process for local changes of the strategy remains flexible and also to ensure a stable and up-to-date development system. In coming years, the GOLF initiative will replace most legacy systems with modern ERP solutions. This enhances the ability of management to make strategic decisions based on current and relevant KPIs across the entire organization.

Benefits

The development of Balanced Scorecards – in conjunction with the introduction of SAP SEM and SAP BW – generated a number of direct and indirect benefits for Norwegian Defense, including:

Standardization of KPIs across the entire organization: With SAP BW and the scorecards as the main source of relevant information, management can spend more time on operational tasks instead of discussing KPIs.

Visualization of strategy: Each unit defines its strategy in SAP SEM and implements it there. SAP SEM is also used as a tool for implementing the required changes. The strategy maps are used to communicate the strategy to all employees.

Management's attention on critical KPIs influences behavior: The fact that the scorecard and its KPI are used by top management had a beneficial effect on the ERP systems as well, leading to an improvement in the quality of the transaction data.

Automatic reports: The entire process of collecting, presenting, and distributing management information is now handled by SAP SEM and SAP BW. This significantly reduced the amount of time that middle management needs to spend on these activities, allowing them to concentrate on operational tasks. *Better communication within management:* The valuations and comments are used to greater extent to improve internal communications. In meetings, managers are more up to date on the topics being discussed. There are also examples of problems that managers were able to solve even before the meeting took place. The valuation of strategy elements by status values concentrates management's focus on those aspects that require their attention.

6.4 Siemens

Company Profile

Siemens AG, a world leader in electrical engineering and electronics headquartered in Munich, is active in more than 190 countries and employs approximately 450,000 people worldwide, with sales of € 78.4 billion (2000). Siemens provides products and services ranging from information and communications, through automation and control, power, transportation, medical equipment, and lighting. Their palette of products extends from memory chips to complete production plants and power plants. In addition, Siemens aims to be an "e-company." This means that topics such as e-commerce, e-procurement, e-knowledge management, e-controlling and marketing of e-business know-how gain increasing significance (Siemens 2000).

Responsibility for worldwide business operations is lodged decentrally in business areas. The exchange of services among the business areas is referred to as "interunit business." In addition, management of marketing for the different product and service divisions is bundled in domestic and foreign companies. Each of these companies has its own external and internal reporting. They are supported by central departments at corporate level that assist in coordinating the co-operation between the business areas. The department Corporate Finance is responsible for financial management (Lochner 2001).

Goals

Financial management faced particular challenges due to frequent acquisition and divestiture and the resulting fluctuating number of companies, which in turn have complex interrelationships. This situation was further complicated by the desire to enter international capital markets.

The tasks of data collection and consolidation were performed in a series of steps. First the foreign subsidiaries reported to Corporate Finance, followed by the domestic subsidiaries and finally the business areas. In step four, Corporate Finance assigned the results of the companies to the reported results of the business areas, and sent the updated data back to them. The fifth step consisted of decentralized elimination of the internal trade relationships between the business areas. This data was then transferred back to Corporate Finance, which then per-formed consolidation for the Siemens group worldwide.

Hermann Giehrl, head of the Information Systems Management area in Corporate Finance, described the starting situation as follows: "Any company that wants access to worldwide capital markets, as Siemens does, must harmonize its financial reporting with international standards. To be listed on the New York Stock Exchange (NYSE), we needed higher-quality data and shorter process cycles. Our existing solutions were insufficient for this purpose, especially since the steadily increasing complexity of our business and constant changes to the corporate structure – such as those resulting from acquisitions – were making our data structures very complex" (SAP 2001a).

To meet these growing needs, Siemens decided to implement the consolidation solution of mySAP Financials. The following were the primary goals for the project (see table 6.1):

Type of Goal	Explanation
Time	Speed up the creation of reports and reduce reporting cycles
Quantity	Reconcile data from approximately 1,200 individual companies worldwide during consolidation
Flexibility	Quickly and easily reflect acquisitions and divestitures of companies or changes in investment relationships
Contribution to "e-company" status	Make use of options offered by the Internet for global collection of reporting data
Quality	Reduce input errors by automating more steps in consolidation

Table 6.1: Project Goals

IT Infrastructure

Over 60% of the software in place at Siemens comes from SAP, with the largest proportion concentrated on handling operational business processes using SAP R/3. At the outset, consolidation involved multiple, heterogeneous information processing systems. Central data storage was non-existent, leading to delays and inconsistencies.

Solution

To attain their stated goals, Siemens started the ESPRIT (**E**nhancement of **S**iemens **P**rocesses in **R**eporting and **I**nformation **T**echnology) project. In terms of the number of decentralized users, it is SAP's largest consolidation project to date.

The project started in 1998 and was implemented in phases (domestic subsidiaries, foreign subsidiaries, management consolidation, company consolidation). The project team consisted of people from Siemens, SAP and the consulting firm, Accenture. Complete consolidation went live in October 2000 (Schuler/Pfeifer 2001).

First the heterogeneous system landscape was done away with. Then a central data pool was installed, in which the approximately 1,200 companies of the worldwide Siemens organization store their data. About 3,200 users currently work with the system (SAP 2001a).

In conjunction with removing legacy systems, the processing steps for data collection and consolidation were also reorganized. All processing steps – from validation, standardizing entries and currency translation to comprehensive automatic consolidation entries – run in parallel and support several hundred users simultaneously. This is a major prerequisite for faster processing times. With security ensured by a controlled authorization concept, everyone involved in the process can access information and use it for various purposes, such as compiling segment information (Schuler/Pfeifer 2001). The main aspects of the new solution are listed below:

Data model

Corporate Finance provides a template for an InfoCube in SAP BW that contains the field structure of the master data of Siemens AG organizational units and the globally standardized Siemens chart of accounts. When shares of companies are purchased or sold, changes to the master data reflecting the new relationships are made centrally.

Data entry

Automatic upload of text files is the dominant form of data entry at Siemens. Since SAP BW was implemented, data is transferred increasingly from the transaction systems using extractors, with real-time update. Manual data entry remains the exception, only coming into play in internal reporting.

Validation

As the first step in validation the system checks whether the data is complete, using approximately 600 validation rules. These checks determine whether posted accounts exist, whether assets and liabilities balance, whether income as reported in the income statement the same as annual net income in the balance sheet, and so on. Each company is responsible for ensuring that its data is processed without errors in the data monitor (see section 5.2.2.2).

Consolidation

As soon as all processing steps are released in the data monitor, the actual consolidation tasks that are relevant for the group as a whole can start. The consolidation monitor (see section 5.2.2.3) is the tool for these tasks, as well as for processing subgroups in parallel.

Output

Information for management initially comes from the SAP Executive Information System (SAP EIS). The reporting functions of the SAP R/3 consolidation solution, SAP EC-CS, generate the consolidated financial statements. In the future, all reports will be generated using SAP SEM and SAP BW.

Benefits

By integrating the individual steps, Siemens can reduce the time needed for closing processes by 90%. And as of fiscal year 2002 they can even disclose their financial statements on a monthly basis. As data is no longer entered and processed manually, the error rate has dropped steeply. An additional advantage is that the system, according to Siemens AG, is extremely flexible and can be easily adapted to their needs. Changes in the organizational structure are immediately visible to all users worldwide.

The introduction of a corporate data pool also lowered IT costs. Centrally operated and maintained hardware and software components are less expensive than decentralized solutions. Data collection has improved, and the costs for updates are lower, as are the costs for IT personnel in the individual companies. The data for internal and external reporting is now consistent, and enables more accurate and more frequent forecasts. Above all, the conversion paved the way to the international financial centers. As of March 12, 2001, Siemens is listed on the New York Stock Exchange (SAP 2001a).

Siemens is relying on the next release of SEM-BCS to solve some problems with functions related to consolidation of investments (Lochner 2001).

7 Conclusion

7.1 Interview with David P. Norton

David P. Norton is president of Balanced Scorecard Collaborative, Inc., a consulting firm dedicated to the worldwide awareness, use, enhancement, and integrity of the Balanced Scorecard as a value-added management process. Together with Prof. Robert S. Kaplan, he developed the concept of the Balanced Scorecard.

Meier: *In your new book, "The Strategy-Focused Organization", you look back at some early Balanced Scorecard users. What experiences have they made in the meantime?*

Norton: The critical idea behind the Balanced Scorecard is that the scorecard describes the strategy of the organization. What you try to do is to build a representation of the strategy and translate it into measures. So, the measures can be used to manage the organization.

The early adopters of Balanced Scorecards - the ones that we documented in our book - did a good job with this. They built scorecards that truly represented their strategy. Then they tied it to the management system. And they began managing with it. Now, it takes a while for strategy to begin to happen, because strategy requires you to have new products, new customers, new cultures. What we have been able to see with the benefit of time when we wrote the "Strategy-Focused Organization" - that was some five or six years after many of these organizations started - we found that everyone of them successfully executed their strategy. This was very impressive, given the fact that typically nine out of ten organizations that start out on new strategies fail to execute them. Each one of these organizations that used the Balanced Scorecard succeeded. That is a big deal. That is really what the book "The Strategy-Focused Organization" talks about, what they did and how they did it.

Typically, the scorecard starts at the top with the executive team, because they are responsible for strategy and they understand the strategy. Building the scorecard at that level really helps them to clarify the strategy and to get consensus as a team. Once they have that, you have to communicate it to all parts of the organization. You have to begin cascading it from the top down to the middle levels and the lower levels of the organization. So, ultimately these organizations had scorecards at every level of the organization. Some of them took it down to the individual, individual people, like truck drivers, people who answered phones and people in hotels who carry your bags to the room. They had their own scorecards. But the key was that their scorecards were linked to the ones at the top. So everyone had the same alignment with the strategy.

Mertens: The Balanced Scorecard is used or just being implemented in many firms. Due to the large number of implementations you probably know about some projects that failed? What are the main obstacles for an implementation of a Balanced Scorecard?

Norton: If a scorecard fails, it is usually because it does not have the support and the involvement of the executives at the top of the organization. The scorecard is not an end in itself. The scorecard is a means to an end and the end that you are shooting for is successful execution of your strategy. The scorecard is a great tool for managing change, for communicating, for aligning the organization, but it is only a tool and so I would say about 90 percent of the cases that have failed - to my knowledge - have been, because there were efforts that have not been sponsored and supported by the executives. There were failed efforts that started in the middle of the organization, where somebody was trying to build a Balanced Scorecard strictly as a measurement program not tied to the strategy. And it did not have the power of the executives behind it to make change happen.

Mertens: In literature referring to the Balanced Scorecard a solution with four perspectives is predominant. Do you think that in hierarchical Balanced Scorecard applications the assignment of these cards to profit centers is sufficient to cover a product view or would it be reasonable for many firms to use a fifth card referring to such a product perspective?

Norton: It seems that there are two dimensions in that question. The first is what should be on a scorecard, and then secondly how will a scorecard differ for different kinds of organizations.

So, the first question is that the scorecard itself as we designed it has these four perspectives. This is an attempt to simplify the real world so that it can be understood. You can have five boxes, three boxes, ten boxes. The question is: Does it help you to simplify, to clarify and to communicate? What we found over the years now - it has been about ten years, and personally I have been involved in maybe 200 cases of building these scorecards - is that you can describe strategy this way in a wide range of organizations from pharmaceuticals to retail, to e-commerce, to governments, to charities.

Because, basically they all have customers, they all have stakeholders, financial stakeholders, citizens whatever. They all have processes to make their products, deliver them, service them. They all have people and they all have technology. So, those four perspectives that the scorecard is built around are essentially a model of how organizations take assets like people and technology and convert them in a process like innovation or customer management to create value for the customer. That ultimately creates financial value for the shareholders. That is the logic of cause and effect. The financial piece of the scorecard is an outcome. To create a financial outcome you have to start with your people and your processes. That simple logic turns out to be quite profound, because it is the logic of value creation. In particular, what makes it profound is the way that the economy in the world has changed in the last 20 years. It has moved from a world of tangible assets and a production economy to a world of intangible assets and a knowledge economy. So, what these four boxes are allowing organizations to do is to define and measure the intangible assets, like the skills of your people, and show how these intangible assets have been converted through business processes to create value for the customer.

As a result, I found that the four perspectives work very well for organizations. They are able to help them to better understand the complex world and communicate it.

The scorecard with the four boxes is a generic tool, it is a generic way of describing value creation. If I take it into an organization and I find division A has one kind of a product, let us say, it makes medical equipment and division B makes turbines and aircraft engines and division C has financial services, you are going to have a different scorecard for each of those products, but the structure of the scorecard will be the same. I will be looking at who is the customer for my jet engine? Who is the customer for my light bulbs? What do they want? How do I give it to them? What skills do I need? So, you have got to use the four box structure to describe how value is created. It is just another strategy, the measures will be different, but the four boxes - the basic architecture - will be the same.

Mertens: Within the scope of the increasing relevance of purchasing functions and supply chain management, how would you value an extra scorecard focusing on suppliers and supply chains?

Norton: Many organizations have in fact done that. What you are trying to do within an organization is to create linkage between different parts. So, if you have a purchasing department you are trying to link the purchasing department to the business units internally. As part of a scorecard program the purchasing department would build a scorecard to describe its relationship with the internal departments and it views the internal departments as its customers. Many organizations just take that logic, turn it around and say, now I have an external supplier, a vendor, I have a relationship with that organization, and I am going to build a scorecard to define it. In effect, the scorecard simply describes what creates customer satisfaction, like on time delivery, low costs, good service and what are the key measures etc. It is a great way to define any kind of a business relationship with a unit and its customers.

The U.S. Government has committed the purchasing function of many of the major departments. The department of energy was one of the first where they used the scorecard to manage the relationships with all of the vendors. They got some excellent results. This case is also described in the "Strategy-Focused Organization" book. There are other organizations, J.P. Morgan for example built a scorecard to manage its outsourced IT and created a partnership with three different organizations. I believe it was Arthur Anderson, CDC and a third. All had a part of the IT responsibility to support J.P. Morgan. They created a scorecard to describe what J.P. Morgan wanted in that relationship. Everyone was focused on the scorecard, because the scorecard became the way in which they represented the strategy of J.P. Morgan which these vendors had to support.

Meier: Where would you see starting points for an integration of Balanced Scorecards and risk management?

Norton: Could you explain to me a little bit what you mean by risk management?

Meier: Risk management means to identify special risks for a company, for example for an oil company a disaster with pollution, secondly to evaluate these risks: Is it a big risk? Is it a small risk? Finally, it means to decide about means to reduce the risks.

Norton: I have seen this in a number of organizations. Typically when you describe a strategy, it is not just one thing like low costs, it is usually three, four, five parallel efforts that take place simultaneously. One piece of your strategy might be to build relationships with innovative partners to develop new products. Another piece of your strategy might be to change the relationship with your customers, so that they view you as a partner. A third piece might be to increase productivity and a fourth might be to identify areas of high risk.

So, managing risk becomes one of several pieces of a strategy. In effect, every strategy should have something about innovation, something about managing the customer value and something about productivity and usually something about society. The risk management piece is treated like that. Once you have identified this as a piece of your strategy, you go down to the next level. What are the key things that I have to do to manage risks? Then those become part of the objectives that you set measurements for and begin managing them.

Mertens: A Balanced Scorecard could be regarded as a periodical reporting system. The alternative in terms of an exception reporting system would be that it triggers by itself a message to the responsible decision maker as soon as significant deviations occur ("information by exception"). Which starting points for further developments in this direction would you see in the near future?

Norton: What is a reporting system? In my view, there is a spectrum of the role of reporting systems. At one end of the spectrum you would find control systems. A control system essentially is an exception reporting system. A premise underlying it is that you know what you want and the system monitors to see that you are within the boundaries. If you are outside the boundaries, if you have a variance, the system can identify it and you act. That is really what budgeting systems and most operational management systems do. But, the premise is that you know the answer to what you want.

On the other end of the spectrum you have reporting systems that are used for communication and for learning. That is where strategy comes down. The strategy is a hypothesis. You think, this is going to work. You think, that if you train your people quality will improve, customers will buy more, and hence you will be more profitable. That is your theory and that is what your strategy is based on. Now, you go out and start doing those things, you train people. But, then the question is, was the theory right? Did the quality result in more sales? So, the reporting system is really designed to force teams of executives to sit down and to discuss the business around those areas of focus. Most of the value comes from those discussions, because it is a process of learning. You have a theory, you define measures and targets. Then the reports come back. The question is, is it working? Is the strategy right? You have to think of it more as a trigger to cause learning. But, this is not by exception, because you would have to know in advance that you have to train your people for 44 hours, so the first exception report would be: "We only trained them for 40 hours – something is wrong!" A second assumption would be that quality would improve and you would have to know how much. But, in reality you do not know the answer to those things. And that is what the system is allowing you to test.

Meier: *The Balanced Scorecard Collaborative has certified a number of software solutions for the Balanced Scorecard. How do you value the SAP solution?*

Norton: The SAP solution is one of the industry leaders. The Balanced Scorecard Collaborative established a set of standards for what we believe a Balanced Scorecard represents. It is based on the philosophy of the Balanced Scorecard and it is based on the best practices that organizations have used. So, the SAP SEM software suite clearly allows it organizations to build Balanced Scorecards and to describe their strategies and allows them to test the theory of the strategy, look at the cause and effect linkages.

But, more importantly, it is integrated in the broader suite of software that SAP represents. So, not only does an executive team have the opportunity to monitor the strategy with the Balanced Scorecard, but they also have the ability to drill down, do analytics in much more detail. It is incredibly powerful. It creates the information environment that organizations need to manage strategy.

7.2 Summary and Outlook

Comparing the SAP solution as discussed in chapter 5 with classical and more recent management methods (see table 7.1), it is clear that SAP SEM/BA represents a significant advance in the use of standard software for management tasks. SAP SEM/BA is thus an important step in bringing today's business management tools to modern management.

SAP Component	Business Task	Business Tool
5.2.1 **SEM-BPS**	2.1.1 Environmental and Enterprise Analysis 2.1.2 Strategy Formulation 2.1.3 Operationalization of the Strategy 2.2 Value-Based Management	3.1.1 Analysis of Potential and the Competition 3.1.5 Portfolio Analysis 3.3.1 Activity-Based Costing 3.3.2 Forecasting Methods 3.3.3 Simulation
5.2.2 **SEM-BCS**	2.1.3 Operationalization of the Strategy 2.1.6 Strategic Feedback 2.2 Value-Based Management	3.3.4 Consolidation
5.2.3 **SEM-CPM**	2.1.2 Strategy Formulation 2.1.3 Operationalization of the Strategy 2.1.6 Strategic Feedback 2.2 Value-Based Management 2.5 Risk Management	3.1.1 Analysis of Potential and the Competition 3.1.2 Benchmarking 3.1.3 Early Warning Systems 3.1.6 Balanced Scorecard
5.2.4 **SEM-SRM**	2.1.7 Stakeholders Communication 2.2 Value-Based Management 2.3 Stakeholder Approach	3.1.1 Analysis of Potential and the Competition
5.2.5 **SEM-BIC**	2.1.1 Environmental and Enterprise Analysis	3.1.1 Analysis of Potential and the Competition
5.3.1 **Financial** **Analytics**	2.2 Value-Based Management 2.1.3 Operationalization of the Strategy 2.1.4 Execution 2.1.5 Operational Performance Measurement 2.4 Customer Relationship Management	3.3.1 Activity-Based Costing 3.2.2 Contribution Margin Accounting
5.3.2 **CRM Analytics**		3.2.2 Contribution Margin Accounting 3.2.4 ABC Analysis 3.2.5 RFM Method
5.3.3 **SCM Analytics**		3.2.2 Contribution Margin Accounting 3.2.3 Break-Even Analysis
5.3.4 **PLM Analytics**		3.2.1 Target Costing 3.2.2 Contribution Margin Accounting 3.2.3 Break-Even Analysis 3.2.4 ABC Analysis
5.3.5 **HR Analytics**		3.2.2 Contribution Margin Accounting

Table 7.1: Realization of Management Approaches in the SAP Components

A positive aspect is that SAP SEM/BA essentially covers the requirements for modern business management application systems specified in section 1.2.

1. SAP BW and SAP Content Management as the central data storage applications in conjunction with the SAP Enterprise Portal improve the organization of planning data and reports and ensure they are consistent throughout the company (information integration).

2. A number of different monitors enable coordination of planning, consolidation, and reporting activities (functional integration).

3. The components are closely integrated with each other (module integration).

4. SAP SEM/BA integrates processes such as planning and control of companies and areas of responsibility, as well as operational business processes (process integration)

5. Web interfaces and the SAP Enterprise Portal enable fast, worldwide access to functions and information.

6. The features of an OLAP system described in section 4.2 were incorporated into the development of SAP SEM/BA. This enables a full range of multidimensional views.

7. SAP placed particular emphasis on an intuitive and easy-to-use user interface for the subsystems intended for upper management, such as the Management Cockpit. While most of SAP's competitors in the area of SAP SEM/BA provide Balanced Scorecards and other approaches for value-based management, the Management Cockpit in this form is essentially only offered by SAP.

8. Great emphasis was also placed on providing different visualization methods.

9. To ensure fast implementation, Business Content is provided in the form of strategy templates (see section 5.2.3.1) along with default settings and examples for data structures and planning or report contents. These can also be used as ideas for individual system configuration.

10. In addition, the concept of roles indicates that steps are being taken toward improved personalization.

The case studies discussed in chapter 6 show that SAP SEM/BA significantly advances both the speed and quality of planning and decision support in actual practice. There are, naturally, still a few gaps to be filled in. The following therefore presents a few ideas for further development.

A particularly difficult aspect is the little-regarded fact that "brilliant product ideas are a propellant that accelerates the enterprise on its course." On the one hand, information processing has its limits in furthering creativity, and there are concerns that information processing systems – at least the way they are normally used – can hinder creative thinking. On the other hand, possibilities open up for taking the pragmatic methods in information processing systems for engineers and product developers, such as those in advanced Computer-Aided Planning (CAP) and Computer-Aided Engineering (CAE) programs, and moving them upward in the management pyramid.

For some functions, computer science and business informatics can supply methods that enable a higher level of automation. An example is the use of text mining to analyze and extract qualitative information from text. Data mining algorithms (see section 4.3) that go beyond the capabilities of CRM Analytics (see section 5.3.2) could also be used in analysis to save time and improve the quality of results.

While the interfaces are normally user-friendly (aside from minor cosmetic problems such as inappropriate line and page breaks), we still see considerable room for improvement in parameter configuration, such as for the planning functions. Increased use of drag-and-drop functions would be a helpful first step. Further development could go in the direction of intelligent help systems that guide administrators through complex situations.

SAP SEM/BA incorporates a number of proposals developed in management science, and consequently exploits the possibilities and limits of information processing. Systems such as SAP SEM/BA assume a certain degree of formalization in the organization, in which management is understood as a process. This determines the definition of processes, events, milestones, and others factors. It remains to be seen whether unconventional and charismatic business personalities will have any problems with this approach.

Those with practical experience and possibly even some theorists who are introduced to SAP SEM/BA for the first time may get the impression that such a complex set of tools will demand even more of their already limited time ("management attention problem"). This objection can be countered by noting that SAP SEM/BA can assist managers in exactly this aspect through elegantly designed simulation experiments that filter out developments and decisions and present them in particularly suitable form.

In fact it appears that coded knowledge in the form of business content is becoming a decisive product attribute on the software market. Collecting this knowledge, structuring it, and making it available to the right people in suitable form is one of the current challenges in management science and business informatics.

Abbreviations and Acronyms

ABC	→	Activity Based Costing
API	→	Application Programming Interface
B2B	→	Business to Business
B2C	→	Business to Consumer
BCG	→	Boston Consulting Group
BEx	→	Business Explorer
BI	→	Business Intelligence
BSC	→	Balanced Scorecard
CAPM	→	Capital Asset Pricing Model
CFO	→	Chief Financial Officer
CFROI	→	Cash Flow Return on Investment
CLTV	→	Customer Lifetime Value
CM	→	Contribution Margin
CMI	→	Capital Market Interpreter
CRM	→	Customer Relationship Management
CVA	→	Cash Value Added
DCF	→	Discounted Cash Flow
DSO	→	Day Sales Outstanding
DVD	→	Digital Versatile Disk
EP	→	Economic Profit
ESPRIT	→	Enhancement of Siemens Process in Reporting and Information Technology
EVA	→	Economic Value Added
FI	→	Financial Accounting
FOX	→	FOrmula eXtension
HST	→	Henkel Surface Technologies
IAS	→	International Accounting Standards
IP	→	Information Processing
IPPE	→	Integrated Product and Process Engineering
ITS	→	Internet Transaction Server

KonTraG	→	German law regarding control and transparency in corporations (Gesetz zur Kontrolle und Transparenz im Unternehmensbereich)
MbO	→	Management by Objectives
MIS	→	Management Information System
MVA	→	Market Value Added
mySAP CRM	→	mySAP Customer Relationship Management
mySAP PLM	→	mySAP Product Lifecycle Management
mySAP SCM	→	mySAP Supply Chain Management
NOA	→	Net Operating Assets
NOPAT	→	Net Operating Profit after Taxes
NOPLAT	→	Net Operating Profit Less Adjusted Taxes
NYSE	→	New York Stock Exchange
ODBO	→	Online Linking and Embedding of Databases for Online Analytical Processing
ODS	→	Operational Data Store
OLAP	→	Online Analytical Processing
OLTP	→	Online Transaction Processing
P&L	→	Profit and Loss Statement
PCA	→	Profit Center Accounting
PDA	→	Personal Digital Assistant
PSA	→	Persistent Staging Area
R&D	→	Research and Development
RCR	→	Return on Customer Relationship
RFM	→	Recency Frequency Monetary Value
ROCE	→	Return on Capital Employed
ROI	→	Return on Investment
ROIC	→	Return on Invested Capital
RONA	→	Return on Net Assets
SAP BW	→	SAP Business Information Warehouse
SAP EC-CS	→	SAP Enterprise Controlling - Consolidation
SAP EIS	→	SAP Executive Information System
SAP R/3 CO	→	SAP R/3 Controlling
SAP R/3 IM	→	SAP R/3 Investment Management
SAP R/3 PS	→	SAP R/3 Project System
SAP SEM	→	SAP Strategic Enterprise Management
SAP SEM/BA	→	SAP Strategic Enterprise Management/Business Analytics
SAPGUI	→	SAP Graphical User Interface
SBU	→	Strategic Business Unit
SCC	→	Supply Chain Council

SCEM	→	Supply Chain Event Management
SCM	→	Supply Chain Management
SCOR	→	Supply-Chain Operations Reference
SEM-BCS	→	SEM Business Consolidation
SEM-BIC	→	SEM Business Information Collection
SEM-BPS	→	SEM Business Planning and Simulation
SEM-CPM	→	SEM Corporate Performance Monitor
SEM-SRM	→	SEM Stakeholder Relationship Management
SHV	→	Shareholder Value
SVA	→	Shareholder Value Added
SWOT	→	Strengths Weaknesses Opportunities Threats
TSR	→	Total Shareholder Return
US GAAP	→	United States Generally Accepted Accounting Principles
VaR	→	Value at Risk
VNA	→	Value Network Analyzer
WACC	→	Weighted Average Cost of Capital

Bibliography

Ackermann, J. (1995) Wieviel Gewinn für wen? Unternehmen zwischen Aktionären und Öffentlichkeit. Neue Zürcher Zeitung Nr. 11, 1995-01-14/15, p. 27

Agthe, K. (1972) Strategie und Wachstum der Unternehmung: Praxis der langfristigen Planung. Gehlen, Baden-Baden

Ansoff, H. I. (1966) Management-Strategie. Moderne Industrie, München

Ansoff, H. I. (1979) Strategic Management. John Wiley & Sons, New York et al.

Ansoff, H. I., Declerck, R. P., Hayes, R. L. (1976) From Strategic Planning to Strategic Management, 4th edition. John Wiley & Sons, New York et al.

Arthur Andersen (1999) STOXX 50 Shareholder Value und Investor Relations im Wettbewerb um institutionelles Kapital. Cited in: Wefers, M. (2000) Strategische Unternehmensführung mit der IV-gestützten Balanced Scorecard. WIRTSCHAFTSINFORMATIK 42/2, pp. 123-130

Babiak, U. (2001) Effektive Suche im Internet – Suchstrategien, Methoden, Quellen, 4th edition. O'Reilly, Köln

Back-Hock, A. (1988) Lebenszyklusorientiertes Produktcontrolling. Dissertation, Nürnberg

Back-Hock, A. (1991) Executive Information Systeme (EIS). Kostenrechnungspraxis 35/1, pp. 48-50

Back-Hock, A. (1993) Visualisierung in Controlling-Anwendungsprogrammen. Kostenrechnungspraxis 37/4, pp. 262-267

Ballwieser, W. (2000) Wertorientierte Unternehmensführung: Grundlagen. Zeitschrift für betriebswirtschaftliche Forschung 52/3, pp. 160-166

Bea, F. X., Haas, J. (2001) Strategisches Management, 3rd edition. Lucius & Lucius, Stuttgart

Becker, J., Priemer, J., Wild, R. G. (1994) Modellierung und Speicherung aggregierter Daten. WIRTSCHAFTSINFORMATIK 36/5, pp. 422-432

Biethahn, J., Huch, B. (1994) Informationssysteme für das Controlling. Springer, Berlin et al.

Bitz, H. (2000) Risikomanagement nach KonTraG – Einrichtung von Frühwarnsystemen zur Effizienzsteigerung und zur Vermeidung persönlicher Haftung. Schäffer-Poeschel, Stuttgart

Black, A., Wright, P., Bachman J. E. (1998) Shareholder Value für Manager – Konzepte und Methoden zur Steigerung des Unternehmenswerts. Campus, Frankfurt am Main et al.

Botosan, C. A. (1997) Disclosure Level and the Cost of Equity Capital. The Accounting Review 72/3, pp. 323-349

Braunschweig, C. E., Reinhold, K. (2000) Grundlagen des strategischen Managements. Oldenbourg, München

Browarzik, R. (2002) Globale Umsatz- und Profitabilitätsplanung mit SAP SEM. Vortrag auf der SAP Conference on Business Intelligence and Enterprise Portals, Leipzig

Bühner, R. (1996) Kapitalmarktorientierte Unternehmenssteuerung. Wirtschaftswissenschaftliches Studium 25/7, pp. 334-338 and 25/8, pp. 392-396

Bühner, R., Weinberger H.-J. (1991) Cash-Flow und Shareholder Value. Betriebswirtschaftliche Forschung und Praxis 43/3, pp. 187-207

Büschgen, H. E. (1999) Grundlagen des Bankmanagements, 2nd edition. Knapp, Frankfurt am Main

Coenenberg, A. G. (2003) Jahresabschluß und Jahresabschlußanalyse, 19th edition. Moderne Industrie, Landsberg am Lech

Copeland, T., Koller, T., Murrin, J. (2002) Unternehmenswert: Methoden und Strategien für eine wertorientierte Unternehmensführung, 3rd edition. Campus, Frankfurt am Main et al.

Deutsche Bundesbank (2000) Wertpapierdepot, Statistische Sonderveröffentlichung. Frankfurt am Main. Zitiert nach: Schuler, A. H., Pfeifer, A. (2001) Kapitalmarktorientiertes Konzernrechnungswesen mit SAP EC, Umsetzung eines effizienten e-Reportings. Vieweg, Braunschweig/Wiesbaden

Dittrich, J., Mertens, P., Hau, M. (2003) Dispositionsparameter von SAP R/3-PP, 3rd edition. Vieweg, Braunschweig/Wiesbaden

Dörner, D., Horváth, P., Kagermann, H. (eds.) (2000) Praxis des Risikomanagements – Grundlagen, Kategorien, branchenspezifische Aspekte. Schäffer-Poeschel, Stuttgart

Drucker, P. F. (1969) The Age of Discontinuity to our Changing Society. Harper & Row, New York et al.

Drucker, P. F. (2000) Die Kunst des Managements. Econ, München

Drucker, P. F. (2002) Innovation and Entrepreneurship, 2nd edition. Butterworth-Heinemann, Oxford et al.

Ehrlenspiel, Klaus (2000) Kostengünstig Entwickeln und Konstruieren, 3rd edition. Springer, Berlin

Entergy (2000) Stock Performance. http://www.shareholder.com/entergy/stock4.cfm [accessed 2004-08-16]

Foster, G., Gupta, M. (1990) Manufacturing Overhead Cost Driver Analysis. Journal of Accounting and Economics 12/3, pp. 309-337

Fraser, R. (2001) Beyond Budgeting - Managing Performance Better without Budgets. Presentation at the mySAP Financials-Kongress, Basel

Freeman, R. E. (1984) Strategic Management: A Stakeholder Approach. Pitman, Boston et al.

Frese, E. (1987) Unternehmensführung. Moderne Industrie, Landsberg am Lech

Fricke, M. (2001) Portal. In: Mertens, P. et al. (ed.) Lexikon der Wirtschaftsinformatik, 4th edition. Springer, Berlin et al., pp. 371-372

Georges, P. M. (2000) The Management Cockpit – The Human Interface for Management Software: Reviewing 50 User Sites over 10 Years of Experience. WIRTSCHAFTSINFORMATIK 42/2, pp. 131-136

Gerke, W., Bank, M. (2003) Finanzierung – Grundlagen für die Investitions- und Finanzierungsentscheidungen in Unternehmen, 2nd edition. Kohlhammer, Stuttgart

Geschka, H., Hammer, R. (1990) Die Szenario-Technik – ein Instrument der Zukunftsanalyse und der strategischen Planung. In: Töpfer, A., Afheldt, H. (eds.) Praxis der strategischen Unternehmensplanung. Metzner, Frankfurt am Main, pp. 311-336

Grochla, E. (1992) Handwörterbuch der Organisation. Enzyklopädie der Betriebswirtschaftslehre, 3rd edition. C. E. Poeschel, Stuttgart

Günther, T. (2002) Unternehmenswertorientiertes Controlling, 2nd edition. Vahlen, München

Hackathorn, R. D. (1999) Web Farming for the Data Warehouse – Exploiting Business Intelligence and Knowledge Management. Morgan Kaufmann, San Francisco

Hackney, D. (1999) Data Warehouse Delivery: Analytical Applications Defined, DM Review. http://www.dmreview.com/master.cfm?NavID=216&EdID=1237 [accessed 2003-05-15]

Hahn, D., Hungenberg, H. (2001) PuK, Planung und Kontrolle, Planungs- und Kontrollsysteme, Planungs- und Kontrollrechnung. Wertorientierte Controllingkonzepte, 6th edition. Gabler, Wiesbaden

Hahn, D., Taylor, B. (1999) Strategische Unternehmensplanung, 8th edition. Physica, Würzburg et al.

Hähne, Y., Schmitz, H., Vetter, A. (2002) Lebenszyklusanalysen mit modernen Software-Tools. Controlling 14/1, pp. 23-28

Hanssmann, F. (1996) Robustheit und Revidierbarkeit von Entscheidungen. In: Pinkau, K., Stahlberg, C. (eds.) Technologiepolitik in demokratischen Gesellschaften. Karl-Heinz-Beckurts-Stiftung, Stuttgart, pp. 68-75

Holthuis, J. (1999) Der Aufbau von Data Warehouse-Systemen: Konzeption – Datenmodellierung – Vorgehen, 2nd edition. Deutscher Universitäts Verlag, Wiesbaden

Horváth, P. (1990) Strategieunterstützung durch das Controlling: Revolution im Rechnungswesen? Schäffer-Poeschel, Stuttgart

Horváth, P. (1993a) Marktnähe und Kosteneffizienz schaffen. Schäffer-Poeschel, Stuttgart

Horváth, P. (1993b) Target Costing. Schäffer-Poeschel, Stuttgart

Horváth, P. (2003) Controlling, 9th edition. Vahlen, München

Horváth, P., Gassert, H., Solaro, D. (1991) Controllingkonzeptionen für die Zukunft. Schäffer-Poeschel, Stuttgart

Hostettler, S. (2000) Economic Value Added (EVA) – Darstellung und Anwendung auf Schweizer Aktiengesellschaften, 4th edition. Paul Haupt, Bern

Hughes, A. M. (2001) Quick Profits with RFM Analysis, Database Marketing Institute. http://www.dbmarketing.com/articles/Art149.htm [accessed 2004-08-16]

Hungenberg, H. (2001) Strategisches Management in Unternehmen – Ziele – Prozesse – Verfahren, 2nd edition. Gabler, Wiesbaden

Inmon, W. H. (2002) Building the Data Warehouse, 3rd edition. John Wiley & Sons, New York et al.

Inmon, W. H., Welch, J. D., Glassey, K. L. (1997) Managing the Data Warehouse. John Wiley & Sons, New York et al.

Janisch, M. (1993) Das strategische Anspruchsgruppenmanagement. Vom Shareholder Value zum Stakeholder Value. Paul Haupt, Bern

Jaros-Sturhahn, A., Löffler, P. (1995) Das Internet als Werkzeug zur Deckung des betrieblichen Informationsbedarfs. Information Management 10/1, pp. 6-13

Kagermann, H. (2000) Strategische Unternehmensführung bei der SAP AG – Erfahrungen und Lösungen eines Software-Unternehmens. WIRTSCHAFTSINFORMATIK 42/2, pp. 113-122

Kaplan, R. S., Norton, D. P. (2001) Die Strategie-fokussierte Organisation – Führen mit der Balanced Scorecard. Schäffer-Poeschel, Stuttgart

Kaplan, R. S., Norton, D. P. (1996a) Translating Strategy Into Action – The Balanced Scorecard. Harvard Business School Press, Boston

Kaplan, R. S., Norton, D. P. (1996b) Using the Balanced Scorecard as a Strategic Management System. Harvard Business Review 74/1, pp. 75-85

Karl, S. (2000) SAP Konsolidierungs-Funktionalität und Kundennutzen. In: Küting, K., Weber, C.-P. (eds.) Wertorientierte Konzernführung. Schäffer-Poeschel, Stuttgart, pp. 549-577

Kilger, W. (2002) Flexible Plankostenrechnung und Deckungsbeitragsrechnung, 11th edition, bearbeitet von Vikas, K. Gabler, Wiesbaden

Kirsch, W., Roventa, P. (1983) Bausteine eines Strategischen Managements. Walter de Gruyter & Co., Berlin et al.

Knolmayer, G., Mertens, P., Zeier, A. (2002) Supply Chain Management Based on SAP Systems: Order Management in Manufacturing Companies (SAP Excellence). Springer, Berlin et al.

Koreimann, D. S. (1976) Methoden der Informationsbedarfsanalyse. Walter de Gruyter & Co., Berlin et al.

Kotler, P., Bliemel, F. (2001) Marketing-Management: Analyse, Planung, Umsetzung und Steuerung, 10th edition. Schäffer-Poeschel, Stuttgart

Kramer, J., Noronha, S., Vergo, J. (2000) A User-Centered Design Approach to Personalization. Communications of the ACM 43/8, pp. 45-48

Küting, K., Heiden, M., Lorson, P. (2000) Neuere Ansätze der Bilanzanalyse – Externe Unternehmenswertorientierte Performancemessung. Supplement to journal Betrieb und Rechnungswesen, n. D./1, pp. 1-40

Lachnit, L., Ammann, H., Dey, G., Lübcke, G. (1989) EDV-gestützte Unternehmensführung in mittelständischen Betrieben. Vahlen, München

Laitko, H. (1999) Risiken der Forschung als Politikum – Zugänge zum Problem. http://www.pds-online.de/agwiss/diskussion/laitko.html [1999-04; accessed 2003-05-15]

Lake, M. (1998) The New Megasites: All-In-One Web Supersites. PCWORLD Online-Ausgabe. http://www.pcworld.com/reviews/article/0,aid,7202,00.asp [1998-08; accessed 2004-08-16]

Lochner, R. (2001) Personal communication, Mr. Roland Lochner, Siemens AG

Lorson, P. (1999) Shareholder Value-Ansätze – Zweck, Konzepte und Entwicklungstendenzen. Der Betrieb 52/26, pp. 1329-1339

Low, J., Siesfeld, T. (1998) Measures That Matter, Strategy & Leadership, p. 24. Cited according to: Wefers, M. (2000) Strategische Unternehmensführung mit der IV-gestützten Balanced Scorecard. WIRTSCHAFTSINFORMATIK 42/2, pp. 123-130

Maani, K., Cavana, R. (2000) Systems Thinking and Modelling. Prentice Hall, New Zealand

Macharzina, K. (2003) Unternehmensführung. Das internationale Managementwissen. Konzepte – Methoden – Praxis, 4th edition. Wiesbaden, Gabler

Markscheffel, B. (1998) Komponenten zur effektiven Bewertung verteilter Informationsbestände. In: Ockenfeld, M., Schmidt, R., 20. Online-Tagung der DGD – Host Retrieval und Global Research. Frankfurt am Main, pp. 129-145

von Maur, E., Rieger, B. (2001) Data Warehouse. In: Mertens, P. et al. (eds.) Lexikon der Wirtschaftsinformatik, 4th edition. Springer, Berlin et al., pp. 131-132

Meier, M. (2000) Integration externer Daten in Planungs- und Kontrollsysteme – Ein Redaktions-Leitstand für Informationen aus dem Internet. Gabler, Wiesbaden

Meier, M., Beckh, M. (2000) Text Mining. WIRTSCHAFTSINFORMATIK 42/2, pp. 165-167

Meier, M., Mertens, P. (2001) The Editorial Workbench - Handling the Information Supply Chain of External Internet Data for Strategic Decision Support. Journal of Decision Systems 10/2, pp. 149-174

Meier, M., Schröder, J. (2000) Integration interner und externer Führungsinformationen in einem Pharmaunternehmen – Probleme und Lösungsansätze. WIRTSCHAFTSINFORMATIK 42/2, pp. 137-146

Mertens, P. (2001) Information – die Ressource der Zukunft. Frankfurter Allgemeine Zeitung vom 2001-08-20, p. 25

Mertens, P. (2003a) Mittel- und langfristige Absatzprognose auf der Basis von Sättigungsmodellen. In: Mertens, P. (ed.) Prognoserechnung, 6th edition. Physica, Heidelberg et al., pp. 157-193

Mertens, P. (ed.) (2003b) Prognoserechnung, 6th edition. Physica, Heidelberg et al.

Mertens, P. (2004) Integrierte Informationsverarbeitung, Band 1, Operative Systeme in der Industrie, 14th edition. Gabler, Wiesbaden

Mertens, P., Cas, K., Meier, M. (1997) Die Integration von internen und externen Informationen als Herausforderung für das Controlling. In: Becker, W., Weber, J. (eds.) Kostenrechnung: Stand und Entwicklungsperspektiven. Gabler, Wiesbaden, pp. 367-382

Mertens, P., Griese, J. (2002) Integrierte Informationsverarbeitung, Band 2, Planungs- und Kontrollsysteme in der Industrie, 9th edition. Gabler, Wiesbaden

Mertens, P., Meier, M. (2001) Controlling als Teil der Informationslogistik. Kostenrechnungspraxis, Sonderheft 45/3, pp. 100-102.

Mertens, P., Rackelmann, G. (1979) Konzept eines Frühwarnsystems auf der Basis von Produktlebenszyklen. In: Albach, H., Hahn, D., Mertens, P. (eds.) Frühwarnsysteme, Ergänzungsheft 2 der Zeitschrift für Betriebswirtschaft, pp. 70-88

Morris, H. (2002) Analytic Applications: Beyond Business Intelligence. http://www.dmreview.com/editorial/dmreview/print_action.cfm?EdID=4988 [1997-08; accessed 2003-05-15]

Müller H. (1995) Konzern-Kostenrechnung, 16. Saarbrücker Arbeitstagung Rechnungswesen und EDV. Physica, Heidelberg 1995, pp. 194-231

Norton, D. (1996) Building A Management System to Implement Your Strategy. Point of View, MA: Renaissance Solutions, Lincoln

Oehler, K. (2000) OLAP: Grundlagen, Modellierung und betriebswirtschaftliche Lösungen. Hanser, München et al.

Oesterer, D. (1995) F- und E-Controlling – Planung und Kontrolle von Forschungsvorhaben und Entwicklungsvorhaben. Expert, Renningen

Oppelt, U. G. (1995) Computerunterstützung für das Management. Oldenbourg, München

PA Consulting Group (2001) Total Shareholder Return. http://www.paconsulting.com/msv/tsrdist.html [2001; accessed 2003-05-15]

Pape, U. (2004) Wertorientierte Unternehmensführung und Controlling, 3rd edition. Wissenschaft & Praxis, Berlin

Porter, M. E. (1999) Wettbewerbsstrategie, 10th edition. Campus, Frankfurt am Main

Porter, M. E. (2000) Wettbewerbsvorteile, 6th edition. Campus, Frankfurt am Main

Procter&Gamble (2002) Annual Report. http://www.pg.com/annualreports/2002/pdf/3.pdf [2002; accessed 2004-08-16]

Publicare (2001) Informationen sind die Währung des E-Business. http://www.publicare.de/www/e/berichte/42efa16.htm [accessed 2004-08-16]

Radke, M. (2001) Die große betriebswirtschaftliche Formelsammlung, 11th edition. Moderne Industrie, Landsberg am Lech

Ram, C., Colvin, G. (1999) Why CEO's Fail. Fortune, 21. Juni 1999

Rappaport, A. (1999) Shareholder Value – Ein Handbuch für Manager und Investoren, Schäffer-Poeschel, Stuttgart

Renner, A. (1991) Kostenorientierte Produktionssteuerung: Anwendung der Prozeßkostenrechnung in einem datenbankgestützten Modell für flexibel automatisierte Produktionssysteme. Vahlen, München

Reuters (1996) Dying for Information? An Investigation into the Effects of Information Overload Worldwide. http:// http://www.cni.org/regconfs/1997/ukoln-content/repor~13.html [accessed 2004-08-16]

Riebel, P. (1994) Einzelkosten- und Deckungsbeitragsrechnung – Grundfragen einer markt- und entscheidungsorientierten Unternehmensrechnung, 7th edition. Gabler, Wiesbaden

SAP (2001a) Konsolidierung mit mySAP Financials – Weltweiter Abschluss – schnell und konsistent, Walldorf

SAP (2001b) SAP Documentation. SAP Strategic Enterprise Management, SEM Release 2.0B, Walldorf

SAP (2001c) SAP Documentation. SAP Strategic Enterprise Management, SEM-BW Release 3.0A, Walldorf

SAP (2001d) SAP Documentation. SAP Strategic Enterprise Management, SEM-BCS Release 3.0A, Walldorf

SAP (2003) SAP Strategic Enterprise Management Release 3.2, Februar 2003 http://help.sap.com/saphelp_sem320bw/helpdata/de/e1/8e51341a06084de10000009b38f83b/frameset.htm [accessed 2004-08-16]

Schierenbeck, H. (2001) Ertragsorientiertes Bankmanagement, Band 2, Risiko-Controlling und Bilanzstruktur-Management, 7th edition. Gabler, Wiesbaden

Schneider, D. (1998) Marktwertorientierte Unternehmensrechnung: Pegasus mit Klumpfuß. Der Betrieb 51/30, pp. 1473-1478

Schönleber, C., Keck, C. (1996) Internet-Handbuch – Techniken, Zugang zum Netz, Dienstangebot, Plattformen. Franzis, Poing

Schuler, A. H., Pfeifer, A. (2001) Kapitalmarktorientiertes Konzernrechnungswesen mit SAP EC. Umsetzung eines effizienten e-Reportings, 2nd edition. Vieweg, Braunschweig/ Wiesbaden

Schwedelson, R. (2001) How To Build a Better House File: Using RFM, Seize Control of a Software Publisher's Greatest Asset.
http://www.worldata.com/wdnet3/articles9_00/How_To_Build_a_Better_House_File.htm [accessed 2003-05-15]

Siegwart, H. (1993) Der Cash-flow als finanz- und ertragswirtschaftliche Lenkungsgröße, 3rd edition. Schäffer-Poeschel, Stuttgart

Siemens (2000) Siemens AG, Geschäftsbericht

Sinzig, W. (2000) Strategische Unternehmensführung mit SAP SEM. WIRTSCHAFTSINFORMATIK 42/2, pp. 147-155

Sinzig, W. (2001a) Moderne DV-Unterstützung für das Ergebnis- und Vertriebscontrolling. Kostenrechnungspraxis, Sonderheft 45/3, pp. 108-110

Sinzig, W. (2001b) Datenbanken. In: Küpper, H.-U., Wagenhofer, A. (eds.) Handwörterbuch Unternehmensrechnung und Controlling, 4th edition. Schäffer-Poeschel, Stuttgart.

Spang, S., Kraemer, W. (1991) Expertensysteme. Entscheidungsgrundlage für das Management. Gabler, Wiesbaden

Stahlknecht, P. (2001) Management-Informationssystem. In: Mertens, P. et al. (eds.) Lexikon der Wirtschaftsinformatik, 4th edition. Springer, Berlin et al., pp. 288-289

Steinhaus, I. (1999) Recherche im Internet, 2nd edition. Koch Media, München

Steinmann, H., Schreyögg, G. (2000) Grundlagen der Unternehmensführung. Konzepte – Funktionen – Fallstudien, 5th edition. Gabler, Wiesbaden

Sterman, J. D. (2000) Business Dynamics: Systems Thinking and Modeling for a Complex World. Irwin McGraw-Hill, Boston et al.

Supply-Chain Council, Inc. (2002) Supply Chain Operations Reference Model, Overview of SCOR 5.0. http://www.supply-chain.org/slides/SCOR5.0OverviewBooklet.pdf [accessed 2004-08-16]

Tischer, M., Jennrich, B. (1997) Internet intern. Technik & Programmierung. Becker, Düsseldorf

Töpfer, A., Afheldt, H. (1987) Praxis der strategischen Unternehmensplanung. Management und Marketing, Band 5, 2nd edition. Metzner, Frankfurt am Main

VBM Resources Center (2002) Total Shareholder Return.
http://www.valuebasedmanagement.net [accessed 2004-08-16]

Wall, F. (1999) Planungs- und Kontrollsysteme. Informationstechnische Perspektiven für das Controlling – Grundlagen – Instrumente – Konzepte. Gabler, Wiesbaden

Wefers, M. (2000) Strategische Unternehmensführung mit der IV-gestützten Balanced Scorecard. WIRTSCHAFTSINFORMATIK 42/2, pp. 123-130

Wenzel, P. (2001) Betriebswirtschaftliche Anwendungen mit SAP R/3: Eine Einführung inklusive Customizing, ABAP/4, Accelerated SAP (ASAP), Projektsystem (PS). Vieweg, Braunschweig/Wiesbaden

Without byline (2001) Hintergrund: T-Mobile leidet unter dem Dilemma der Mobilfunkwelt. http://www.handelsblatt.com/hbiwwwangebot/fn/relhbi/sfn/buildhbi/cn/bp_artikel/strucid/PA GE_200012/pageid/PAGE_201197/docid/445291/BMNAME/0/CN/bp_home/CNCT/1/CT/b p_contextnew/CTLINK/0/IPV/0/MM/bp_main_menu/ [accessed 2004-08-16]

Zingel, H. (2000) Produktlebenszyklus und strategisches Marketing. Phasenbezogene Konzepte und Methoden des Produktmanagement. http://www.zingel.de/pdf/09prod.pdf [accessed 2004-08-16]

ZVEI (1993) Unternehmens-Controlling: Planung, Kontrolle, Steuerung in Unternehmen der Elektroindustrie. Sachon, Frankfurt am Main

Glossary

The glossary contains terms that refer directly to SAP applications and/or have a special meaning at SAP.

Administrator Workbench	Tool for controlling, monitoring, and maintaining the processes involved in data procurement and processing within the →Business Information Warehouse (SAP BW)
Advanced Business Application Programming (ABAP)	Programming language developed by SAP for developing →applications.
Application	In SAP usage this refers to either →SAP SEM/BA as a whole, to a component such as SEM-BPS or SCM Analytics, or to a complete task within a component, such as personnel planning.
Application system	For SAP, an application system is a physically installed →application.
Business Analytics	Encompasses functions required to control business processes running within a company or company units. →SAP SEM/BA
Business Application Programming Interface (BAPI)	Interface defined according to business principles to enable data exchange between SAP components and between SAP components and external systems. →Business Framework Architecture
Business Consolidation (SEM-BCS)	Component of →SAP SEM for consolidation according to legal principles and for consolidation for internal management purposes.
Business Content	Predefined role and task-related information models that can be suited to company-specific requirements.
Business Explorer (BEx)	Reporting tool in →SAP BW.
Business Framework Architecture	Open software architecture for the technical integration and commercial data exchange between SAP components and between SAP systems and systems from other providers. Major elements are the →Business Application Programming Interfaces (BAPIs).
Business Information Collection (SEM-BIC)	Component of →SAP SEM that gathers information from internal and external sources and assists in structuring and editing this information and linking it to internal data.
Business Information Warehouse	Data warehouse product from SAP. Major components are the →Business Explorer (BEx), the →Administrator Workbench, and →Business Content.
Business Planning and Simulation (SEM-BPS)	Component of →SAP SEM for planning, budgeting, forecasting, and simulation, both company-wide and for specific areas of responsibility.
Cause-effect chain	Part of →SEM-CPM that provides an overview of the entire strategy of a company or company unit. Cause-effect chains define and visualize the causal relationships between the objectives in a Balanced Scorecard.

Characteristic	SAP umbrella term for structuring transaction data, such as company code, product, customer group, fiscal year, period, or region. The combination of characteristics specifies evaluation objects, enabling differentiated results and planning. The permitted forms of a characteristic (characteristic values) are managed as master data in the system, for example, for the characteristic Region: North, Central, South.
Consolidation Monitor	Component of →SEM BCS that graphically represents and manages the status of consolidation data processing.
Content Management	SAP's document management system
Corporate Performance Monitor (SEM-CPM)	Component of →SAP SEM, divided into the areas of →Strategy Management and →Performance Measurement.
Customer Relationship Analytics (CRM Analytics)	Component of →SAP SEM/BA that focuses on the analysis of customer relationships.
Data Monitor	Component of →SEM BCS that graphically represents and manages the status of consolidation data reports.
Drag&Relate	Function that simplifies the execution of transactions across different systems. On a graphic interface, the user selects a business object (for example, a purchase order) by clicking on it and dragging it into another object (for example, a logistics system). The system then executes a context-sensitive action (for example, displays the delivery status of the purchase order).
Editorial Workbench	Component of →SEM-BIC that controls the research for external information and assists in structuring and editing this information and linking it to internal data.
Enterprise Portal	Role-based and personalized Web portal from SAP. Users only need to log on once (Single Sign-On) to get access to individually configured functions, services, and information from different systems.
Extractor	Extractors select data from transaction systems and format it for transfer into a data warehouse.
Financial Analytics	Component of →SAP SEM/BA that focuses on the cost and revenue management analyses of measures for improving customer payment behavior, safeguarding liquidity, and working capital management.
Flexible Upload	Method of transferring data from an external system into an SAP system.
Human Resource Analytics (HR Analytics)	Component of →SAP SEM/BA for analyzing employee information.
InfoCube	The central objects on which reports and analyses in SAP BW are based. An InfoCube describes a self-contained dataset for a commercial area. This dataset can be evaluated with a →query.
InfoObject	Umbrella term in →SAP BW for a combination of characteristics and key figures. InfoObjects are used in →InfoCubes and the structures relevant for the data request (extract, transfer, and communication structure).

Information Request Builder	Part of →SEM-BIC that enters research requests in a structured way.
Internet Transaction Server (ITS)	Software system that enables users in the Internet and intranet to communicate with SAP systems directly. To do this it starts business transactions, function modules, reports as Internet applications.
In-Place technology	In-Place technology provides direct access to data in SAP systems from external systems.
Key Performance Indicator (KPI)	Measures that play a key role in measuring the performance in specific areas, such as in Customer Relationship Management or Supply Chain Management.
Management Cockpit	Part of →SEM-CPM, a concept based on the requirements of higher management for presenting management information. The presentation is similar to the displays in airplane cockpits.
Measure Builder	Part of →SEM-CPM that helps the user define complex measurements for valuating company performance and set up extensive business measure systems.
Measure Catalog	Part of →SEM-CPM used to manage measures in the →Measure Builder grouped according to business criteria. In addition to user-defined measure catalogs SAP also includes catalogs with measures that can be added to user-defined catalogs.
Measure tree	Part of →SEM-CPM used to illustrate the calculation of complex key figures.
Metadata	Metadata describes the format, origin, history, and other aspects of data.
OLAP processor	Part of →SAP BW that executes multidimensional queries.
Operational Data Store (ODS)	Storage area in →SAP BW. An ODS object stores cleaned transaction data at document level.
Oros ABCPlus	ABC Technologies software for which →SAP SEM/BA provides a special interface. The program simulates process models and thereby investigates activities carried out within a company for rationalization potential from a process-oriented view.
Performance Measurement	Area of →SEM-CPM that contains the →Measure Builder and the →Management Cockpit.
Persistent Staging Area (PSA)	Essentially an "inbox" in →SAP BW where data is cleaned up and transformed by transfer rules before reaching the →Operational Data Store (ODS).
Planning workbench	Analytical tool in →SAP SEM/BA used to define companywide planned data structures and planning functions.
Powersim Studio	Software from Powersim Corporation for which SAP SEM/BA provides a special interface. The program simulates dynamic process flows within a company and derives planning measures from them.
Product Lifecycle Analytics (PLM Analytics)	Component of →SAP SEM/BA that focuses on the analysis of the activities from the original product idea to marketing (New Product Development and Introduction).

Product Lifecycle Management (mySAP PLM)	SAP product that creates product and process data for the entire lifecycle of a product, maintains it, and makes it available via the Internet.
Query	Collection of a selection of →characteristics and key figures (→InfoObjects) for analyzing the data of an →InfoCube or →ODS object in the →SAP BW.
Retractor	Retractors select data from a data warehouse and transfer it back into the transaction systems.
SAP BA	→Business Analytics
SAP BW	→Business Information Warehouse
SAP R/3	SAP system for operating business processes.
SAP SEM	→Strategic Enterprise Management
SAP SEM/BA	→Strategic Enterprise Management/Business Analytics
SAPGUI	SAP Graphical User Interface. Standard user interface of SAP systems.
SEM-BCS	→Business Consolidation
SEM-BIC	→Business Information Collection
SEM-BPS	→Business Planning and Simulation
SEM-CPM	→Corporate Performance Monitor
SEM-SRM	→Stakeholder Relationship Management
Staging engine	Part of the →SAP BW that processes the data transfer from source systems.
Stakeholder Relationship Management (SEM-SRM)	Component of →SAP SEM for communication with stakeholder groups.
Status and Tracking System	Part of →SEM-BPS that monitors the progress of the different planning tasks like a workflow management system.
Strategic Enterprise Management	SAP Strategic Enterprise Management (SAP SEM) supplies the functions needed for corporate strategic decision making. → SAP SEM/BA
Strategic Enterprise Management/Business Analytics (SAP SEM/BA)	SAP SEM/BA provides a full range of functions for corporate management. →Strategic Enterprise Management (SAP SEM) and →Business Analytics form one software product (SAP SEM/BA).
Strategy Management	Area of →SEM-CPM where the Balanced Scorecard plays a central role. The system also provides modules and business content for value-based enterprise management, particularly value driver management. The area also includes instruments for Risk Management.
Strategy map	→Cause-effect chain
Strategy Template	Part of the Business Content for the Balanced Scorecard. Strategy templates consist of predefined strategies, perspectives, objectives, and measures, as well as a →cause-effect chain for each strategy.
Supply Chain Analytics (SCM Analytics)	Component of →SAP SEM/BA that focuses on the analysis of activities within collaborative vendor networks.

Technical name	Language-independent name of an information object that can be used as a search criterion.
Value Driver Tree	Instrument for value-based company management that visualizes and interprets the influence of operational value drivers on strategically relevant measures.
Visual Assignments	Analytical tool in →SAP SEM/BA used to define relationships between objects (for example, cost centers) graphically, and thereby create clearing models.
Web Survey	Technology for creating and statistically evaluating electronic surveys. A beneficial feature here is that the input fields of the Web page are directly linked to the corresponding data fields of SAP systems.

Index

A

ABC analysis 50
Accenture 185
Account determination 92
Accumulate balances 92
Acquisition of new customers 154
Activity input planning 152
Activity type 151
Activity-Based Costing 52, 163
Activity-Based Management 162
Additional financial data 107
Administration system 2
Advanced Business Application
    Programming (ABAP) 97
Aid program 75
Air transportation market 6
Analytical application system V, 73, 146
Analytical tool 83
Analyzing the competition 35
Application software 78
Associative analysis 155

B

Balance sheet planning 93
Balanced Scorecard VI, 30, 41, 109, 111,
    124, 134, 152, 160, 170, 187, 193
Balanced Scorecard Collaborative, Inc.
    187
BAPI (Business Application Programming
    Interface) 80
Baseline strategy 113
BCG (Boston Consulting Group) 19, 40
Benchmark provider 127
Benchmarking 36, 127, 169
Beta factor 32
Beyond budgeting initiative 16
BI (business intelligence) 71
Boehringer Ingelheim 47
Boston Consulting Group (BCG) 19, 40
Break-even analysis 49
BSC Wizard 111
BSC-Wizard 182
Budgeting 152
Bundling Management 156
Business Analytics 80

- Customer Relationship Analytics
    (CRM Analytics) 152
- Financial Analytics 143
- Human Resource Analytics (HR
    Analytics) 166
- Product Lifecycle Analytics (PLM
    Analytics) 163
- Supply Chain Analytics (SCM
    Analytics) 159
Business Application Programming
    Interface (BAPI) 80
Business area consolidation 102
Business Consolidation (BCS) 102
Business Content VI, 8, 78, 194
Business Dynamics 58
Business Explorer (BW BEx) 81
Business Framework Architecture 83
Business informatics 194
Business Information Collection (BIC)
    138
Business intelligence (BI) 71
Business Planning and Simulation (BPS)
    85
Business to Business (B2B) 159
Business to Consumer (B2C) 159
Business unit level 5
BW BEx (Business Explorer) 81

C

CAE (Computer-Aided Engineering) 194
Call center 153
Call center script 153
CAP (Computer-Aided Planning) 194
Capital asset pricing model (CAPM) 22
Capital investment calculation 60
Capital investment planning 93
Capital market driven enterprise
    management 5, 18
Capital Market Interpreter 89
Cascading Balanced Scorecards 41
Cash flow 92
Cash flow return on investment (CFROI)
    19, 24, 125
Cash value added (CVA) 19, 24
Cash-to-cash lead time 161
Category Management 156
Causal factors 162
Cause-effect chain 59, 112